sports
talk

sports talk

A JOURNEY
INSIDE THE
WORLD OF
SPORTS
TALK RADIO

ALAN EISENSTOCK

POCKET BOOKS

New York   London   Toronto   Sydney   Singapore

POCKET BOOKS, a division of Simon & Schuster, Inc.
1230 Avenue of the Americas, New York, NY 10020

Eisenstock, Alan
   Sports talk : a journey inside the world of sports talk radio /
Alan Eisenstock.
      p. cm.
      ISBN: 0-7434-0694-X
      1. Radio broadcasting of sports—United States. 2. Talk shows—United States.
I. Title.

   GV742.3.E58 2001
   070.4'49796'092—dc21
   [B]   2001034026

First Pocket Books hardcover printing October 2001

10 9 8 7 6 5 4 3 2 1

For information regarding special discounts for bulk purchases, please contact
Simon & Schuster Special Sales at 1-800-456-6798 or business@simonandschuster.com

Printed in the U.S.A.

FOR BOBBIE, JONAH, KIVA, AND Z

We did it again.

CONTENTS

sports
talk

I.

how i got hooked
on smack

i drive.

It is November of 1973. I have been living in Los Angeles for barely two months. I am alone most of the time. My wife has just begun a grueling Ph.D. program while I stay home in our small one-bedroom apartment, trying to write screenplays on my IBM Selectric, which rests on a desk made of two black metal file cabinets and a plywood door. To be honest, I spend most of my day reading mystery novels by Robert B. Parker, Michael Z. Lewin, and Loren D. Estleman, featuring lone-wolf detectives who spend their nights trailing beautiful blondes and bad guys into bad neighborhoods, and their days sitting alone in closets doubling as offices, chain-smoking, their hands wrapped around a bottle. I don't smoke or drink hard stuff and I don't know any blondes or bad guys. But I know the night.

And so I drive, cruising Sunset and Wilshire and Olympic and losing myself in the voices of the darkness. The voices that pour out of the car radio.

I have heard these voices all my life, beginning when I was a boy. They were the companions who calmed my night fears. They were the voices of DJs like Crazy Joey Reynolds, who once locked himself in his studio and played "'Til There Was You" over and over, for four hours straight, while he honked aah-ohh-gah horns, rang cowbells, and cracked jokes in the background. What thrilled me was how Reynolds broke the rules. He was daring and irreverent, and what resulted was nothing less than theater of the mind.

Even before Crazy Joey, there was baseball, where long luxurious pauses in the action allowed my imagination to soar. Although I lived in New England, Red Sox territory, the powerful night signal from New York brought me the sound of the Yankees. Mel Allen, all Southern comfort, unconditionally in love with the Bronx Bombers, midnight pitchman for Ballantine beer and White Owl cigars, described the Yankees in his honey-soaked tenor: "How *about* that?" and "It's going, going *gone!*" Phil Rizzuto, known as the Scooter, the former vacuum cleaner of a shortstop, he of the timely hit and high-pitched chatter, jabbered happily alongside Mel. What a team they made! At ten, as I snuggled in bed, Mel and the Scooter visited me through a clunky brown console perched on my nightstand. I closed my eyes and was transported out of my room like the boy in Maurice Sendak's *In the Night Kitchen,* afloat over a magical baseball diamond, envisioning my own lush green field of dreams. Mel Allen is gone now, a victim of the bottle, murderer of many a night owl. Rizzuto is still part of the Yankee broadcast crew, but I've heard that lately the Scooter has started to slow down. On a recent TV telecast, sitting next to Bill White, a thin, sturdy former Yankee himself, Scooter looked directly into the camera and, obviously reading cue cards, said with a smile, "Hello, everybody, and welcome to another big Yankee game. I'm Bill White."

In '73, as I creep across the night streets of L.A., I swivel my head at each corner, peering for evidence of nightlife, of any life. There are 3 million souls in this tinsel city but not one single person on the streets. A deserted, empty urban terrain. Dark, eerie, and cool. Cooler than you'd expect. The smog has lifted but the emptiness leaves you with a chill. It's just past ten, but as I crawl through a green light, the only car on Pico Boulevard heading downtown, it feels like it's last call and the city is closing down.

I flick the knobs on the radio of my humpbacked, baby blue AMC Gremlin, blinking my eyes, looking for voices, hearing . . . a comforting drone . . . unbelievably . . .

Don Drysdale!

Grinning at me through the chrome glow of the dash. Six feet six, black wavy hair sculpted backward into a ducktail, guy looking like a "hitter" in Dodger blue, a lilting monotone in a slow, flat Sacramento drawl as he takes a call. Drysdale, the intimidator, who insisted that you have to pitch inside, that if a guy goes deep on you, you throw *at* him next time, bury one in his side, is now nice as can be, a voice beaming warmly at you, like a host at a sedate dinner party offering to take your coat.

"Big D, this is Cal from Long Beach," a caller offers up, his voice a nasal crackle right down the middle.

"What's on your mind, Cal?" Big D asks, pleasant, inviting, the perfect gentleman, no glower in his voice, no effort to intimidate, every effort to accommodate. This is *Dodger Talk,* where you get to talk one-on-one with Big D. What a thrill. What an *honor.*

"Well . . ." Cal from Long Beach launches into a stammer. He swallows, wanting to dislodge the something on his mind. Then a deep breath and with a whoosh: "I think we need a new manager. We have the goods—Cey, Sutton, Buckner, Lopes, and this kid Garvey—but Walter Alston is—"

"Now hold on there, Cal," Drysdale says, his voice rising a little. This caller is out of line. This caller has to be *told*.

"You have to understand the *game*, Cal," Big D says, steady. No high hard one, but *smoke* on the inside corner, a lesson. "Walt Alston has been managing a long *long* time. He knows his players better than *anyone*, believe you me. If ever there was a manager who deserved to be in the Hall of Fame, Walter would be it. His experience, I mean, the word *genius*—"

"Well," Cal the Caller says.

I'm tooling back on Franklin, slow, like an unmarked car looking for suspects. I turn the radio up. I'm looking for drama in the dark.

"Still"—Cal swallows—"I think the game might have passed—"

I don't hear the rest. No one does. Big D has shut him down, gone for the seven-second delay. Did the caller curse or did he just kick metaphorical dirt on Big D's cleats? We'll never know because true to *Dodger Talk,* true to all sports talk, Drysdale dodges controversy. Sidesteps it like a mound of dog shit on the sidewalk. But gracefully. Without missing a step. This is 1973. The voices through the radio are soothing, agreeable, smooth, melodious. Talk Muzak.

"And now let's talk to Phil from Whittier. Hey, Phil, you're on with Big D . . ."

No mention of Cal from Long Beach. He's long gone, slain, a victim of stepping out of bounds. It's oddly unsettling to me. I wanted to hear Cal and Big D get it on. Wanted to hear them *rumble*. I remember Joey Reynolds and the chances he took and how thrilling it was to be a witness to his free-form radio experiment. Pissed, unrequited, I slam my foot down on the accelerator, hang a right toward Sunset, angling onto the Strip. I hit a light, cool my heels. Trying to find my balance in this new town, this new life.

My hand slides onto the radio tuner. I've heard enough of Drysdale and *Dodger Talk*. I search for night sounds, something more meaningful. Find it.

Roy Orbison singing for the lonely . . .

Night falls the next day at five o'clock. A cool clean late-afternoon breeze. I leave the apartment windows open, soaking in the black night air. I've hammered out a couple of scenes to a screenplay, read them over carefully, balled them up, and slam-dunked them into the trash. I've air-guitared a riff to *Captain Fantastic* and collapsed onto the secondhand couch, my cat Lou curled up with me, a mystery novel his pillow, his motor rumbling in my lap like a semi.

I want to hear voices. The TV is not my friend. Too self-centered, too demanding. Maybe later I'll be in the mood. Find a good trashy made-for-TV movie, hopefully something with Linda Blair. Right now I feel like bullshitting about sports. I want to escape. Get lost in a discussion of football or basketball. I wouldn't mind a little sports emoting either, the kind you read in columns by the hilarious Jim Murray in the *Los Angeles Times* or the always steady Frank Deford in *Sports Illustrated*. I'd even give an opinion if I could, invisible in the womblike sanctity of the dark. I reach over and absently tune to KABC, home of *Dodger Talk,* and "sophisticated talk of Los Angeles."

And I hear it.

Not an echo but a scream.

A voice with the consistency of sandpaper. A guttural celebration of phlegm. The voice of a man who sounds as if he's just staggered into the studio from a barstool.

"Look at it this way," the voice wheezes. "All you people out there, get it *straight*. It goes like this. Life is a department store and sports is the toy department."

I sit up. My cat hops off my lap.

"My name is Ed Beiler," the voice through the radio roars. "I know that doesn't mean anything to you right now. So let me tell you who I *really* am. I am *your* voice, the voice of the fan, the everyday Joe who can't afford a, a, a fancy box seat at the ballpark, who sits in the bleachers with a, a, a beer and a hot dog and shouts bloody murder from the first pitch to the last out because . . . *I paid for my ticket and I am entitled! That's right!* I'm the guy who boos the umpire when he makes a, a, a lousy call. I'm the guy sitting behind you who screams like *hell* when a Dodger player boots a routine grounder or turns an easy fly ball into an adventure. I am also the first guy on my feet when Davey Lopes steals a, a, a base, when Don Sutton strikes out the other team's best hitter, and when Steve Garvey hits one out of the *park!* I am your best friend and management's worst nightmare! I am . . . *Superfan!*"

I'm riveted.

"I'm the guy who's ticked off at the prices you have to pay to see a Los Angeles Rams football game or a Los Angeles Lakers basketball game. I'm the guy who is ticked off at how much you have to pay for a Dodger dog. I don't like owners who charge too much, coaches who make bonehead decisions and play the wrong guys, and players who make more money than I'll ever make in my life and cry about it. If you're like me, you got a lot on your chest. So let's talk about it, folks. Come on. Call me up. I'm gonna be here every afternoon from now on to take your calls. I'm not a radio DJ or a, a, a former player or anything like that. I, am, *you.*"

I am hallucinating. I must be. Super*fan?* On KABC, the home of sophisticated talk . . . ?

"Yeah? Supe?" The caller sounds like he's at a construction site.

"Yep."

"What do you think of Alston? Isn't it time for a change?"

"Heck *yeah!*" Superfan bellows. "Walter Alston is *old*. He used to be old and good. Now he's just old! Too old to manage the Dodgers. The team should be looking elsewhere. He's had a great run, done a lotta good things, but the Dodgers need someone who can communicate with the younger players. Throw him a nice farewell party, give him a, a, a gold watch and retire his jersey, give him a free pass to Cooperstown, because he belongs there, but let's move *on.* "

I turn the radio up.

"Okay, let's take another call. Ron from Glendale. You're on with Superfan."

"Hey, Superfan! This is great! What do you think of the Rams?"

"The Rams? I think you mean the *Lambs,* don'tcha? They *stink!*"

And so it goes. For two straight hours, the man called Superfan rants, rages, screams, shouts, whines, taunts, and wails. He hangs up on callers and hollers at players. He challenges owners to call him and explain where they get the *cojones* to charge obscene ticket prices and virtually eliminate the very fan who made them rich. It is astonishing radio. It is both fresh and a little bit frightening. I feel like I'm overhearing a drunk in a bar screaming and slurring his opinions until he either throws a punch or passes out. On the radio, Superfan is the vocal equivalent of a train wreck. I know I should turn the dial, but I just can't take my ears off him.

The next day, a Tuesday, I tune into KABC just before five and settle in with a beer and a bag of chips, the perfect Superfan snack. No way I'm boiling up a pot of chamomile tea while I listen to this guy. Bill Ballance, the host right before Supe, intros him curtly, then grudgingly reveals that all of Superfan's phone lines are lit up, blazing. Callers are backed up, on hold, waiting like they're on line to get Springsteen tickets. If he notices, Superfan doesn't let on. He just wants to pick up his rave where he left off.

"Hey, everybody, it's me again. Superfan! We gotta talk. I wanna talk about the ugliest eyesore in town. The biggest pit. The absolute worst, the poorest excuse for a, a, a stadium in the *world*. But what choice do we have, folks, if we wanna see a professional football game? In Cleveland they have the Mistake by the Lake. We have the Screw-Up by USC. I'm talking about the Los Angeles Memorial Coliseum! Have you *been* there? What a joke. First of all, I don't know about you, but I can only afford the cheap seats. But I love football. So I went to the game Sunday. You know where I sat? In the very last *row!* Have you ever sat in the, the, the last row? *Huh?* Lemme tell you something about sitting in the last row of the Los Angeles Memorial Coliseum. *You can't see the game!* You are a million miles up! You look down and the players look like, like, like a *buncha ants wearing football helmets!* You know what? I want my money back! I'll tell you what else. We oughta find the right politicians, call them up, and tell them this: tear down that pit and *build us a new stadium!* We deserve it! What do *you* think? *Huh?* Call me! Get it off your chest, folks! This is where you can let off steam. Right here. On my show. Because, remember, I, am, *you!* And I am . . . *Superfan!*"

Wow.

I feel as if I have been slammed backward into the wall by a blast of gale-force wind. I remember Big D from the other night, recall his solemn devotion to the Dodgers, and it feels like a dream.

Now, every afternoon, with increasing arrogance and assurance, Superfan booms his broadcast through my twin KLH speakers standing guard on either side of my bricks-and-boards bookcase. Listening to him is my new ritual; he becomes a legend in my living room. In the real world, in the world that tracks his dollars-and-cents success, his first ratings come out. The L.A. radio community is stunned. Superfan *owns* the afternoon drive-time slot. Sports columnists and TV pundits don't know what to make of him. We, the legion of his followers, don't care. Hell, we're not even sure *we* like him. We certainly don't always agree with him. But we always, *always* tune in.

I wonder if he is unique. I wonder if other markets across the country have their own Superfans. I call around. Talk to friends in Detroit. Pittsburgh. The Bay Area. Nothing like him anywhere. Finally, I speak to a friend in Boston. No broadcasting barkeep like Supe in Beantown, but there is something else. Every night from seven until eleven. Three guys who talk sports, with an edge. The *Sports Huddle*.

My friend sends me a tape and a picture of the Huddle. Two balding guys with narrow arrogant smiles flank a beefy, dark-haired guy with thick black geeky glasses that make him look like a welder. This man, the one in the middle, is the legendary Eddie Andelman. He sits behind a WEEI microphone and wears a major shit-eating grin. Sports radicals. I know I'm going to like this. The tape is a mishmash of hilarious arguments, outrageous one-liners, and prank phone calls, including a call to room service at Howard Cosell's hotel in Detroit during which Andelman orders a double prune juice—straight, no chaser—for Cosell's breakfast. The Huddlers make no bones about it: they rifle the sports pages in search of the punch line. They're intelligent and shameless, the Firesign Theatre of sports.

At one point, they talk about the America's Cup, the most important yachting race in the world. The Cup had been won most recently by Australia, but this year yachting mavens believe that the Americans have an excellent chance of bringing the Cup back home.

"Who *cares?*" one of the Huddle guys howls on the tape. "I mean, the America's Cup? This is a sport? This is a waste of everybody's time."

"I don't know," one of the other Huddle guys says. "I think

it's us. I'm sure the America's Cup is a big deal everywhere else in the country. We're just in the minority."

In the background a phone rings as the guys place a call.

"Who you calling?"

"I'm calling a Mr. Stevens, who is a forest ranger at station number eleven in . . . I can't read this, I think it says Hairy Knuckle, Texas. Can that be right?"

"Absolutely."

"Why are we calling this guy?"

"Testing your theory."

"*Hello.*"

A voice dipped in brine. A Lyndon Johnson soundalike.

"Ranger Stevens?"

"Yes?"

"Sir, we're calling from WEEI radio in Boston, Massachusetts. We want to get your opinion on the big upcoming sporting event this weekend. You're on the air. Okay?"

"Well, I guess—"

"Great. So who are you picking in the America's Cup?"

"The which?"

"The America's Cup. Who do you like?"

"I'm not familiar—"

"You rooting for the white guy in the blue yachting cap or the Caucasian in the blue yachting cap?"

"Or the blue guy in the Caucasian yachting cap?"

"Caucasian? Oh, we're talking *golf*—"

High-pitched, contagious laughter, mine and from the guys of the *Sports Huddle,* drown him out.

Months go by. I flip the radio dial. I hear sports being talked about, usually right before or right after the Lakers, Dodgers, and Rams games. Team house men and station shills humming along.

You gotta love the Dodgers' chances this year Lakers looking good every player on the same page very positive attitude in the locker room clubhouse dugout hum hum hum . . .

But in the afternoon on KABC, seven ninety on your radio dial, Superfan rails against the rickety bleacher seats in the Coliseum left over from the 1936 Olympics; inconvenient, unsafe, and overpriced parking; concession stands located too far from your seats serving lousy, overpriced food; and overpriced crybaby players caring more about their stats and their salaries than winning a ball game. He shouts down anyone who disagrees with him; he blathers, bellows, and brays. Okay, it's one note. But it's a high note. A helluva high note.

Then two unexpected things happen.

First, I get a job.

A guy reads a screenplay I wrote, passes it on to another guy, who hands it off to Carol Burnett's husband, Joe Hamilton, who happens to be the executive producer of a one-hour Smothers Brothers television special. I am hired as a writer for the show. Which means, gulp, I have to leave my house.

I adjust. For the next several months I am crammed in a small conference room with Tom and Dick Smothers and ten other comedy writers who scream sketch ideas at the top of their lungs and desperately try to be funnier than everyone else in the room. We break for lunch at noon, go to a famous Beverly Hills hangout, bitch about the business and the Brothers Smothers, and try to be funnier than everyone else in the restaurant. I leave the office after seven each night. I've got a migraine from the smoke and the tension and the junk food and the flying one-liners, some of which hit me head-on, most of which just graze my scalp. I can use a friendly, soothing voice. I punch in KABC but I'm too late. Superfan's show is over. He is done for the day, no doubt wobbling back to his barstool. I'm surprised at how disappointed I feel. Is it possible that I actually . . . *miss* him? On my way home, or on my way downtown to have dinner with my wife, I tune my car radio to a game, jazz, NPR, or slide in a tape, Springsteen, Peter Gabriel, The Police. It's a settle. I want to unwind with Superfan.

In spring of 1974, the Smothers job ends. I am back home, unemployed, scratching my cat's back, catching up on the new Parker. At five o'clock there is nothing but sun. The night is a season and a lifetime away. But it's okay. I take my chances, indoors, with the radio. I tune in Superfan.

And hear unexpected thing number two.

He's not there.

In his place are two second-string baseball announcers politely taking phone calls in an even more sanitized version of Dodger Talk, if that's possible. Where is he? Where is Superfan?

I find out a week or so later.

He's in jail.

Busted by the IRS for fraud. Something to do with an illegal trucking operation. The word *racketeering* is thrown around. The charge seems bogus to me, trumped up. They got Supe because he told it like it is. Locked him up because he took on the sports establishment. Threw him in the slammer because of his big mouth. A few days later, I find out that this is his second tour of duty. KABC not only hired a virgin broadcaster, they hired a convicted felon.

The afternoons go by in slow motion. The boring baseball guys are replaced by a hideous sports call-in show hosted by a human sleeping pill nicknamed The Steamer. Maybe because they can't find anyone better, or they just give up, the station leaves The Steamer on the air. Weeks later, I learn that the ratings in Superfan's old time slot have plummeted. I, too, feel myself falling into a void.

I miss Superfan's rants. I miss his passion. I miss his convoluted opinions. I even miss his volume. I know he's not clever or subtle enough to inspire a dialogue of any intelligence or insight. I know I'm not really challenged or engaged. In fact, I'm provoked and often annoyed. I know all this. But Superfan was instinctive enough to say the harsh, honest things about sports that smarter, slicker, and more melodic voices were too afraid or too blind to utter.

Man, I got the itch.

I hear the hum; I want the buzz.

And then, miraculously, he's back. Just like that. Four and a half months into his jail sentence, he's let out on parole to do his radio show. Nodding off to The Steamer one day, I hear simply, "Hello, everybody. It's time to reopen the toy department."

I sit up.

"I done my time."

Pause. A sniffle.

"*Ahhh.* Sometimes ya gotta let it out."

Superfan. A super fan and a sensitive man.

"I made a, a, a *mistake.* Big time. I got mixed up in some, some, some *things.* Ran around with the wrong crowd. I've suffered. My family's suffered. My bosses here have, have, have *suffered . . .*"

Sniff.

"Okay. Enough. I just want to say thank you to KABC for letting me back on the air. And I want to tell you—no, I want to *promise* you—all of you, that that part of my life is behind me. Yep. That is a promise. So let's take some phone calls and get back to what it is we're here for . . . *sports!* Let's talk to Jim in Van Nuys! Yo, Jim!"

"Supe! Great to have you back!"

"Great to be back, Jim."

"Hey, about those Dodgers, did you see the game last night?"

"*See* it? I was *there!* Talk about no clue! What was Alston *thinking?* He leaves the, the, the guy *in?* A blind man could see that Messersmith was done, cooked! Your pitcher's arm is hanging like a wet noodle, you got a, a, a lefty batter coming up, you bring in your *lefty!* Managing one oh one!"

Superfan's voice rises in indignation. I envision him thumping his chest in triumph, released for good behavior into the recognizance of his program director. I picture prison guards and parole officers getting choice box seats during the pennant drive. I see the warden sharing the owner's box during the World Series. I guess my two months in show business have made me cynical. Superfan's return reeks of a superstar's preferential treatment, a backroom deal.

A few callers express this opinion. Supe cuts them off, changes the subject. His stammer becomes more pronounced. His anger boils. He is clearly thrown by those who don't welcome him back, don't *want* him back.

"Can you believe that guy? Listen, pal, you don't like that I'm back, fine, but don't call my show with that, that, that *crap*. I suppose you're a perfect citizen, right? *Huh?* None of us is perfect. None a you is perfect. How about this? Call me up if you're perfect, if you never made a mistake. Awright? *Huh?* Now let's get back to the phones . . ."

Supe's off and running, but not without his share of side-stepping and backpedaling. He is a brawler, though. No surrender in him. I can hear him in clinches with callers, on the defensive, hanging on, desperate for this round to end.

The negative calls keep coming the next day. Superfan's screeners are ready. They shoot most of them down before they hit the air. Supe himself is uncharacteristically subdued. He seems less interested in mouthing off, and more interested in being indignant. He raps now, incoherently, about sports and life, bleating about society. He's out of his league.

"Stick to sports," I say into my radio. "Rant about the Dodgers' weird play at the plate last night."

But he doesn't. I'm not sure what Superfan is talking about anymore. I tune him in each afternoon, but what I hear is pure babble. Maybe the shock of the talk has worn off. Maybe I have spent so much time with my ears glued to Superfan that I've been dragged below the surface. The surface, unfortunately, is pretty thin. Superfan is loud and obnoxious, the guy behind you at the game, screaming at every batter who comes up. But like the guy behind you, by about the third inning, the screaming gets old.

I have an option. I can turn him off. Which is what I do. Instantly, the two hours between five and seven become found time. I work, take up running, and am even inspired, on occasion, to cook dinner. My head feels surprisingly clear. I am drawn back into music. When I crave talk on the radio, I find myself listening to *All Things Considered* on our local public radio station. After a couple of months, I become a subscriber.

One afternoon, bored stiff by a report about new forms of edible algae found on the ocean floor, I fall off the wagon. Fondling the free coffee cup I'd received for sending in my twenty bucks to the NPR pledge drive, I switch back to Superfan.

He's on a mission. A suicide mission.

"Have you ever really *tasted* a Dodger dog? *Have you?* Do it. I dare you! Hold the pickle, hold the relish, hold the mustard, no chili, no ketchup, no *bun!* Just eat the damn hot dog! You know what? It's *garbage!* Everyone loves 'em and I don't know why. I'm stumped. Now, I'm a big man! I love to eat! I eat all kinds of, of, of *garbage,* all kinds of, of, of *crap!* But I will not eat a Dodger dog! No way, no how, no sir! You could put a gun to my head and I will not do it! I'll tell you why. I wanna know what's *in* those things! Beef? Pork? Meat and meat by-products? Wood shavings off the floor? *Animal droppings? What?* I'm afraid to think about it! I am going to do all of southern California a big favor. I am going to make those rich owners, the people who sell us Dodger dogs, replace them with something *edible!* I want all-beef franks! That's the least they can do! I guarantee you that Peter O'Malley, and all the rich guys up there looking down on us pee-ons, don't eat Dodger dogs! No way! I bet they're laughing like hell at us while they're sitting in their box seats, sipping their champagne and, and, and eating their roast beef sandwiches! I promise you they are not eating them disgusting Dodger dogs!"

Well, in fact, they were. And like most of the fifty thousand plus fans at each game, loving them. To KABC management and the owners of the Dodgers, Superfan had gone too far. Disrespecting them was one thing; disrespecting Dodger dogs was a sacrilege.

In short, Dodger ownership and KABC management had heard enough. I thought Supe's harangue against Dodger dogs was classic, vintage Superfan. But KABC fired him on the grounds of a conflict of interest. Apparently, he had been warned previously and repeatedly. This recent rant was part of an ongoing campaign against the unfortunate, unsuspecting wiener. It was the last straw. Superfan was kicked off the air without ever having the chance to say good-bye.

Once I knew he was gone for good, I spun the radio dial feebly in a halfhearted effort to find him again. I heard voices in the early morning, late afternoon, and into the night, baritoned stoners introducing acid rock, sultry seductresses breathily announcing freeway pile-ups, and a bunch of screamers trying to be funny. This was 1974. Howard Stern was still in college, Don Imus was not yet clean and sober, and Rush Limbaugh hadn't been invented yet.

As Superfan vanished, sports talk radio took a deep breath. The genre needed to examine itself. Programmers needed to find out what their audiences wanted. They knew their listeners wanted serious stuff—scores, stats, highlights, and analysis. But sports freaks didn't really want to hear oddball personalities and their crazy opinions, did they? They certainly didn't want to mix sports with humor. And they definitely didn't want to combine shock talk with sports talk.

Wrong.

We know now that audiences wanted all of it, all the time, twenty-four hours a day.

No one knows what became of Superfan. There are rumors that he went back to his original career, selling liquor to wholesalers, or that he became a bartender. There is also a rumor that he died.

A few years after Superfan's last broadcast, I lie in bed, bleary-eyed, channel surfing with my remote. I breeze by a local eleven-o'clock newscast. The anchors are stereotypes: a white male with a chiseled chin and a mane of perfect white hair camped next to a bubbly black woman wearing eye makeup that looks like it was put on with a roller. They are laughing hysterically. When did the news become so funny?

Catching their collective breath, they introduce a new sports guy who's subbing for their regular sports guy who's covering the Lakers downtown. The sub sports guy is a wide truck-driver type, short, stubby, thick around the neck. Stuffed into his pants is a gut much more accustomed to pancakes than sit-ups. His face is flat and ruddy, his hair close-cropped army-style. Pockmarks dot his skin. He looks a little like Robert Parker, the mystery writer, whose books have sustained me through many a dark and lonely night.

The sports guy starts to talk, and within three seconds I know who he is. His voice gives him away.

It is none other than Superfan.

As proof, the words "Ed 'Superfan' Beiler" appear superimposed beneath his formidable skull. Supe peers uncomfortably into the camera and reads the sports scores haltingly: "The a, a, a, Dodgers beat the Pirates tonight over at the Stadium, five to a, a, a, *three . . .*"

It's obvious that Superfan has a face made for radio. He has no business here. Who was the genius who thought he would work on television? Maybe he needs the money and someone is cutting him a break. I stare, pained, praying for the sportscast to end.

He finishes his report. His forehead is swimming in sweat. His cheeks are deep crimson, two shades short of a stroke. The two chuckling, oblivious news anchors press on, trying to entrap the former Superfan into an opinion.

I can't watch. I want Superfan to stay tucked in the corner of my memory alongside those thrilling moments of radio that reside there still—several World Series and playoff broadcasts, DJs going off the deep end, live coverage of news events that became theater of the ear such as Watergate, the Clarence Thomas confirmation hearings, and Bush vs. Gore at the Supreme Court.

Today, nearly thirty years after Superfan's first blast on the radio, I am still obsessed with sports and addicted to *smack,* loosely translated as sports trash talk. But the phenomenon of sports talk radio would not exist without Superfan.

The book that follows is a journey, a trip through time and space and countless hours of conversation. The journey represents a year of travel and discovery. I trekked through the studios and control rooms of some of the craziest, most respected, and most popular sports talk radio hosts around, including Mike and the Mad Dog, the number-one sports radio team in the country, broadcasting on WFAN, the number-one billing station in the world. I was welcomed into the lives of radio legends and spurned by one of the biggies, Jim Rome (the man who coined the term *smack*). In addition to hanging out with the hosts, I hung with their program directors, producers, engineers, screeners, Update-and-Flash guys, wives, children, pets, and neighbors. I had coffee and dinner with some of their most notorious callers. The result is a fan's notes, a character study, or more correctly, a study of characters.

It is, most of all, a book of voices, the voices I hear.

One voice, the loudest voice, echoes throughout the book. It belongs to Arnie Spanier, the Stinkin' Genius. Arnie is not yet rich or famous or held in high esteem by his colleagues or critics. But as one sports talk radio host said, "Arnie is there, at the four-star restaurant, waiting for his table."

Arnie is also a typical middle-class American, busting his hump every day, fighting the good fight, struggling to make a living and provide for his family. He just happens to have an atypical job in a fierce and fickle business, an industry that relies on scrutiny and stealth and that believes, as another talk show host told me, "You're nobody unless you've been fired."

As the book unfolds, Arnie finds himself in a make-or-break situation. If things go well, he will be a hero. If not, he becomes the goat. How it all turns out is part of the story.

But why Arnie?

I think because he reminds me of someone else, another voice in another time, clear but distant, the voice that started it all for me thirty years ago. The voice that got me hooked on *smack*.

The voice of Superfan.

He's back.

Except now his name is the Stinkin' Genius.

discovering genius

ARNIE SPANIER:
THE STINKIN' GENIUS

thirty years later.

Monday night. Poker night. Ten-fifteen P.M.

I drive.

Heading home on the Santa Monica Freeway, crawling along, hugging the slow lane. Last hand, as usual, was called at nine forty-five. A couple of the guys, Danny and Doc, have to get up early for, gulp, *work*. I stayed, as usual, and helped Gary put away the chips. Otherwise I'm home before the kids are in bed. Don't want to give the game of poker a bad name. Keep the image alive of green eyeshades and a cloud of smelly, brown cigar smoke hovering over thousands of dollars' worth of chips at four in the morning. The truth is, our maximum bet is two bucks and we serve herbal tea and fresh popcorn from the Beverly Hills farmers' market. Ah, California.

I fiddle with the radio, realize I'm on FM. Some British

techno crap stinging my brain. Sounds like music played with a Hoover and a chain saw. What is this? My wife has *every* station programmed to NPR? Jesus. Finally. There it is. AM 1540. The hit I need.

One-on-One Sports Talk from Chicago.

And there's the voice in the night to soothe me more than a cognac. Arnie Spanier. Sounding like a bookmaker gargling with glass. Arnie, you Stinkin' Genius, take me home. I settle in, listen to a caller with a lisp named the Professor. Richard Simmons with a gambling problem.

"Arnie, I'm telling you, I just bet a million dollars on the Eagles taking the nine points. I *swear* to you."

"Hold on, Professor, now *hold on!*"

The Stinkin' Genius's voice, both the croak of his perpetual sore throat and the sheer volume of his scream, knocks my head back.

"You didn't bet a million dollars in Vegas! *Because no one in Vegas will take a million-dollar bet!*"

"Not on the Strip but downtown—"

Soft, sibilant, hurt.

"You want me to believe you? Fax me a copy of the betting ticket? *Fax me a copy of the stinkin' ticket!*"

"Okay. Maybe it wasn't a million dollars," the Professor utters, defeated, his voice dissipating into a sea of static. "But it was a *lot*—"

"Yeah, *right.* I don't have time for this. Let's go to New York. Joe the Waiter. What's shakin', Joe?"

A painful sigh breathes through the radio. *"Ohhhh.* Meester Arnie."

My fingers reach for the volume. I can sense it. Something is about to happen.

"What's the matter, Joe?"

"Meester Arnie, I have so much trouble."

That accent. It can't be real. The guy sounds like Martin Short in *Father of the Bride.*

"What kind of trouble, Joe?"

"Same kind. The gumbling." Gambling. I should have known.

"What am I gonna do with you? How bad?"

Joe the Waiter lowers his voice. Whispers across the country. "Last veek I lose ten thousand."

"No!"

"Meester Arnie, I'm telling you."

"Did your wife find out?"

"Ohhh, she find out. I slip in bussment."

"You fell in the basement?"

"No, no, Meester Arnie, I *slip.* "

"What the hell are you talking about?"

"I *slip* in *bussment,* " Joe the Waiter howls, impatience crowding his cartoon accent.

"You *sleep!* You sleep in the *basement!* "

"Yes, yes! Dat's why—"

"Not to worry, Joe. I'm gonna straighten you out right now. I'm gonna give you my picks, you're gonna get even, then you're gonna cool it for a while."

"Oh. I get even then I no gumble."

"That's right. Now just play these picks and you'll be all right. You got that?"

"Yes, Meester Arnie, I write down."

"Okay, good. Here we go. Write these down. Tulane minus the six against Louisville. Got that?"

"Yes, yes. Tulane. Vot about Michigan? I *luf* Michigan."

"Forget Michigan. Who said anything about Michigan?"

"Okay. Cancel Michigan."

"Take Arizona minus five against Washington State."

"I'm writing down. Arizona minoose five. How about Texas? I *luf* Texas."

"*Texas?*"

"Yes, Texas, the Lunghorns—"

"Forget the Lunghorns!"

"Okay, okay, I cancel."

"No wonder you owe ten grand, you don't *listen!*"

"Okay, okay, I sorry, no more. But vot about Ohio State? I *luf* the Buckeyes!"

"*What are you doing?*"

"Okay, all right, I cancel Buckeyes. I cancel right now. There, see?"

"No, I can't see. This is the radio!"

"I know is radio. You so funny, Meester Arnie!"

"Okay, okay, let's do the pros. Take Tennessee plus the three."

"Tennessee plus the tree. Good. I cancel all the rest. *All,* Meester Arnie."

"Finally."

"But Meester Arnie, Miami Dolphins laying only a deuce? I *luf* the Fish!"

"No *Fish!*"

"I cancel Fish. No Fish. Dead Fish."

"*For cryin' out loud, you're gonna be sleeping with the fish!*"

I'm not sure when I pulled over to the side of the road, but I have. And the radio's up and I'm laughing out loud, a loony on the freeway, glued to sports talk radio as an actor, *has* to be an actor, calling himself Joe the Waiter, argues football picks in a fake foreign accent with the Stinkin' Genius.

No way this guy's for real.

"Oh, Joe the Waiter's for real," Arnie Spanier assures me. "He lives in Queens and he actually is a waiter at some fancy restaurant in Manhattan."

"Huh," I say.

I am momentarily frozen. *None* of this seems real to me,

especially the fact that I am actually talking on the telephone to Arnie Spanier. Partly I'm stunned because he sounds so subdued. I strain to hear the shrillness, the hard edge, the high volume that drives his show for four hours a night. Instead, as we talk, I hear a softness that surprises me. Then I say something that he finds funny and I hear that signature laugh, that guttural volcano, and I am able to relax. Yes, it's him. I got the Stinkin' Genius on the line.

It happened in a flash. Tuning in to Arnie one night, I heard the unimaginable: he announced he was leaving the network. He wouldn't reveal his plans, wouldn't say where he was going, but implied that he would resurface in a new and exciting place.

"Don't know exactly when my last show will be," he offered mysteriously. "So I might not get to do a good-bye show."

That was it. The next night he was gone, replaced by a string of temporary hosts who couldn't carry his headset. Then I heard that the new and exciting place was L.A. and that the Stinkin' Genius was granted afternoon drive on KXTA 1150. I called the station, asked for Arnie, and left a voice mail telling him that I was writing a book about sports talk radio, that I was a fan, and that I wanted to include him in the book. Arnie called me back the next day.

"This is great. How about we meet at Mort's Deli?"

"Perfect," I say. "It's right near my house."

"Mort's a friend of mine. I took his daughter to the prom. He's still not talking to me! Ha ha *ha!*"

We arrange to meet for breakfast. We hang up. I pace, start formulating questions.

The phone rings.

"Alan, hi, this is Beth, Arnie's wife."

"Hi, Beth. Nice to meet you."

"Same here. Listen, Arnie didn't realize that he has a conflict tomorrow. See, we take our son, Shea, for a swimming lesson every Tuesday morning. So he has to reschedule the interview."

"Not a problem."

"He really wants to do it," Beth adds quickly.

"Great. How's Wednesday? Same time, same place?"

"Perfect," Beth says. There is genuine relief in her voice. And something more. I listen for a moment, see if I can pick it up. Oh. There it is. Got it.

Power.

The woman has power.

I like her instantly because I know her. Know what she's about. This woman drives the bus.

"Just curious, Beth," I say. "Why did you call me back? Why didn't Arnie?"

"Oh, listen, you don't know Arnie. He wouldn't call you back. He *couldn't.*"

"Why not?"

"He's too shy."

I don't get it. "It's no problem changing the interview. Really."

"Oh, I know," Beth says. "It's just that, well, Arnie . . . he was just too afraid to call you."

"So," I say, sorting it out. "Here is a guy who makes his living talking to people on the *phone* and he's too shy to call me back?"

"You got it. You know all that shouting, that bluster? That's a *character.* Arnie is playing a part. You'll see."

Arnie and I are seated at a table in the corner of Mort's Deli in the heart of Pacific Palisades, California, a sleepy village on a bluff overlooking the ocean. Mort's reminds you of a coffee shop in Las Vegas. Television screens tuned to *SportsCenter* are posted at each corner of the dining room. Brown flat deli tables flank a center food-preparation area. In the front, by the generically rude cashier, you can buy a paper, the *Trades,* or a lottery ticket. Occasionally celebs spill out of the cafeteria line juggling food trays and cell phones as they circle the sit-down area looking to claim a spot where they're sure to be seen.

"I'm from the Bronx," Arnie says.

He has kind brown eyes, a hefty body, wears a blue University of Michigan sweatshirt and an easy smile. In the flesh, his voice is even thinner, less gravelly; the microphone clearly buffs it up.

"I lived in New York until the sixth grade. My dad used to have a stationery shop. He wasn't really making a go of it so he decided to fold up the store and come out to California. So thirteen years old I came out here. No money, no nothing. We lived in an apartment in West L.A. My dad finally got a job and then slowly but surely . . ."

He grins, lowers his head slightly.

"Kinda like the *Beverly Hillbillies.* One day Jed's shooting at some food and up comes some oil? One day my dad's looking for a job, he gets a *great* job, and before you know it, he's got part of the company, and he's rolling in money. We moved out of the apartment and bought a nice house in Brentwood. My parents still live there. I got one brother. Six years younger. Mighta been a mistake, I dunno."

He reaches back and roars, *"Haaa,"* loud, causing heads to turn.

"Did you play sports?"

"Yeah. I was always good enough to make the teams but never good enough to take it to the next level. Like in high school, I went to school with Steve Kerr. I was a better shooter than he was. He'll be the first to tell you."

No laugh this time; he's looking right at me. No fantasy either. He's dead serious.

"How'd you get into sports talk?"

Arnie sighs, gets comfortable.

"After college, I was working for Chiat-Day Advertising. I didn't know what I wanted to do. I was like a temporary employee, you know, by the week. One day after work, I went to see my little brother play basketball at Palisades High. I'm sitting in the stands, I got my sweats on, and I'm watching them set up the cable. They're gonna film the game. I'm waiting and waiting and I see they got no play-by-play guy. I walk over to the guy in charge and I go, 'Where's your play-by-play guy?' He says, 'He didn't show up.' I say, 'I'll do it for you. I know the Palisades team. I don't know the other team real well, but give me a sheet and I'll improvise as I go along.' So I did it. After that they started calling me to do the Loyola Marymount games. I became a play-by-play guy on local cable. This was the Hank Gathers, Bo Kimble era. It was very exciting. They didn't pay me, but it was very cool. Then I started doing stringing work, getting like six bucks an hour."

He pauses, takes a sip of water. His lips caress the rim of the glass as if the hazy tap water of Mort's is some mysterious elixir.

"I decide to hit the road. Gonna get in my car and drive around the country, see what I can find. I get a job in Boca Raton doing weather. I go up to Ukiah, California, and become a country-music DJ. Hollywood *Haazze. H* double *a,* double *z,* one *e.* These jobs only last like three months."

I scratch my forehead with my pencil, smile. I picture the Stinkin' Genius at twenty-three, on the road, schlepping from town to town in a dirty, battered Plymouth, tapes and crumpled newspapers riding shotgun.

"I just did what I had to do. Called up stations. Stopped in. Played my tapes. Went everywhere. I went to Iron Mountain, Michigan. I went down to the Keys in Florida. Worked there for a week or two. Nothing was really happening. Finally decided just to come back to L.A. Moved into my parents' house in Brentwood."

Behind us in Mort's a busboy upends a tray of plates. Dishes and flatware careen across the linoleum floor. A stream of swearing in Spanish. Focused, Arnie barely reacts to the noise.

"I was stringing for XTRA 690, then for SEN, the Sports Entertainment Network, out of Vegas. All for free. I finally decided that I wanted a show. And I wanted it on SEN. So I called my boss. Rod Stowell. I said, 'Rod, this is Arnie. I've been doing stringing work.'

"'Yeah, I've heard you. You're pretty good.'

"'I want to do a show. Fill-ins, weekends, nights, anything.'

"'Where have you done a show before?'

"'I'll be honest with you. I've never done a show.'"

Arnie pauses, tilts his head, channels Rod Stowell:

"'What, are you *crazy*? You're gonna be on nationally. I can't do that. Go to Arkansas. Get some experience. But you know what? I think you're funny. Call me back in September. Maybe we'll have something.' I call him in September. Nothing. I call him in October. Nothing. November, nothing. In December, a call comes. A week before Christmas. It's Rod. I'm still stringing, and not getting paid of course. Rod says, 'I got a show for you. Christmas Eve, Christmas, New Year's Eve, New Year's. Midnight to six. You drive yourself to Vegas. We'll put you up at this cheap hotel where all the hookers hang out. We'll pay for your food. You got a problem with any of this?'

"'Nope. I'll be there.'

"'Then come on and do the show.'"

The road to Vegas. The break.

Arnie and a friend, a guy with a car, drive five hours through the desert, air conditioner erratic, conking out near Barstow, windows cracked the rest of the way, dry saunalike air busting hard against their faces. The friend, stoked about Christmas in a casino, a lump of fifties in his pocket secured with a sea-blue rubber band ripped off from a neighbor's Sunday *Times*, blasts a Led Zeppelin tape until the air conditioner dies. Arnie, caught up in the frenzy of his impending future, ignoring his inability to carry a tune, screeches a painful harmony on "Whole Lotta Love," then, for the next couple of hours, with the car wilting in the heat, retreats into silence and sleep, waking to sad sandy hills looking like overcooked sponge cakes looming on both sides of the Nevada border.

At the hotel, dodging roaches, Arnie showers in a minute. His friend drops him at the radio station and heads toward downtown, Arnie in the distance hearing the humming of "Deck the Halls" through a slice in the driver-side window. Arnie slides through a dingy anteroom passing for a lobby, mounts a cement staircase, and quietly enters the control room. He glances at a shadowy figure behind a microphone in the tiny studio across the glass and begins to write down some thoughts on a yellow legal pad. It is just six o'clock. Arnie is eager; hell, he is six hours *early*, but this way he has time to plan his show and stake out the promised land.

An hour passes. Very little movement. A silent guy in a Kiss T-shirt slouches in, swipes an armful of tapes from stacks on either side of Arnie's head, then disappears into the dark. The guy across from him, Mr. Six to Midnight, plods through his show, never acknowledging him, grim-faced behind oversize tinted glasses, resembling Roy Orbison on a good hair day.

Eight o'clock passes, then nine. Arnie stretches, wonders when Rod Stowell's going to show up to show him the ropes.

Ten o'clock. Arnie wandering in search of a soda machine. Finds two vending machines down a hallway, next to a row of lockers. One offers candy and soup, the other, soda and soup. Las Vegas, land of gambling, neon, nudity, and . . . *soup?*

Eleven o'clock. Arnie figuring Rod's on his way. Probably'll arrive right before the show, tell him what to do, stay with him until he gets the hang of it.

Eleven-thirty. A door opens downstairs. Heavy footsteps on their way up, slowly, wearily. Arnie stands, smiles, and greets . . . the night janitor.

"How ya doin'?"

"Arright."

The janitor, appreciative and thrown that someone has actually noticed him, grins through a mouth of five scattered gold teeth. He moves off in search of his mop. Arnie slumps back down. Should he try to call his boss? Don't have the number, don't know his whereabouts. His leg starts to twitch like Elvis.

Twelve o'clock. No Rod. Six to Midnight signs off, shakes his head free of his headset. He stands, yawns, swings open the door to the studio, and signals to Arnie. Arnie shoots out of his chair, approaches Six to Midnight with a slight—where did this come from?—limp.

"Your turn. Bye."

"My turn, *bye?* What do I *do?*"

"You never done a show?"

"No."

Six to Midnight waves Arnie into the studio. He points to two square switches on a console. "This is how you turn *on* a caller, this is how you turn *off* a caller. Here's a headset. That's all you're getting from me."

And he evaporates like a mirage in the desert.

In Mort's, a dozen years later, Arnie smiles, a shy smile curling around a hint of triumph.

"I had no idea what to do. No idea what you bump back with, music numbers, nothing. I'm flying by the seat of my pants. It was really just the way we're talking. About an hour into the show, I'll never forget this, the Philadelphia Eagles were playing the Saints in a playoff game. The Saints had never won a playoff game. I gave my prediction. I say, 'Maybe the Saints win their first playoff game.' I get a call from Philadelphia. This guy starts *ripping* me. 'You don't know what you're talking about. How the hell do they let assholes like you on the air?' I just lost my marbles. I started *screaming*. *'Who the hell are you? What the hell do you know?'* We're going back and forth. And that's how the whole thing started with the screaming and the energy. After that, I picked up the pace and got really animated, kinda took this on as my new style. I finished the two weekends, packed up my stuff to go home, and went into the office Monday morning. I tell Rod thanks, appreciate it, I'm going back to L.A. I have a tape now, maybe it'll lead me to something. He says, 'Wait right here,' and he goes into his office. He comes back a minute later and tells me two people quit. He offers me the noon-to-three shift. I work it for two weeks, then I hear, 'The boss likes you.' I guess he did because he put me on three to six. And that's how I got my first regular gig."

"And 'the Stinkin' Genius' . . . ?"

Arnie's whole face widens into a grin.

"It started in Vegas when I was picking games. I was on a terrible losing streak. Everything I said went into the toilet. I said Anthony Young of the Mets was gonna be the next Doc Gooden. He lost twenty-three in a row. I said the new San Antonio franchise was gonna win the Canadian Football League. The franchise folded two weeks later. Then, all of a sudden, when I started picking college football, I got hot. It was unbelievable. I was on a roll like you've never seen. One day when I was on the network, in Chicago, I remembered Nebraska kicking the crap out of Arizona State the year before.

31

I said, 'Mark this on your calendar for next year: Arizona State, no matter how good or bad they are, are gonna kick the crap out of Nebraska.' We were on in Lincoln and I like to get the people riled up there so I said, 'Not only are they gonna beat you, they are gonna wipe you out! *In fact, they're gonna shut you out, twenty to nothing!*"

Arnie pauses.

"The score was nineteen nothing. I got on the air and I started shouting, 'This is beyond genius!' and people started calling and saying, 'You're a *stinking* genius!' I rolled it around and thought, *'Stinkin' Genius?* That's perfect.' Every talk show host needs a cool nickname, right? I got mine!"

From the outside it's just a contemporary, boxy, accordion-glassed office building in Burbank. But step into the faux-wood-paneled elevator, watch the doors slide shut, and you begin your ascent into a mind trip. The elevator hesitates, stops, plops in place, the doors open like a theater curtain and you are dumped into a scrunched lobby, every inch of wall space slapped and overlapped with rock 'n' roll posters. You have entered the radio universe of KIIS-FM, 102.7, L.A.'s reigning rock giant, home of Rick Dees, a thirty-year fixture at the station who drinks from the same fountain of youth as Dick Clark; KCDA-FM, 103.1, alternative rock, live acoustic concerts in Studio C, my FM station of choice; and KXTA-AM, 1150, home of the Dodgers, UCLA basketball, and Arnie Spanier, the Stinkin' Genius, new kid on the block.

I shake hands with Art Martinez, Arnie's engineer, and follow him into the control room, the walls of which are lined with hundreds of royal blue tape cartridges. Each one has the name of a product or company smudged on its side—IBM, Seagram's, California Federal Bank.

"Commercial carts," Art explains as he lands on a swivel

chair in front of a dizzying grid of switches, knobs, buttons, and lights. This is "The Board." Art caresses a joystick and heaves it up toward the moon. I settle in next to Brian Blackmore, Arnie's producer, a baseball cap tucked into his headset. Brian barks into a telephone cradled against his left ear.

"XTRA Sports, hello? . . . What do you think about the Lakers? . . . No, what's *your* opinion? . . . Okay, what's your name and where are you? . . . Hang on, buddy. XTRA Sports, hello . . ."

A commercial for *your* Southern-California Lexus dealer blares over speakers jutting from each corner of the control room. Around to my left, barely in view, Arnie sits in a tiny glass booth, the studio. He adjusts his headset, palms a lighted square switch. His voice booms Big Brother-like over another set of speakers somewhere.

"Hey, can anybody hear me? I need my headset volume turned up. . . . That's better."

"You wanna hold on, buddy?" Brian brays to a caller. "We're talking mostly Lakers. . . . Okay, hold on, buddy. XTRA Sports. What do you want to say?"

A stinging electric guitar lick screams above us, then abruptly cuts out.

"Got sound here," Art announces in the clear.

"Hey, Leo," Brian squawks into the phone. "I'm gonna put you up first."

Electric lick down a level, Phil Jackson's deep bass voice rumbles overhead: "Dis*eased*. That word is almost two words. We're not at ease right now. We have to figure out how we want to play as a basketball team and get cohesive again."

"That's *Phil Jackson*," Arnie shrieks above us. The Stinkin' Genius is on the air! "That's the coach of the Lakers, talking about the game last night against the woeful Cleveland Cavaliers . . ."

"XTRA Sports, hello?" Brian says, more urgency in his voice. "What's your name? . . . Pierre? . . . What? You're in a *jail* facility? . . . Oh, you're a *deputy*. What do you want to say about the Lakers? . . . Hang on, Pierre. XTRA, hello . . ."

Brian leans forward, edge of his seat. In front of him is a large monitor, maybe nineteen inches. As Brian talks, he types two-fingered fast on the keyboard. The monitor displays two columns, telephone lines one through six on the left side, seven through nine on the right. Brian talks, pounds his keyboard. I watch the sentences dance across the screen: "Lakers in first, but still worried. Dwight in car." Below that flashing in hot pink: "No one else is playing better. Mike in Covina." Further down the column, line four: "Agrees Shaq is a liability. Gene in Northridge." And so on, to the bottom of the screen, spilling over to the right side. All lines lit, flashing-pink Barbie neon, Brian trying to keep up typing, callers calling, the producer not quite able to handle the volume of calls, can't stop the endless stream of voices screaming for Arnie or the sweat beading up beneath the brim of his cap.

"What do you wanna say to Arnie? . . . Okay, turn your radio off and roll your window up. Hang on, man. XTRA Sports, hello."

"Where *are* you people?" Arnie hollers. "All of a sudden you Lakers fans are *gone*? Are you kidding me? I got phone lines *open*? What's the matter with you people? Look at that, Brian, the phone lines are stinkin' *open!*"

"Hold on, buddy. XTRA Sports, hello."

I lean over, confused. All nine lines are lit and flashing. I look at Brian for a reality check.

"The lines aren't open. Are they?"

"He's just fucking with them. XTRA Sports, hello. . . . Hey, Greg, where you calling from, man? . . . What's your beef with the Genius? . . . Hang on, buddy."

Brian turns to me, a look of awe and exasperation clouding his face.

"Thank God we only have nine lines. It goes like this his whole show. *Bloop bloop bloop bloop bloop.* All nine lines, never stops. I'm like, man, can't we have a slow show for once?"

"So it's like this every day?"

"Every day. The six years I've been doing this, I've never seen anything like it."

Brian pounds a finger into a phone line. "You there, Pierre? . . . Okay, bro, you're up next. Let him have it."

Arnie's voice booms over us: "This is Arnie Spanier on XTRA 1150 . . . ," and I find myself oddly relaxed. Arnie, fully in character now inside his tiny glass theater, the mouth that roars, takes on all callers, most of whom argue lamely in favor of the Lakers. Arnie shouts back, bazookas them all, stopping only to pepper us with a scream-of-consciousness commercial for an herbal weight loss supplement I'll call "Lard-Off."

"Lose weight while you sleep with Lard-Off. I'm telling you, this stuff is amazing. The best thing is, you don't have to do *anything.* Don't have to go on a diet, don't have to exercise, *nothin.'* And this stuff *works.* I've been taking it for what, Brian, a couple of weeks now? And it's really starting to pay off. I look *great.*"

"Oh, yeah, Arnie," Brian mumbles.

"They're calling me Fabio around here."

"Ten seconds, Fabio."

Arnie wraps it up, chugs some soda as Terry Bradshaw on tape hawks a commercial for laser eye surgery. Music up then and Arnie rocks on. During breaks, Arnie shoots out of his glass booth and joins us in the control room. Other people arrive, all young men in T-shirts, all trying to look busy, most just wanting to hang. Nachos with waves of yellow cheese slathered on them, diet drinks, and slices of pizza magically appear. The pungent odors of perspiration and flatulence float through the control room. When Arnie leaves, the noise in here rises to a wall of sound that literally drowns out Arnie and his show. But as soon as he's got a break, he's right here with us, the ringmaster, laughing loudly, then casually seeking validation. *Am I off base about the Lakers? I never said they sucked. I'm not making this shit up. Was that last call funny? Who was that Pierre guy? Sounds like he was calling from a lockup.*

It all sounds fine to us. We grab for the nachos, the diet Slice, and belch happily. I feel like I'm reliving my sophomore year of college.

"Thirty seconds."

Arnie hustles back into his tiny glass chamber, soda in hand, all business. I lean back comfortably.

"Hey, you listen to me, people. You got something to say, you call *me, don't call my boss!* He comes running down the hallway going, 'What are you doing? You're pissing everybody off! I'll give you two hundred bucks if you don't take any calls for one hour!' I say, 'No way, put your money back in your pocket.' 'Okay,' he says, 'I'll give you a *thousand dollars!*' People, do me a favor? *Don't call my boss!*"

An hour ago I would've looked around for a guy in a suit. Now, of course, I know that it's all part of the show, par for the course, the illusion of radio.

"I'm a talk radio guy."

The likable pear-shaped man in the loose-fitting suit leans back in his chair and addresses me in a pleasant tenor.

"I believe that this format, sports talk, needs to program to the average fan, which is, by the way, who I am. This is where we've had difficulty with some people who are sports purists and hard-core fans. Especially people in the print media. Most columnists around the country do not like sports talk radio. First of all, any sports talk show host who calls himself a journalist is a fraud. What we do is bullshit for a living."

I am sitting behind closed doors with Mike Thompson, operations manager of KXTA Sports 1150 AM and Arnie Spanier's boss. Thompson jabs at his tie and absently runs his fingers, comblike, through thinning brown hair. His head bobs and weaves when he talks as if he's a point guard preparing a move toward the hoop. He sits behind his desk, his eyes constantly monitoring a computer screen for incoming E-mails.

In the business, Mike Thompson is known as a fixer, a sports talk radio doctor. His most recent triumph was at KTCK-AM 1130, The Ticket, a previously information-oriented, buttoned-down sports talk station in Dallas. Thompson removed the straightest, least-compelling hosts, moved a jokester duo calling themselves The Hardline from midday to drive time, and instituted a frat-house, sometimes raunchy "guy talk" format. The local print media was appalled. One writer referred to the new Ticket as the "Schticket." But the audience was listening. The station's ratings instantly skyrocketed.

KXTA in Los Angeles is Mike Thompson's next challenge. He has been here for fifteen months and has found that turning this ship around, in one of the most competitive radio markets in the country, is going to take all he has. One of the recent moves he has made, a move that he believes is the first step to shoving the station into prime earshot in the L.A. market, is hiring Arnie Spanier out of Chicago. Fifteen months does not seem like a long time to perform a programming miracle, but in the do-or-die world of radio, it is a lifetime. And the clock is ticking.

"My goal is to get the most amount of people listening to this station. And I can do it with guy talk. Who says someone can't be knowledgeable, credible, *and* funny? These are the people we gravitate toward in real life. Unfortunately, some stations have gone away from personality and become more NPRish."

Thompson makes a pyramid with his fingertips.

"This is the only art form that is completely extemporane-

37

ous. These guys are on an open microphone for three or four hours straight. It is a *tough* job."

He studies his fingertip pyramid, taps his index fingers.

"Talk radio is about this moment in time. In my opinion, one of the things that bad sports talk radio does is what I call the interview circle jerk."

He lets this sink in, then busts his pyramid, scoots his chair forward.

"We should only be interviewing sports breakers. Newsmakers. Guys that are happening right now. I believe that, A, big stars don't necessarily make informative or entertaining radio. B, it makes no sense to interview somebody who has nothing to say. And C, he has to be from the A-list. A lot of hosts think they're bigger in stature because they can get, I don't know, Jim Palmer on the telephone. I get tapes and résumés from hosts who just list the people they've interviewed like that means something. That is one of the *diseases* of this format."

Thompson bounces on his chair, bangs a palm on his desk.

"If you have a great host who has a personality, this is his column of the airwaves."

"What is a great host?"

"It really is so simple. It's like when you meet someone and you say, 'Hey, I like that guy.' It's someone who is engaging, smart, has a good sense of himself, some knowledge, and can speak off-the-cuff. Frankly, sometimes it helps if they're a little nutty."

A bob of the neck, a slight head feint.

"Ultimately, what makes great sports talk radio, and great columns as well, is people. Human issues. That's why the NFL in most cities is the driving force behind sports talk radio. Because it's perfectly tailored to talk radio. You got a week between games and the most amount of players and coaches who can fuck up."

We both laugh. My laugh is shorter, more compact. Mike, a big man, a man who I think thrives on *excess,* roars. My instinct tells me that Mike Thompson works long and hard, plays harder, likes his challenges large and his drinks often. He's relaxed now. I creep toward the edge of my chair. I'm energized, feeling as if I'm sitting across from a brilliant mass com professor who loves to perform.

"A lot of people in this format misplace the use of the telephone call. Years ago, when talk radio started, there was something called a busy counter. It told you how many callers got through. In the sixties, the hot button issues were what, the death penalty, the war, abortion. Blink blink blink blink *lights.* Okay? So here are all these hosts and they see the stimuli, the lights. Hey, look at all those lights! Abortion abortion abortion, lights lights lights. Then they picked up the ratings. Whoosh. The bottom fell out."

Mike wipes his mouth with the back of his hand. I almost think he's going to order a drink right now. But he edges closer, letting me in on a secret.

"At that point they realized, wait a minute, the caller is not the listener. Less than one percent of any talk radio station's listeners actually *call.* "

Thompson points at me now as if I work for him. "When you surrender your programming to the people on the telephone, you are not hitting what's on the mind of most people. You've got to trust the host. He's got to say, here's what's happening, here's what I think. The calls simply embellish his point. They are a programming *tool.* Here's what bad talk radio, in my opinion, sounds like."

Thompson clears his throat, places a fist in front of his mouth, and assumes a character. He deepens his voice and sits ramrod straight.

"Good afternoon, everybody, and welcome to Sports Talk.

Call me up with a sports question.' Or, 'It's *Open Forum.*'"
Thompson chuckles, goes back to his professor's tenor.

"I mean, what is this question shit? Have you ever heard
Larry King say, 'Call me up with your questions about Bosnia
now?' No! People *comment.* The first thing I heard when I came
to this format was, 'Hi, I'd like to know who was in the starting
backfield of the 1955 Longhorns. I'll hang up and listen.'
That's not anything. That's the *answer* man."

Thompson's peripheral vision spots an urgent incoming
E-mail. His fingers fly over the keys in reply, his eyes still somehow locked into mine. I peek at his desktop. Piles of memos,
today's *Los Angeles Times,* a ratings book. Radio listenership is
rated on quarter hours. The key is not necessarily the number
of listeners, but who they are and how long they listen. Sports
radio boasts a core of listeners who spend among the longest
time tuned in, not touching the dial, often exceeding twenty-
three hours a week.

Mike folds his hands in his lap. A beep signals another E-mail.
Thompson ignores it.

"Sports talk is a representation of what we do in real life.
Hanging out in a sports bar. Giving our opinions. The journalists say we're not serious, we're not *journalists.* "

And now Mike Thompson leans forward and actually whispers. "No, we're not."

I pause, let the whisper echo in the room. I want to ask him
about the task at hand.

"You said one of the things that drives sports talk radio is an
NFL team. There's no team in L.A."

"I know. It's a challenge." Mike massages his forehead. "This
is the hardest form of talk radio. Anyone who is a great sports
talk radio artist could hit the ball out of the park if they went
into regular talk radio. Think about it. Pick up the paper."

He grabs the *Times,* scans the front page, and reads at random, "'Pupil Promotion.'" Thompson slaps down the paper, assumes his talk show character once more. Deep voice, military-straight back. "'Damn it all! No one is going to be promoted to the tenth grade unless they pass!' Now. Whata we got in the sports page?"

He flips to the sports section, glances through it, and mumbles, "We got the Lakers, the Kings, blah blah blah. It is harder to find *meat* here. A lot of times sports talk hosts have to make something out of nothing."

Mike Thompson is a lifer. He was born with radio blood. While still in high school, Mike had a paid radio gig, on the air, reporting news and sports on a small radio station in Philadelphia. He enrolled at Temple University and, naturally, became a communications major. At the end of his sophomore year, while studying for his communications theory final, he had a revelation. He had left a paying job, on the radio, so he could go to college and study communications in order to get a job . . . *on the radio.* He had given up what he wanted to achieve. It seemed rather backwards. He then did what he figured was the sensible thing: he quit college and went back to radio.

"I've always been fascinated by talk radio. As a kid I loved to listen to Jean Shepherd, guys like him. I did what we call DX-ing, going up and down the dial. I found Pete Franklin in Cleveland. These guys were *characters,* that's what they were. That's my challenge. Finding people like that."

Mike Thompson looks at me, shrugs. "People like Arnie."

Arnie's boss squirms in his chair, considers me, taps a forefinger lightly against his cheek. It's five o'clock, dark outside, a perfect L.A. winter day. A lifetime ago this was my time to be alone with Superfan.

Mike shakes his head. "God, I really love this format."

Thompson smiles, cooling down his motor. He is suddenly quiet, intimate, as if he is on the radio and I am his only listener.

"Radio, unlike TV, is very personal. You flip it on at home, in the car, you say, it's *my* station. TV now is desperately trying to create brand. NBC 'Must See TV.' But nobody says, 'I'm gonna go home tonight and watch NBC.' With radio though, it's 'Hey, eleven fifty, man, that's my station.' It is this way because every day you hear a new performance. And tomorrow it's wiped away and we start all over."

Mike Thompson's credo is to program what he believes the listener, called in the business the end-user, wants to hear. In this case, in his opinion, the end-user wants guy talk.

"We're *men*," he says, as if there is some doubt. "Everything that comes up in our lives is intermingled with sports. We are re-creating what happens when a bunch of guys sit down in a barroom. It's real. We don't sit down and say, 'Okay, we are now going to have the sports part of our conversation, now we're going to have the pussy part of our conversation. It's all blended. And I'm well aware"—Mike applies the finishing touch with no less than a British accent—"this is not proper sports journalism."

In the last six years, Mike Thompson has lived in New York, Atlanta, Dallas, Philadelphia, and Los Angeles. He has bypassed relationships, given up planting roots. Like a hired gun, he hits a town, cleans it up, and rides on. He is forty-six. He has no kids and no responsibilities. His life is his work; his work is his life. For fun, he listens to the radio and tries to remember, then re-create, what brought him here.

"Fuck the guests. Ultimately, the great performers can walk into a studio without a single call or single guest"—Mike Thompson claps his hands. I jump a mile—"and it's magic."

He closes his eyes for an instant, breathes in a tiny silent prayer. Then he smiles at me crookedly.

"Arnie is almost there."

• • •

Welcome to the Power Hour of the show. Arnie is wrapping it up, buzzed on diet Coke. Brian, his producer, is right there with him, keeping pace, thankful though that we're in the clubhouse turn. The control room is thick now with the smell of cheap aftershave and mozzarella cheese. The air crackles with the feeling of a football game during a rout. We're up 54–7 but we've still got a quarter to play. Bring us home, Arnie!

"Hey, Robert, what's shakin'?"

"Arnie, you stinkin' genius, you're freakin' killin' me." Words slurred, drunk as a skunk. "I'll tell you why Shaq's not a liability this year. Because Phil Jackson is a freakin' genius."

"How come Phil hasn't been able to teach him how to shoot free throws yet?"

"Arnie, you're *killin'* me. You can't teach Shaq how to shoot free throws."

"Why not?"

"Arnie, that's like trying to teach a whale how to fly."

"XTRA Sports, hello," Brian says. . . . "Yeah, okay, turn your radio off. . . . Turn it . . . *owwww.* Call me back. Ohhh, *man.*"

Brian, cringing, whips off his headset, gives me a "They don't pay me enough for this shit" look, jams the headset back over his baseball cap, and is right there on it, "XTRA Sports, hello," wanting, I think, with such a big lead to just fall on the freaking ball.

"Who is this fucking guy?"

The heavy, metal control-room door flies open as if it's made of plywood, and Mike Thompson charges in. His cheeks are flushed but he's nowhere near angry. He's grinning, his body jouncing; he wants to join the party. He points to Arnie.

"He's drunk, Arnie! Lose him!"

Thompson smooshes his mouth against the glass wall of the studio and makes a face. Arnie laughs, waves at his boss, keeps going with Robert the caller, trying to find the fun in a discussion of Shaq's free-throwing ability with a guy who's half in the bag. Thompson dances a little, then turns around, presses his ass against the window, and drops his pants. Arnie breaks up. Mike throws his head back and howls, a long, shrill hyena screech.

The show's still got fifteen minutes to go but we're heading toward the elevator. Behind us, Brian is rerunning Arnie's interview with Jack Snow, St. Louis Rams color man, so Arnie can make the UCLA-Arizona basketball game on time.

"Thompson's a great guy. I'm lucky to have him for a boss."

"Does he moon you often?"

"That was a first. And hopefully the last." A midsized Arnie laugh, more of a grunt amid a gush of air after four straight hours of hollering. We wait for the elevator to arrive. Arnie watches the numbers descend, then thinks aloud, "I think Thompson's grooming me for big things. At least that's what he says."

"He believes in you."

"I have a chance to do great here. I really do."

"Who would you put at the top, the best there is?"

"Mike and the Mad Dog," Arnie says, no hesitation. "They are everybody's number one."

The elevator doors open. We get in and we both sag against the back wall.

"But other than them, who else is there?" Arnie asks. "Rome, sure. Used to be the Sports Babe. No more. Who else? Hacksaw? I like him, but we're totally different. JT the Brick is up-and-coming. I hear he's a good guy. I mean, I say to myself, why can't I be one of the top guys in the country?"

I shrug. Why not?

The elevator doors shimmy shut, hurtling us down, fast, toward the parking structure.

III.

morning drive

EDDIE ANDELMAN:
THE GODFATHER OF SPORTS TALK

Why the hell do you want to talk to *me*?"

Boston accent thick as chowder.

"Because I think you're the guy who started sports talk radio as we know it today."

"Well," Eddie Andelman says, "that's probably true."

Boston. Thursday evening, March 2, seven o'clock.

The journey begins.

I am scrunched on a harrowing commuter flight from New York. Twelve angry men, all in suits except for me, reeking of manhattans and digital cell-phone breath, are stuffed into a rickety corridor with wings, wheels, and propellers, pretending to be a plane. Ice is caked on the windshield. I know because I'm practically in the cockpit. The pilot, thirty-something with sandy hair and a sinister smile, makes a feeble joke about the plane needing snow tires as we fishtail to a stop on the icy runway in Boston. I'm not laughing because there's something stuck in my mouth. Oh, yeah. It's my *heart*.

I also awoke this morning with the sports talk radio host's nightmare.

I have no voice.

I am able to speak only in a hoarse whisper.

I locate my suitcase and crash through the doors from baggage claim. Outside it's cold, and snow flurries dust me like dandruff. A Cadillac the size of a yacht is parked at the curb, trunk up. A woman in her fifties, blond hair, stylish, perfectly done, wearing a long winter coat, is screaming at an airport cop.

"You have not heard the end of *this!*" she promises.

The cop, overmatched, backs away.

"Looking for me?"

A short round man in a gray blazer appears. His thick hair is unruly, flying in twelve directions at once. He smiles, revealing gaps in his teeth that make him look like a little kid. The grin is warm and disarming. He wears thick glasses. He is maybe five-ten and 250. He wrestles the suitcase out of my hand.

"We've been circling for a while. I tried to park here, but there was an incident with the police—"

"Oh, no, I'm sorry," I croak.

"Not your fault," Eddie Andelman says, tossing my suitcase into his trunk. "These Boston airport cops are notorious. Judi's fuming."

I slide into the front seat and introduce myself to Judi, who sits in the back, arms folded, beyond pissed.

"Edward," she says, "you'd better talk about this on the air tomorrow."

"Oh, I intend to. You bet."

Eddie Andelman eases into traffic. The Caddy has a more intricate dash than the prop job I just got off.

"You like Chinese food?"

"Sure," I gurgle.

"Good. We're going to the best and biggest Chinese restaurant in the world."

"Sounds great," I whisper.

"And when we get home, we'll take care of that throat," Judi promises.

Eddie grins.

Kowloon in Saugus, on Route 1 just north of Boston, bills itself as "New England's Premier Oriental Dining and Entertainment Complex." Eddie maneuvers the Caddy into the parking lot. I have seen smaller parking lots at ballparks. Someone leaves and we steal the space, first row, twenty yards from the door. Eddie herds Judi and me inside. I'm assaulted by a whoosh of Popsicle colors and a concert of laughing voices, clanging cash registers, and the whir of a thousand Lazy Susans. The *first* dining room we enter is the size of center field. We are greeted by Bobby Wong, the general manager, who escorts us to Eddie's booth, right up front. Bobby hands Judi and me menus. Eddie waves his off.

"Look inside," Eddie says.

Judi shows me: *Eddie Andelman Lo Mein.* Sautéed shrimp and vegetables over soft noodles. I wonder if they can amend it to scallops instead. Judi looks interested.

"That sounds good," she says. "I'm a little tired of the Eddie with the shrimp."

Eddie orders. Bobby sits down with us.

"You've been here before," I grunt to Eddie.

He smiles. "A few times. I've known this guy since he was a baby. Right, Bobby?"

"Yeah. Used to call him Uncle Eddie."

"Biggest Chinese restaurant in the country, am I right?"

"True," Bobby admits.

Bobby leaves as the first course arrives. Eddie serves. He

has small hands and stubby fingers, hardened not by years of hard labor or catching knuckleballs but by years of lunging for the lo mein with coarsened chopsticks. We settle in. My throat is raw and the noise is throbbing, but the food is killer.

We talk a little Eddie history. How he got Barbara Borin hired in 1974, the first woman sports reporter ever in Boston. His friendships with Rick Pitino, Bob Cousy, Red Auerbach, John Havlicek, Marvin Hagler, and Pedro Martinez. His feud with some of the Boston media, reflecting the ongoing enmity between newspaper reporters and sports talk radio hosts. The truth is, Eddie Andelman has outlasted all of them. He has been on the air for over thirty years.

"A big part of this whole thing is whether or not you can withstand the critics. There have been terrible things written about me. I have thick skin. I'm fat, I wear glasses, I'm Jewish and proud of it, and I don't give a shit what they say."

He shakes his head, reaches for the lo mein with his name on it.

"These guys *claim* to be gentlemen."

I pour him and Judi some tea.

"Thanks. See, a lot of sportswriters are negative because they don't know how to be anything else. Listen, I'm proud of everything I've done. I really am."

"So many charity things," Judi says.

"Every year we do the Hot Dog Safari," Eddie says. "All the hot dogs you can eat, plus about ten other kinds of foods, kids are free, adults are ten bucks, and we do an auction, that sort of thing. The profits go to the Cystic Fibrosis Foundation. We hold it at Suffolk Downs Race Track. And next week we're going down to the Dominican Republic with Pedro Martinez. We're gonna give away a whole bunch of bats and balls to the kids down there. I saw film footage of all these little kids playing baseball with sticks and no gloves, so we're gonna give 'em at least the proper equipment to play with."

He twirls a string of lo mein with a flick of his wrist. Guy's a pro.

"You know, I've had a great career," Eddie says. "I believe you have to give back."

"He's a very generous man," agrees Judi.

Bobby comes over. "Everything all right, Eddie?"

"Great. As usual." He sneaks a credit card onto the table, sleight of hand.

"Let me get this," I protest.

"No way." Bobby whisks the credit card away.

"That's another thing," Eddie says. "I spend time with my sponsors. I make sure I go out with all my steady guys. I've had people with me for thirty years. I really care about the people I do business with. I use the products I sponsor. And I would never do an ad for a product or a service that I don't believe in. I have integrity that way."

"And when people hear that, they know he's *real,*" Judi says. "They might not like him, and plenty of people don't, but they know he's telling the truth."

In the Caddy, heading home. Home is Lynnfield, a Boston suburb of sprawling homes on multi-acred rolling lots. After the din of Kowloon, the quiet of the car is otherworldly.

"If this station could've gotten rid of me five years ago, they would've."

Eddie stares straight ahead, his hands giving the wheel a light finger massage, his mouth swirling an after-dinner mint.

"They would rather have somebody making minimum wage who would lie and say he was making a million dollars a year. It's not that I break any rules. I don't. I don't drink, do drugs, or swear. But what I know is funny, the program director is afraid to try. And that's rocking the boat."

A moment of silence. Or reflection. I can't see in the dark.

Eddie continues, "No matter what type of talk you're

doing, sports talk or regular talk, it's the same ingredients. You'll never replace hard work, you'll never replace being prepared, and you've got to be ingenious. You've got to invent things. I don't allow callers to ask me, 'What do you think?' I hang up on them. I want to know what the hell *they* think. And you know something? When someone gets critical, I let it go. I know how to milk it. Call me a fat pig, I don't give a shit."

"Do they do that?"

"Oh, sure. And different days are different callers. Friday afternoon you get a lot of salesmen. They leave early, they say, 'I'm going to Poughkeepsie on a call.' But they're really going to play golf or to the track or to a bar, and on the way they call sports talk radio."

"I've never heard it broken down like that."

"Yeah, well, I'll tell you this. Sports talk radio is only gonna last if it's entertaining. And entertaining is not doing toilet jokes."

Nothing but phantoms behind us, but Eddie clicks on his left-turn signal as he pulls into his driveway. A large two-story colonial looms over us, set in a cotton ball of snow. Eddie presses a stubby finger into the visor and the garage door opens. Eddie pulls the Caddy inside. We walk through the garage into a utility room: treadmill ("That's for Judi"), bookshelves, awards, plaques, and pictures celebrating Eddie on the walls. The basement level features another room, an office/library with a desk and more bookshelves. We go upstairs and walk into an open, cheery kitchen, which spills into a family room.

"Let's take care of that throat," Judi says.

She opens a cabinet as I peek at one of several framed family photographs. The Andelmans have three grown sons. Big, strapping, dark-haired handsome boys. Eddie beams as I look from the picture to him, back to the picture. How the hell did he get his three sons to look like Freddie Prinze Jr.?

"Here," Judi says. She offers me a small wicker basket filled with throat lozenges and sprays.

"I like these," she says, selecting one that's shaped like a tiny football. "They're from England." I take it, unwrap it, and pop it into my mouth. Tastes like Scotch. How bad can it be?

Eddie calls one of his sons, Michael, on the telephone. Eddie wears a wide smile from hello. The conversation is intimate and affectionate. Finally he says, "Wanna talk to Mom?" and passes the phone to her.

"Come on, I'll show you to your room," Eddie says.

We go up the main staircase to the second floor.

"That's our room at the end of the hall. Got the big-screen TV in there. The bathroom. And here's your room."

He swings open a door to what must have been one of the boys' rooms. Small and narrow. On the bed are several magazines and two books: *Sports Fans of the World, Unite* by Eddie Andelman and *On Three: Inside the Sports Huddle* by Herman Weiskopf.

"I thought you might want to take a look at these," Eddie says.

"Thanks, I would."

"Okay. I'm gonna go prepare for tomorrow's show. You need anything, holler. We're leaving here at eight-thirty *sharp.* Breakfast is at eight."

"I'll be there. Again, thanks."

"No problem. Good night."

He pads down the hall, goes into his bedroom, and closes the door.

Within seconds, I hear the big screen roar.

Show prep.

I stay up past midnight reading *Sports Fans of the World, Unite,* which is a book of humorous essays by Eddie about various sports-related subjects. As a writer, Eddie is unsubtle, opinionated, and uproariously funny. No surprises there. I drift off to sleep and wake up around seven. My throat is even worse.

I go downstairs at a minute after eight. Eddie and Judi are camped at the kitchen table. Eddie sips an orange juice as he studies the sports section of the *Boston Globe,* which is sprawled on the table in front of him. Judi reads the front page. *Good Morning America* hums from a television set in the family room. Occasionally, Judi glances at Diane Sawyer.

"How'd you sleep?" she asks as I come into the room.

"Fine," I croak.

"Your throat sounds worse," Eddie says.

"Yeah, it's not so great."

"Come on, eat something. There's coffee, cereal, toast, muffins."

"I feel like I'm at a wonderful New England bed-and-breakfast."

Eddie grins. "My wife." He shakes his head. "She's the best. I got lucky here, I tell you."

"You're not kidding," Judi says. "Edward, don't eat that onion bagel. Are you crazy? You know your stomach's been acting up."

"Just a cornah—"

Judi yanks the bagel away from him.

"It's true," he sighs. "My stomach's been on the blink for a few days."

"A few days. More like a week."

He rolls his eyes. Jesus, do I feel like I'm home.

"You all set there? You need anything?"

"No, I'm fine. The coffee's great."

"Look at this." Judi points to the television.

Ironically, *Good Morning America* is doing a feature about the kindness of strangers. One of their reporters, a "pregnancy pillow" stuffed under her shirt, recently rode the subways during rush hour in four cities—New York, Boston, Chicago, and San Francisco—to see how many people would get up and offer her a seat. Astonishingly, New York finished first. Boston finished last.

"I've got to talk about that," Eddie says.

"Don't forget to mention the airport police," Judi reminds him.

"I won't, dear." Another glance in my direction, then, "Come on, pal, we've got to go."

It is a perfect March day in New England, clear, crisp, and bright. Eddie drives slowly.

"I was a decent athlete in high school. But I was on the wild side. I used to cut school all the time to go to the ball games. I learned how to forge my mother's name perfectly."

We pass through Lynnfield, crawl by a series of majestic homes nestled in snow.

"I had no intention of ever being on the radio. My father was great. He was very smart. When I went to Boston University, he made me take the accounting curriculum. It was the only curriculum at the school that was tough. It was a struggle for me because I wasn't much of a student. When I got out, I decided I'd better get serious about life, so I enrolled at Northeastern night school for an MBA. Took me four years, twelve months a year. After I got my MBA, I started my own insurance company. I did really well. Then I met Judi and I got involved in real estate. I got into malls at the very beginning. In particular, I bought drive-in theaters and turned them into malls. I was actually the first one in the country to do that. I still keep my finger in that pie."

We pull onto the freeway. Eddie's on a roll.

"Around then, I started a sports radio show on a small station in Boston. At the time, there really weren't any telephone talk shows. There were sports shows, you know, where three guys sat around. They had one in Miami, couple of sportswriters were on. Eddie Pope was one. It was a good show. We had one in Boston called *The Voice of Sports* with Don Gillis. But no one took calls. We started taking calls and the thing exploded. I knew we had something good because it was a very small station and people were calling from everywhere. People I knew from high school, from college. It was unbelievable."

Morning commuter traffic heading into downtown Boston crowds us on both sides like a police escort.

"I like to get in around nine, an hour ahead of time, and go over the show with my partner, Dale Arnold. Like this morning, we have Dennis Byrd from the Jets. The paralyzed player. He's coming in live. He's promoting a charity. I keep preaching this. You've got to serve the community. At least every three, four months, you should do something."

"So . . . a lot of guests?"

"Guests are very important. You're doing a four-hour show. You don't want strictly calls. There are some days when it's okay. If there's a big baseball trade and that's all anyone wants to talk about, that's fine. But people want to talk to and listen to the athletes they root for. That's the number one thing. Another problem with these shows is they want you to believe that these guys are *inside. Let me tell you the story, I know the real story.* That kind of crap. And when they talk about contracts, it's almost funny. None of them understand front-end loading, back-end loading. All they know is, *no one's worth five million dollars a year.* I personally know people in the real estate business who make ten times, twenty times, *fifty* times a year more than that. I know lawyers in that position, businesspeople who make more than any athlete who's ever lived."

I wonder if Eddie Andelman is a businessman doing a sports talk show or a sports talk radio host with a passion for business. I steer the conversation back to sports.

"What do you think of Jimy Williams?" I ask. "Is he a good manager?"

"I thought he was a hick. I've since apologized to him because I think he's done a great job with the Red Sox. He's got over ninety wins the last two years. I think the players really like him. Basically, if I had to sum up the Red Sox managers over the last forty years, I would say ninety percent of them were outrageous drunks."

Ah. Eddie Andelman *lives.*

We drive past miles of torn-up concrete and ripped-up roadways guarded by menacing bulldozers, metal jaws dripping mud. This is the Big Dig, a fifteen-year project designed to turn Boston into, according to Eddie, "The best city in the world."

"Boston's been good to me," Eddie says quietly. "And I think I've been good to it."

"Did you grow up in a close family?"

"Not really."

Eddie Andelman blinks.

"It was a strange situation. My father never even made a living until he was fifty. And then he hit it big. He was a real estate developer. He got into warehouses. Way before his time. He really hit it good. But by then I had my own career."

We don't speak for another minute.

"I lived on my own really since I was seventeen. I left for college."

Eddie's voice cracks.

"I never came back."

"So you moved out of the house at that point?"

"Seventeen years old. I never stayed another night. Not that I didn't love my mother and father. I had the greatest mother in the world. I'd come home for, you know, supper, Friday nights . . ."

His memory trails off. Another minute of silence. I can't speak. And Eddie doesn't want to.

Eddie rolls into the studios of WEEI like a human bowling ball. Today he wears a charcoal gray sweater over a pink Brooks Brothers shirt. His hair remains a jumble, a small gray unkempt lawn. He veers into his office, three desks in a row set off in a corner. His partner, Dale Arnold, arrives a few minutes after we do. Dale is fortyish, stocky, a mop of brown hair atop an eager, friendly face. Dale does play-by-play for the Boston Bruins on a local cable channel. Eddie and Dale begin talking about today's show in hushed voices as if they're spies.

"After Byrd, I think we should talk about Pitino," Eddie suggests.

"I agree," Dale says. His voice is high-pitched with just a hint of Maine. "Then we'll have the Football Chicks come in."

"Yeah, we're packed," Eddie says.

Eddie excuses himself while he and Dale record a spot for their show. I sit at Eddie's desk, sip a Styrofoam cup of Lipton. I tune in to the commotion around me—violent laughter billowing from a tall earringed string bean balancing an armload of tapes; the scraping of metal chairs on hardwood floors; the whap whap whap of running shoes spanking down the hall; the smell of cologne and three-day-old coffee.

Eddie and Dale return. Dale heads into the lobby where Dennis Byrd waits with a couple of his former teammates. Eddie taps his fingers on his desk.

"I'm gonna call Pitino," he says, punching the phone.

It's been a rough week for the Celtics coach. After losing a heartbreaker to the Raptors on a last-second Vince Carter shot, Pitino apparently exploded, cursed at a ten-year-old fan, and stormed off the court. The Boston media, smelling a deliciously

bloody story, descended on him like a school of ravenous pira-
nha. Eddie, alone, has remained staunch in his support.

"It's unfair. He's under a lot of pressure. *Jeff?* Eddie. . . .
Okay, you? . . . Listen, I want to see if he'll come on the show.
I'm fighting here alone. If he could do ten or fifteen
minutes . . . you know how I feel. I really like him. . . . All right,
well, we'll be on until two o'clock. And I'm not out to do a
hatchet job, you know that. Awright? . . . These things go away.
Tell him I said to keep his pecker up."

He pauses, grins.

"Yeah, I do. Here's the good thing about it. I went to a
hockey game the other night, the first time in eleven years. You
wanna know something? I'm back to basketball. What a *joke.*
Anyway . . . I really would like to have him on for a little while.
Because I think he should clarify some things. . . . I know, I
know. These people with that *he told my kids to drop dead* type of
shit they're saying on the station. It's irresponsible. It's the
Howard Stern type of mentality that's rampant everywhere. . . .
Yeah. It's fucking unbelievable. They had him beating little kids
yesterday. Anyway . . . it was a tough game. So I would certainly
like to have him on. It would be good for me and it would be
good for him. What could be better than that? . . . You got the
inside number, don'tcha? . . . Good. Thanks, Jeff."

Eddie gently hangs up the phone.

"Do you think Pitino will call?"

"Oh, yuh. He knows I can be tough, but at the same time he
knows I'm not there to hang him. Rick Pitino happens to be
one of the terrific people in sports. I've known him twenty
years. I was at his son's funeral. There is no way Rick Pitino
would tell a kid to drop dead. Or call a kid a little asshole.
There's just no way it would ever happen. I'd bet my life on it.
He's too smart and he loves kids too much. Never *ever* happen."

He lowers his voice to a whisper.

"Certain hosts say things just for shock value. Because they know they can get away with it. It's partly because the FCC doesn't have the power it once had. Nobody pays attention to them anymore. Stations do what they want. We had a meeting here and we were told, *'Pissed off* is a good word. It's a guy buzzword.' If that's the extent of your contribution to the program . . ."

Eddie massages his forehead and absently musses his hair. That explains the look.

"I'll tell you right now—"

Voice even lower.

"The demise of sports radio as we now know it will happen because it's not creative or interesting enough."

He bends his head upward toward the wall clock.

"It's time to go in."

Music up.

Sister Sledge wanna-be wailing *I'll tell you* over and over to a techno-soul-dance beat. A familiar sports talk announcer's voice intros on tape, *"The* A Team *with Dale Arnold and Eddie Andelman!"*

"Here we go, here we go, here we *go,"* the producer sings.

"Sports radio eight fifty, WEEI," the announcer booms.

I'll tell you I'll tell you I'll tell youuuuuu.

"It's a little tough for people in the heart of Patriots country to sit in a room with so many former New York *Jets,* but it is for a good cause," Dale says. "We don't normally start with guests right at the top, but there is a *spectacular* event going on tonight here in Boston . . ."

Dale proceeds to describe the charity event and introduces Dennis Byrd, who sits in his wheelchair next to Dale, then introduces three other players in the studio.

Finally Eddie speaks. "Dennis, I would have to say that

you're a favorite among sports fans for many reasons. Even though you were once a despised Jet, the fact that you've come back, and what you've done, everybody is impressed. You've got a lot of character."

Eddie and Dale then plug the event, occasionally popping in a football question about what it was like to play for Bill Parcells, and the Jets chances for the coming year. At the end of the segment, off the air, Eddie thanks Dennis Byrd and the other former Jets for coming, praises their commitment to charity work, then reaches into his pocket and hands Dennis a hundred-dollar bill.

"A small donation," Eddie says quietly. "I happen to believe in what you're doing."

Dennis is stunned by both the gesture and the fact that Eddie's donation is given off the air. The talk show host had the perfect opportunity to grandstand and he chose not to. The Jets leave and Eddie waves me into the studio, a small, tight space. Eddie sits in the center of the room, hands folded on the console in front of him like a Jewish Buddha. Dale is sprawled out, a tangle of nerve endings in search of comfort, coiled, absently twirling the microphone cable. Eddie is reserved, calm, radar up, sweeping the landscape for smart, tough opinions and sharp one-liners.

Back after the break, Eddie and Dale fall into an argument about the status of Boston Bruins defenseman Ray Bourque, a fixture on the team for twenty-one years. Bourque is rumored to be gone by the afternoon, headed to Philadelphia, the result of a trade that he himself has requested. Dale is certain that the loss of Bourque will have an adverse impact on the Bruins ticket sales.

"A businessman knows full well if Ray Bourque asks to be traded out of here, it's going to affect ticket sales, concession sales—"

"Dale," Eddie says, "Ray Bourque is like a John Havlicek. They don't sell tickets."

"I disagree with you."

"Great boxers don't sell tickets. It's the thugs, the bums, the knockout artists. That's who sells tickets. Not a gentleman athlete like Bourque."

Dale Arnold backs down, disarmed by Eddie's embrace of Bourque. The conversation segues from the Bruins to the Celtics and the plight of Rick Pitino. Now the soul of Eddie Andelman comes hurtling forward.

"I really feel for Rick Pitino. He has fallen into a situation that is impossible to cure. I think he knows that now. I think he feels great guilt over the money he's getting. It's the first failure of his life. But I truly believe, Dale, that they *can* rebuild. They have to accept three years where they're terrible—"

"You've changed your tune in that regard, though—"

"Well, I've been *hoping*. I've been hoping like everybody else."

Eddie stops for just a tick, then with his thick, chowder-soaked South Boston drawl dripping with a passion that *grips* you, he says, "See, I will never turn away from being a Celtic fan. Never. They've won more than everybody else put together in this town. I have great memories. I've met so many people whom I truly admire. Havlicek, Cowens, Auerbach. I'll never change. Because I know, in my heart, that they will raise championship banners here again."

"I don't see it," Dale says. "Not in the foreseeable future. Rick Pitino thought he could come in, redo it a little, tweak here, pull there, and in a couple of years he'd be playing for the championship. He didn't realize he had to start at the bottom."

"Well, the Lakers did not go to the bottom. They had sharp management—"

"Ah. So the Celtics don't have sharp management."

"If you had to give them a report card, you'd have to give the Lakers an A and the Celtics an F. But what are we supposed to do? Do we cut off Rick Pitino's fingers? Do we force him to humiliate himself publicly? Do we stone him?"

Dale, angry, says, "You know, Eddie, your Celtics bias shows here—"

"I admit it—"

"My point is, if it was Red Sox management that failed, you'd want them gone. You'd want them *fired.*"

We're off and running. For the next five minutes, Eddie and Dale go at it like two brawlers in a downtown bar.

The argument peaks.

"They're still working from handicaps," Eddie shouts. "They're still working from the death of two players—"

"Oh, come on, the death of Len Bias is not affecting *this* team *now.*"

"Except you don't know who Len Bias might have been traded for. You don't know what would have happened, Dale. This is like *It's a Wonderful Life* with James Stewart."

"Oh, please—"

"Dale, if you think I have Celtics bias, you're right up there and maybe even a nose ahead with the Bruins."

Music up. We go to a break. Eddie and Dale remain frozen in tableau, Eddie sitting statue-still, hands folded, Dale slowly twirling the microphone cable like a lasso.

"That's our big argument," Eddie says eventually. "Basketball and hockey."

Dale smiles, looks off, but he doesn't really look angry.

"Was that staged?" I grunt.

"Well, no, we both believe in our positions," Eddie says. "But put it to you this way. Right now they think two guys arguing is the secret to success."

On *they* Eddie jerks his head in the direction of the hallway.

"It's so ridiculous," Dale mutters.

"But was that real?"

"Look, I've been a Celtic fan all my life. Dale's dream job since he was a kid was to do play-by-play for the Bruins."

Back to the tableau. But just for another moment.

"Hey," Dale says, "I liked our interview with Terry Funk yesterday. He really was neat, wasn't he? What a nice man."

"Yuh," Eddie says, then turns to me. "The other thing now is that you can get faxes and E-mail. It's great. You don't always get the same moronic callers. People tend to say more in faxes and E-mails."

Back for the first segment of calls. All four lines are lit. The first caller, Bruce on a car phone, attempts to break down the salary cap and contract structure in the NBA and NHL. Dale, thumb resting on the caller eject switch, listens intently and engages Bruce in conversation. Eddie is noticeably silent. Finally, he gives me a look, shrugs, and says, "All right. I don't understand a word you said, but I'll go along with you."

I laugh. Dale smiles and picks up another call, Brian from Quincy, who wants to discuss John Rocker. Actually Brian from Quincy wants to *defend* John Rocker.

Wrapping up his one-minute rant, Brian from Quincy says, "I love New York City to death, but John Rocker was totally right—"

"Was John Rocker totally right when he came on yesterday to apologize? Was he totally right then? You *bigot.*"

Click. He's gone.

"We're on a roll already, aren't we?" Dale says.

"Yuh," Eddie says. "Two for two."

Dale reads a commercial. Eddie purses his lips. "We've had as much bad news in sports the last two years as we've had in the last *twenty*. It just seems like bad news is happening every single day."

He grimaces stoically and doesn't move a muscle.

●　　●　　●

Eddie Andelman is a typical Boston sports fan, which means he takes every win and loss personally. A win by the Celtics or Sox puts Eddie in a good mood for the day; a loss makes him downright ornery. A string of losses has him begging on the air for an end to the misery.

"But what would you *do?*" Eddie asks Tommy from Quincy, who's called up to complain about the Celts. "Let's say you were the owner of the Celtics, what would you *do?*"

"I don't know," Tommy admits sadly.

"See, nobody has a solution. That's what's so *frustrating.*"

Eddie sighs deeply. All of greater Boston feels his pain.

"Have to lighten things up," Eddie concludes an hour into the show.

"The callers are so emotional about their teams," I say.

"Yuh. They're so used to having the Celtics and Bruins be contenders that this is truly painful for them. And for *me.*"

Dale is about to pop in another call.

Eddie waves a stubby finger at him. "Before we get on with the calls . . . has anyone had to pick someone up at the airport in the last six months? I would now rate Boston's Logan Airport as the worst airport in *history.* It is so dumb there and stupid. It's a wonder any tourist comes here. If you want to come to Boston, you better come by train."

Eddie winks at me.

"Eddie has edge."

So says Jason Wolfe, the program director of WEEI.

"The secret to his success is that he is first and foremost very entertaining. And second, he attracts more than just your average sports guy. Which you have to do to be successful."

Jason is in his early thirties, welcoming, and steady. He occupies a large corner office with a great view. The furniture is solid but not showy, a lot, I figure, like him.

"It's that edge," Jason repeats. "It's such a factor. People either love him or hate him. We just did a research project here and they asked this question for each of the shows: 'What do you like best about the show and what do you like least?' Eddie was the number one answer for both. Best and worst. But that's great because even though half the people said he's the worst thing about the show, they *listen*. They're not going away. You have to listen because you want to hear what he's going to say. In that way, he's kind of like Howard Stern."

Lunch arrives, takeout from a local taco place. Eddie ruffles through a grease-soaked wrapper and offers me a mushy brown thing. A *Boston* taco? I pass. Eddie's with me. Grumbling, he forages around the control room, a bear in a Brooks Brothers shirt, in search of edible tree bark.

Dale, oblivious to any of this, plops a couple of chicken tacos down in front of him and digs in.

"How long have you two been a team?"

"Four and a half years, I guess," thinks Dale. "Didn't they stick us together, what, four and a half years ago, Eddie?"

"And it's the happiest four and a half years of your life?"

"God, no, the show would suck if that were true. Who would want to listen to *that*? We'd be like Ozzie and Harriet in there."

Dale pauses, takes a bite of the questionable chicken. He winces, dabs at the corner of his mouth with a soggy napkin.

"The difference is, we know it's a *show*. I think half the people listening don't understand that. What you hear is real. We honestly disagree about things. But we don't take it personally. I'm not calling his house at night saying, 'Goddammit, how could you say that?'"

"Do you guys hang out?"

"Sure. We actually have dinner together once in a while."

Dale plows through the tacos in front of him like he's just coming off a fast.

More calls, chugging toward the final hour.

"Mark on a car phone. You're next up on the *A Team,*" Dale announces.

Mark whines about the Celtics, refers to Pitino as a captain going down with his ship.

"Speaking of captains going down with their ship," Eddie says, "I saw the movie *Titanic.* Those were the stupidest violinists in the world. To be sitting there playing music and not jumping ship? Boy, were they stupid. Usually violinists are pretty clever. Mark, let me ask you a question. Who was the greatest violinist ever to play professional sports?"

Dale grins, and I rasp out a laugh.

"They're just not getting it done," Mark on a car phone moans. "It's a breakdown of fundamentals—"

"Have you noticed they haven't scored as many points as the opposition?"

"I'm not sure *what* it is—"

Click. Mark's gone.

"Trying to lighten it up a little bit," Eddie explains.

"Derrick from Newton," Dale says. "You're on the *A Team.*"

"The problem with the Celtics and Bruins is simple. It's *both* coaches," Derrick says.

"How about if we switched them?" suggests Eddie. "Let Pitino coach the Bruins."

"Can he skate?" Dale wonders.

"You don't have to skate to be a coach."

"Oh, sure, you do."

"You do? Huh. I never realized that. You know, there's also the wardrobe and hair factor. Rick dresses really sharp—"

Dale rolls his eyes, the caller presses on, and I choke with laughter.

• • •

"You can't just know sports," Eddie says during the next pause. Eddie's eating a banana from home. Dale's carving up an enchilada.

"You've got to be a little more well-rounded," Dale agrees. "A little more well-read."

"Definitely," Eddie says. "In talk radio, I'd want to know, do people read? Are you literate? But, ah, they don't care. You know why? Because they're not educated themselves. Howard Stern went to Emerson—"

"He went to B.U., too," Dale says.

"Well, all right, but . . . Dale, you just dropped something on your shirt."

"I know. I saw it." With his thumb, Dale scrubs a small red blotch beneath his shirt pocket. "I already tried to get it off and failed."

"Well, put some water on it *now.*" Eddie's tone is concerned and fatherly.

"I'll go home and change it anyway," Dale mumbles, but he dashes into the control room, stretching his shirt like a tarp.

"Anyway, Stern used to come up to my show, years and years ago. Skinny kid with an Afro. He can't really expand at all. He's got the perfect job and the perfect audience—"

Music up, Dale hustles back in, a large *wet* blotch beneath his left pocket now—an odd look, like he's lactating.

"Heads up," Dale warns.

The team clamps their headsets into place, heading for home.

Andy on a car phone tries to explain the fans' frustrations with Rick Pitino.

"The thing is, he promised that we'd be in the playoffs. Now everyone has an expectation—"

Eddie interrupts, "I would hate like hell to think that any coach or manager would say, 'We don't have a chance of making the playoffs.'"

"Of course he wouldn't," Dale says, his voice rising. "But why would you say we're going to be a playoff team this year unless you know you are? You don't promise what you can't deliver, that's all."

"What if a guy says, 'This car was owned by a little old lady and only driven eleven hundred miles.' It's really caveat emptor," Eddie says.

"No, it's a lie."

"Oh, stop it."

Andy on the car phone tries to cut in. "When they got rid of David Wesley—"

"I want to pick Dale up on this," Eddie says.

"Wait a minute!" Dale shouts. "If a guy lies to you about a car, it's a lie! It's not caveat emptor. It's a *lie!*"

"Let me ask you a question, Dale. Can you recognize the difference between a sports fib, salesman's puff, and a lie? Because if not, then just call Rick Pitino a liar."

"I really think—" tries Andy on a car phone.

"I will give you a thousand examples out of the sports pages that is salesman's puff. You can't say because he's using a strategy that he's a liar. You can't say that, Dale," Eddie says.

"I don't think I called him a liar. *You* tried to get me to call him a liar."

"No, Dale, you *said*—"

"I said, a lie is a lie—"

"It's *not.*"

"Wait a minute. You walk into a parking lot to buy a car and the car dealer lies to you and says some little old lady drove this, it's not a lie? It's caveat emptor? Explain that to me!"

"The law explains it very carefully—"

"It's a *lie.*"

"No. It's salesman's puff."

"No, it's *not,* Eddie—"

Eddie chuckles and literally throws up his hands.

"Look at some of these games the Celtics have lost," Andy on a car phone says, undeterred, doing his own show. "Chicago, Atlanta, the *Clippers*—"

Dale sits across from Eddie, arms folded, red-faced, frustrated. I'm not sure he's even listening.

And I doubt they'll be going out to dinner tonight.

After the show, Eddie insists on driving me to the airport.

"Dale actually seems like a nice guy," I say.

"Oh, he is a nice guy," Eddie says. "I only go so far with him. Sometimes he's a goody-two-shoes and I'm the mean bastard. But we take on different roles. If I do a show by myself, it's a different kind of show. You've got to mix it up."

He pauses, sucks on a lozenge. "Next week I'm gonna do a whole thing on jelly."

I'm not sure I've heard him right. "Did you say *jelly?*"

"Yuh. You know how you go into a restaurant and they have those little packets of jelly? There's apple jelly, grape jelly, honey jelly. Who the fuck eats them? Everybody likes *strawberry* and they're always out of it."

"You know, you're right."

"I know it. I'm going to make a big thing out of that. Who manufactures this stuff? I might even call Smucker's or whoever and ask why they even make honey jelly."

"I actually think grape is the worst."

He grins. And I smile back.

A discussion of little plastic packets of jelly.

Now that's sports talk.

IV.

line one

THE SMELL OF BASEBALLS

Who listens?

And who calls?

Based on the wave of commercials you hear for speed-reading courses, herbal weight-reducing supplements, creams preventing hair loss, and penile-enlargement procedures, the typical sports-talk radio listener is a dumb fat bald guy with a small penis.

Richard G. is an investment banker. He is not dumb, fat or bald, and I have no knowledge of his genitalia. I do know that his mother taught elementary school in Manhattan and his father was a New York beat cop. Richard is now in his late forties and lives in Santa Monica, California. He has a great sense of humor, a nice bunch of friends (I'm one), and is the guy you call when you need something lifted or repaired. Richard can't sit still. He always needs a project; he'd much rather spend a Sunday cleaning out the garage than taking a nap. He is, by all accounts, a normal guy, someone you've met at the gym or at the school holiday sing. The guy right over there in the nice suit, the one who drives the classic 320i black Beemer, the man with the glasses and the big, breathy laugh.

What even his close friends don't know is that Richard is not only a devoted listener to sports talk radio, he is also a caller. He has called *Dodger Talk* and several of the hosts on KXTA in L.A. He has also phoned the *Jungle* and run *smack* with Jim Rome.

Super Bowl Sunday. Richard and I sit at his round, antique oak table in the sunny kitchen of his sprawling Spanish house. We are surrounded by kids' art taped to the walls. Our coffee cups stick to place mats also made by his kids. The kitchen smells of lemon.

"Why do you listen to sports talk radio?"

He shrugs. "Because I'm in the car," then he adds quickly, "I also listen to classical music."

"Come on. You listen to a *lot* of sports talk."

It's like I caught him stealing.

"Okay, yes, I listen to a lot of sports talk."

"Is it what you go to first?"

"Yes. I typically go there first."

"And if you're not happy with what show's on, do you switch around?"

"Constantly. Between three stations. I'd say these days my favorite is Jim Rome. Second place would be Hacksaw."

"Let's talk about Hacksaw since Rome won't see me."

"Why not?"

"I don't know. His agent asked me how this book would help his career."

"Really? That is lame."

"I thought so. So Hacksaw?"

"Hacksaw has good information. He's also a caricature. He's funny to listen to. He doesn't try to be funny, but he comes off funny."

I hadn't realized before that Richard has a deep resonant broadcaster's voice. In sports talk jargon, he's easy to listen to.

"No guy talk for you."

"No. Only hard-core sports."

"Do you listen other than in the car?"

A mischievous smile. "Occasionally I sneak it at work."

"At work, too, huh? So how much time each day do you listen to sports talk?"

"No more than an hour a day. Tops."

"What if these guys aren't on? You still listen?"

"Oh, yeah. I listen to shitty guys, too. I tune in on the weekends as well, even though my favorites aren't on, to get scores and updates. And at night, when I'm working at my desk, I have my radio tuned to sports talk."

"I think it's more than an hour a day."

"It could be." He blows out a laugh.

"An hour a day," I say. "You are so busted."

"Okay, okay, I admit it."

"It's a small vice, Rich. It's not like you go to work wearing your wife's underwear."

He loses it. He's laughing so hard he has to stand up to catch his breath.

"Okay. So."

We're calm. Back to business.

"How did you get started listening?"

"I do a lot of driving in my job. I was hopping around stations and I started listening to Joe McDonnell and his partner. Very bitter guys. I didn't like them but for some reason I kept listening."

"Do you ever listen to Arnie?"

"Occasionally. When there's nothing else on. I find his voice annoying."

"When you go back to New York, do you listen to Mike and the Mad Dog?"

"Sure."

"So, no more music. No more NPR. Only sports talk. Any straight radio talk? Imus, Howard Stern . . . ?"

"Dr. Laura? Nope. None of them. I tried Howard Stern. Didn't like him."

"Okay. Now . . ." I feel like a lawyer trying to bleed out a confession. "You are not only a listener, you are also a caller."

"Well . . ." Richard shifts noisily in his antique oak chair. "I have called."

"You remember the first call?"

"I started with postgames. First the Dodgers. Then the Lakers. I called Stu Lantz. Then I made my first call to Rome."

"Why did you call?"

Richard rubs his chin, remembers. "It was just a fun thing to do. You always think that you can feasibly be in the running for the Huge Call of the Day. I felt I could do better than any of those other clowns who were on."

"Was there something you were dying to say on the air?"

"No. I forced myself to think of something. Like on Rome, I knew he gets very few tennis calls, so I thought I could get in with a tennis take. My first call was about Pete Sampras in the U.S. Open."

"Did you write it down?"

He is offended. "No."

"You can tell the truth."

"I didn't write it down."

"Okay, all right. How long did you wait on hold?"

"Only about twenty minutes. I called on a cell phone. See, car phones go to the front of the line. So I would just call from my cell phone and say I was in the car. I'd be here hanging out."

"Did he rack you?"

"No. I think I was a little too nervous. But he didn't hang up on me so I consider the call a huge success."

"What about your other calls? Did you vary it, talk about different subjects?"

"Oh, yeah. I remember talking once about Bucky Dent smelling baseballs."

"*What?*"

"I forget the details exactly, but it was quite the topic of conversation on the sports talk circuit."

"Nice. And again you waited on hold only for about twenty minutes?"

"Oh, no. A few times I probably waited on hold for over an hour. But you're listening to the show so it's productive time."

Now we both laugh.

"Rome isn't taking many callers now," Richard says finally. "He's absolutely correct. It's a lot better when he doesn't have callers. There is just a handful who are any good. Sometimes I think about calling Hacksaw. Particularly when my son is in the car. I want to break him in. Have the next generation enjoy the experience."

I ask if he agrees with Mike Thompson, who says the listeners are not representative of the callers.

"Oh, absolutely. The listeners *have* to be more intelligent than the callers. These people will call a show and say, 'How do you think the Giants are going to do this year?' That's not a question. They just want to hear themselves on the radio."

"Other than Rome and Hacksaw, do you think these hosts are any good? Or are they schmucks with microphones."

"Schmucks with microphones. Definitely."

"What's the number one thing you want to know about these guys?"

"What they look like."

"Okay. Tell me what you think Hacksaw looks like."

"My guess is that Hacksaw is a relatively short guy. Clearly he wears a toupee. He's about five six. Kind of short and stocky. And very hairy."

"Why do you say he wears a toupee?"

"Because it sounds like he wears a toupee. Actually, the other hosts joke about it. One of those guys says he has a lot of black hair all over his body."

"Age?"

"He's gotta be in his midfifties."

"Facial hair?"

"None. Clean-shaven."

"Glasses?"

"No glasses. Apparently wears Bermuda shorts, black socks and shoes. Nerdy."

"What about Arnie?"

"I would say Arnie is in his late fifties. Thin build. Wiry. Very high energy."

"Papa Joe?"

"Papa Joe's gotta be the fattest guy on the air. That's what he sounds like. He's a lunk. Fifties. I think they're all in their fifties. Maybe Papa Joe is in his seventies."

"Okay. You're pretty much all wrong."

"I know I'd get Rome right because I've seen him on TV."

"Let me ask you the big question."

"What?"

"Do you ever fantasize about doing a talk show."

"I would love to do a talk show."

"I think you'd be good at it."

"I have a lousy voice."

"You have a great voice. You have a *radio* voice. Some of these guys don't have good voices at all."

He considers this. "Peter Brown has a great voice. I hate Papa Joe's voice. And I can't stand Arnie. I'd like to stab him a million times."

"Is it him or his voice?"

"His voice. It's terrible. Also he's whiny. He's your classic New York whiner. I grew up next to that guy."

Richard starts drumming his fingers on the table. This is my signal. He's getting antsy. Gotta wrap it up so he can change the oil in his car or caulk his bathroom.

"Do you think sports talk radio is a fad?"

"No, unfortunately, I think it's here forever."

"What about XTRA Sports in L.A.? Arnie Spanier's station."

"I hate that station. It's awful."

"If you were Mike Thompson, operations manager, what would you do to turn it around?"

He thinks for a moment.

"I'd blow it up and change to popular music."

V.

midday

MIKE NORTH:
MONSTER OF THE MIDDAY

hey, buddy, it's Mike North. Sorry I missed you. I've been in England, doing my show. So when you wanna hook up?"

"I can't do it, Mike. My plane leaves first thing in the morning. I don't want to change it because of the blizzard that's coming in."

"Okay, listen to me." Pause. *"You cannot do a book about sports talk radio and not put me in it.* It's that simple. Not only am I maybe the biggest guy in the business, but I have the best story. Bar none."

"But the blizzard," I say weakly. "It's supposed to be the Perfect Storm with snow."

"You won't be sorry," Mike North promises.

I call the airline and change my flight.

Mike and BeBe North live in Park Ridge, a suburb of Chicago made up of a cozy downtown filled with weatherworn brick buildings and a residential area tucked under shady trees lined up like a thousand green, leafy umbrellas. My cab pulls up in front of a huge corner Tudor. My kind of house.

Mike North and his dog, a black Lab mix with a bandaged back leg, greet me. Mike is six feet or so, stocky and athletic, and is a dead ringer for the actor Robert Wuhl on TV's *Arli$$*. He pumps my hand while his dog clumsily tries to jump up on me. Giving up, she herds me into the Norths' kitchen.

Wolfgang Puck couldn't have a better kitchen. The main feature is a smooth, black-and-brown-speckled granite center island so shiny you could shave in it. BeBe, Mike's wife, rushes toward me and grips my hand. She is thin with sharp features, black hair the color of an eight ball, and a smile that can light up the night. The dog barks, kind of a half-assed bark really, and plants a paw on my knee.

"Aw," BeBe says, her eyes filling up.

"That's Licorice," Mike says, introducing the dog. "She just had surgery."

"Aw," I say, and bend down and pat her.

Mike points to a leather couch in the den just off the kitchen, and BeBe joins us with a tray of bagels, buns, sweet rolls, and a pot of coffee.

"Thanks for comin'," Mike says.

He sinks into the couch. He wears socks, no shoes, and plants his legs on the coffee table.

"So," Mike says.

He takes a swig of coffee and tosses himself back into his couch. He runs a palm across the top of his head and smiles. He is wide-eyed, kidlike, and reveals a matching pair of dimples. Licorice wiggles her ass like a cat.

"No, Licorice, don't jump on the—"

"Couch," I say, but it's too late. The dog snuggles into her spot and gives me a look of sheer misery.

"She's not supposed to jump," BeBe says.

"Yeah, but try and stop her," Mike says. "Poor thing." He ruffles the hair on the back of her neck. Licorice scrunches her jaw. Her eyelids start to droop shut.

My educated guess is that Mike and BeBe don't have kids.

Click.

Mike North lands his coffee cup in the center of his saucer.

"I started out as a hot dog vendor. Did it for sixteen years. In 1989 I had three hot dog stands in Chicago. I always wanted to be in radio. I used to listen to the sports in this town and I thought it was so *vanilla*. I was thirty-seven. These two guys used to come in to eat. They were the manager and general manager of a rock station. They told me about a station that leased time. WSBC. They had a wattage of like two hundred. I rented time there for two years. I paid two hundred bucks an hour, plus a hundred for a producer. What I did was, I sold advertising each week to the people who came into my hot dog stand. A guy from General Electric, a guy from AAMCO auto parts, a guy from Vienna Beef, a guy from a wrecking company. I made seven hundred bucks each week. I said, this is nice, I can do this forever. To make a long story short, somebody from WLS heard me. Guy drivin' home was flippin' around the dial. I used to tape the show eight in the morning on Saturday, then go to the hot dog stand. The show would be played at eight at night. I handicapped the football. LS needed a guy to fill in for a week. They called me. I hosted one week—"

He stops on a dime. Whips his head around to the kitchen.

"Bee, was it one week or one day?"

"On LS? One *day.*"

"That's right. St. Patrick's Day. No calls or nothin'. So I did three hours of just talkin'. I was givin' out volleyball scores, lawn bowling, anything." He takes a sip of coffee. "They never called me again."

North's got a Chicago street guy's twang and a comedian's timing.

"I can't really blame 'em. Then the rock station I was tellin' you about? I find out the owner was thinkin' of makin' it a country-music station or a cool-jazz station. I told 'em one day at the hot dog stand, you guys should start a sports station. I go, 'Denver's got 'em, Kansas City, Los Angeles, New York. They all got 'em except Chicago. You'll make a mint.'

"'Ah, nah, we don't think so.'

"I go, 'Come *onnn.*' 'Cause I figure, if they do that, they owe me at least a tryout. September comes around, I hear they're startin' a sports station. I have all my tapes from all my shows that I've done. I sent in my tape. Three hundred other people tried out. They were lookin' for a street kid, you know, a natural guy. They had all the other hires. They called me. I went for three, four interviews, then, from there, they put me on the radio. They put me on with Dan Jiggetts, a former Bear. Harvard guy. They said, 'You're only gettin' six months.'

"I said, 'Fine.'"

Another sip of coffee. Another pause.

"After six months, they come to me and they wanna talk. I was gettin' like"—a shrug, like he's brushing away a mosquito with his shoulders—"I don't know, forty-five thousand at the time. They gave me a thirty-thousand-dollar raise. Not bad after six months. I figure, hey, you know? They give me a new contract and they put in the deal that no station in Chicago could compete."

A lean back into the leather fold of his couch. A sly smile. Not mean, not smug. *Satisfied.*

"What they didn't know was two years later Mark Chernoff from WFAN in New York was coming through Chicago on some business trip or somethin'. He said he wanted to meet me at the O'Hare Hilton. I thought the guy was BSin' me. Well, I met him. He offered me and Jiggetts a far, *far* more substantial contract to take over for Mike Lupica and Len Berman. I had to go back to my station, the Score, and tell 'em. They never dreamt that somebody from out of town would want us. They *never* dreamt that. My station here had to meet the FAN's money. It was all starting to snowball for me. Now, eight, nine years later, here I am, solo on the radio, living in my dream house. Finish your coffee, I'll show you around and stuff."

"This house is unbelievable."

"Yeah, thanks. We lived in a four-room apartment for the first ten years of our marriage, then we moved to a town house. I always wanted to live in these suburbs. When I was kid, I used to ride my bike through here, thinking, you know, someday. I'm from the North Side of Chicago. A real poor area. As a kid, I used to deliver all the newspapers. Now I found myself on the front page. And in the sports pages. I've had like over a thousand articles written on me. Big ones, little ones. It's amazing. The beautiful thing about it is that I grew up here. I was born here. See, the other thing is, I dropped out of high school."

"Wow," I manage.

"Yeah. Dropped out my sophomore year. I did not like school. My dad was real strict. A hard-drinkin' Irishman. He passed away. My mom is a beautiful, petite Italian woman. So it was an Italian-Irish household. It was a tough house. But I helped make it tough because I didn't go to school. . . . I wasn't a criminal or anything but I . . ."

His voice trails off. He circles his fingers around his coffee cup.

"After I quit school, I bounced around for three or four months, just hangin' out. Then my uncles got me a job workin' with the city."

"What kind of job?"

"Pickin' up paper and rakin' up fish on Lake Michigan."

Mike's voice softens and slows and cracks.

"I had a dose of reality then. I'd see people I knew walkin' down the street and I'd hide. I was ashamed of the job I had. Then I got drafted. They made me an MP. I was supposed to go to Nam in three weeks. But I got a break. Nixon put the freeze on. That was in '72. What was good was I got my GED. From there, I came back out and went to Truman Junior College. I played basketball for them. I didn't like it. Lasted about a year. Then I went to acting school at the St. Nicholas Theatre Company."

"Mamet," I say.

"That's right. I wanted to be the next Steve McQueen. The army paid for that, too. Two guys who were in my class, two guys who became my friends, were Joe Mantegna and William H. Macy. Lemme tell you, the criticism in acting is, oh my God—"

"Worse than in sports?"

A wave of the head. "Thirty times worse. I couldn't do nothin' right. None of us could. But the guys who stuck it out made it. I did it for a year. I was just *lookin'*, ya know? All these things helped. Performing in front of an audience. I perform in front of an audience every day. Selling, being in the hot dog business. The same guys would come in every day and we'd argue sports. To this day, I handle my callers the way I handled my customers.

"'Aw, you don't know what you're talkin' about, Jim. I'm tellin' you, Maddux is gonna be good.'

"'You're crazy, buh-ba-ba.'

"'Okay, we'll see. Here's your beef. Have a great day, take care of yourself, I'll see ya tomorrow.' That's how I leave all my callers. I don't leave bitter. We never left bitter. Because you wanted the customer to come back."

Get the customer to come back. The key to sports talk.

"Hey, Bee, bring the dog some water. She's crying."

"Ohhh," BeBe says, and fills a metal water bowl.

Mike lowers his face, goes nose to nose with Licorice. "What are you crying about?"

"What's the matter, Licorice?" I ask in her face.

She gives me a look that says, *My leg is killing me, forget the water, I need morphine and get outta my face.*

"Here, baby," BeBe says, laying the water at Licorce's feet. The dog regards it skeptically, looks up at BeBe, then, I think to make her happy, laps at the water a few times.

"You ever pinch yourself?"

"Every day," Mike says. "I was just in London doing my show. I never thought I'd get out of Chicago to do *anything.* I've been all over. I pinch myself every day. Like my dad. He never saw this house. He would've loved this house. I have everything I ever wanted."

"Plus you're doing what everybody who loves sports would kill to do. Talk sports for a living."

"I either wanted to play second base for the Sox—because Nellie Fox was my idol—or play wide receiver for the Bears. I *love* the Bears. But doing this? It's unbelievable. I mean, I'm the number one sports guy in Chicago. And I came from nowhere to get there. The ratings speak for themselves. I've had the highest numbers almost the whole time I've been here."

"What's your secret?"

"My philosophy on sports radio is, when you go into a sports bar, you'll talk sixty percent about sports, ten percent about women, ten percent about politics, ten percent about religion, and ten percent about what's goin' on in the world. That is why the show's been successful. I don't think there's been one show I've done where it's been a hundred percent sports. Lemme show you what I have charted for today."

He slides over toward me, a yellow legal pad clutched in his hand. "Now here." He has scribbled some names down in blue pen and drawn a line down the center of the page. "I have for today Kukoc. That's the main one. DePaul, last night. And women's soccer is gonna have a league. Can they make it? Those are my three topics. For sports. To start the day off. What happens sometimes is, like, Jim Miller may sign today with the Bears as their quarterback. Two hours in, he may sign. Do you think it was a good signing? *Buh-ba-ba.* So that comes in. That stuff is gravy. It hits ya outta nowhere. But I also keep a list here of stuff in case. And I go by the lights. I had a program director tell me that doesn't mean anything. Ninety-five percent of the listeners don't call."

"I've heard."

"You wanna know something though? If I'm only gettin' *one* light goin' out of a six-light bank, that's my gauge that there's lack of interest. I don't wanna hear this ninety-five percent deal. There's no proof of that. My feeling is every listener's a potential caller. I get first-time callers every day. I've been on eight years and I'm still getting first-time callers. Now. Back to this."

He shows me the legal pad and what he has written on the other side of the blue line.

"If you had it to do all over again, what would you do in life? Last good movie that you saw. What business other than the one you're in would you get into? Just stuff like that to fall back on."

"Ever have that blank-page nightmare? Where you can't think of anything to say?"

"Well, you know what used to happen to me?" Mike North lowers his voice. "I used to be a heavy drinker."

He speaks now in a whisper. His voice is hushed, as if in prayer.

"I used to drink a lot. I used to drink every day. The first four, five years of doing this I was living a dream. I'd get off at two o'clock. I was workin' ten to two. There were times I was drinkin' a bottle and a half, two bottles of champagne, a bottle of vodka a day. No more. I quit."

"What made you stop?"

Mike sighs deeply. "I got tired of feeling like shit. Plus it was a challenge going off on my own, without a partner. If I wanted to be the best, I knew I had to stop. Another thing. When I first came on the air, I never had notes. Never wrote anything down. I just talked off-the-cuff like I was at the hot dog stand. But. I'd be out at night and somethin' would go on. Or I'd read somethin' or see somethin' on TV. I'd say, I'll remember that for tomorrow. The next day, I didn't remember it. So that's when I started writing down notes. I'd come home at night with eight or nine cocktail napkins filled with stuff I wrote on 'em. I'd transfer those notes onto my yellow pad. Finally, I just went straight to the pad. That thing has saved me. Lemme tell you somethin' else. Tony Kukoc got traded yesterday. I know for a fact that right now on the station they're talking about it. By the time I get on at twelve o'clock, that topic is gonna be talked about from six o'clock this morning. I have to come up with a different angle."

He rips the corner off his bagel and kisses the air. Licorice's ears twitch like Mr. Spock's. Mike lobs the piece of bagel into a high arc, slow-pitch softball style. Licorice studies the bagel's descent, leaps at the last second, and snatches it an instant before it would plop onto the peg-and-grooved floor. Minimal effort, maximum grace. Dog played that bagel like Clemente used to play right field.

"Nice catch."

"Yeah. She's good. She's a great Frisbee catcher. Shame she can't play no more. Anyway. Today I'm gonna come on the air and talk about Krause and how I think he's underrated. I'm gonna ask our listeners to give Jerry Krause a grade. What would you grade Tony Kukoc? See? Different angle. We're not asking you the same stuff the previous hosts asked you from eight to noon. I always make sure I break it up. Want some more coffee?"

"Yeah, thanks."

He pours me a cup from a sterling-silver pitcher. The movement looks out of place in Mike North's rugged blue-collar fist. Street kid posing as Professor Higgins.

"I don't think you're one of those shy guys who becomes outgoing on the air, are you?"

"Bee!" he shouts over his shoulder.

"Yeaah?" BeBe singsongs from the kitchen.

"Shy or outgoing?"

A beat.

"Am I shy or outgoing?"

"I'm sorry?" BeBe hears the question. She doesn't believe it. "He's out*going.*" For emphasis. "Mike's never been shy in his life."

"I think I'm the same off the air as on."

"Would you say so?" I ask BeBe.

"Oh, yeah," she says, gliding into the room. "The only thing is, some people get the impression that because he's so outspoken and honest, he might be tough to deal with. He's not. He is *so* nice. People love working with him."

"Do you listen to the show?"

"Oh, yeah. I listen all the time. I love listening to him."

"She does the show with me once in a while."

"He's fun to listen to."

"But I'm very competitive." Holding hands with BeBe, gently rubbing her wrist. "I want to win."

Mike North pops in a videotape, aims the remote, crashes back into his couch.

"Buncha interviews I did at the Super Bowl on Radio Row. You're gonna like this."

Fade up on Mike talking to Randy White, former Dallas Cowboy defensive-line terror and member of the Pro Football Hall of Fame. They are discussing calf-roping.

"I gotta tell ya," Mike observes. "I'm an animal lover. I don't like it when the cowboy ties up the calf's legs. To me that's cruel."

"Welll," White drawls. "It may seem a little cruel. But look at the alternative. He could be—"

"A steak," says North.

I crack up and Mike changes the subject. He brings up the Bears' 44–0 drubbing of the Cowboys. White says he doesn't remember the game.

"Come on," North says, "you gotta remember it."

"Who was the quarterback? Flutie?"

"No. Steve Fuller."

"Where did we play that game?"

"In Dallas."

"In *Dallas?* Are you sure Flutie wasn't the quarterback?"

"Were you taking painkillers?" North wonders.

Randy White blows out a stream of air as he bursts out laughing.

"You have gone about as low as a guy can go," North says. "You are pretending you don't remember that game."

"I don't remember. Would you remember if you got beat forty-four to nothing?"

"Nah. Probably not."

And Randy White, former scourge of NFL quarterbacks, is laughing so hard he has to bend over to brace himself so he won't fall over.

"I try to do all my interviews like that," North says, stopping the tape. "People are tired of hearing athletes talk about X's and O's. I give 'em that, too, but I like to have fun."

"Doesn't seem like you're intimidated by anyone."

"I'm not. One time Mike Ditka came up to me and he said, 'You seem to be the only guy who's not scared of me.'

"I go, 'Well, I grew up with Don North.'

"He goes, 'Who's Don North?'

"I go, 'My father. You're just a football coach. I had to live with Don North every day for nineteen years. He woulda given you a run for your money.' No, believe me, I'm not afraid of anybody."

Mike fast-forwards through another three interviews. "You know George Young?"

"Know of him. Former GM of the Giants, now a higher-up in the NFL."

North nods. "Ya gotta see this."

George Young appears on-screen, a bear in a rumbled brown suit. High, tinny voice, thick glasses, maybe a dozen strands of brown hair standing at attention, nose stuck way, *way* up in the air. North waves at the TV with the remote. He beams.

"Do you pay to go to the games?" Young accuses North.

"Hey, buddy, I got DirecTV," Mike answers.

Young smirks. "You don't even pay to go to the games."

"Hold on for a second. Let me tell you somethin'.."

"Complain when you're a paying customer."

"That's right." Joe Theisman, appearing out of nowhere. "I agree with that."

Young's pumpkin-shaped face spits out, "I love these guys who get in free and then—"

"Hold *on,*" Mike North says. "We *don't* get in free. How'd you like it if everybody watchin' at home *canceled* DirecTV? We *pay* to go to the games. Because I *pay* to watch every Sunday. I saw that game. I buy the advertising—"

"Let me explain something to you," Theisman cuts in. Slow, soft, condescending. Suddenly taking the role of George

Young's hit man. "The league already has their seventeen billion committed. They don't care whether you buy DirecTV or not. Let's put an end to this conversation right now."

Mike North completely ignores Theisman. The move says, *This is my show, buddy.*

"Where you from, George?"

"Baltimore" trickles out of George Young's mouth.

"Let me tell you something, George. Without the fans of the National Football League, you'd be selling hot dogs in Baltimore right now."

I've seen George Young interviewed before. Every other host has rolled out the red carpet, then lobbed in a bunch of softball questions.

Everybody kisses George Young's ass.

Mike North kicked his butt.

In a December 31, 1999, *Chicago Tribune* column entitled "10 Who Helped Mark the Broadcast Decade," Robert Feder lists, along with Oprah Winfrey, Mike North. Feder calls North the "undisputed star of WSCR-AM," asserting of him: "no one better symbolized the rise of sports talk radio as a legitimate genre in the nineties or the democratization of sportscasting."

Mike and I look at Feder's column spread out in front of us on the coffee table. Mike smoothes out one of the corners that has dog-eared up slightly.

"This means a lot," he says. "I've won a lot of awards. But to be put with those people. Oprah Winfrey and Bill Curtis."

He blinks once.

"This is something," I say.

"Yeah."

He nods, blinks again. "You know, I'm very, very, uh . . ."

Mike sucks in a breath, then lets the air out like a smoke ring.

"I think most radio people are insecure. I really do. It takes a lot to admit it, but I'm insecure. I work hard every day, thinking that if I don't, someone's gonna tap me on the shoulder and say it's time to go back to the hot dog stand, you had a good run."

Beat.

"I don't know how to put this . . . it's not bragging . . . but I believe I'm the best going. By far. I believe that I am the best talk show host in the country. If I didn't believe it, I wouldn't be doing it. The only guys who I would consider formidable, if they came opposite me, would be Mike and the Mad Dog. The only guys. I've heard 'em all. Hey, you wanna see the house?"

He stands and rubs his hands together in a gesture of pure glee.

"There was a ranch-style house here and we bulldozed it. I just bought the house next door, too."

"Whoa. You are doing okay, Mike."

"Well, I can tell you what I make, but it can't be in the book."

I shut off the tape recorder.

He tells me what he makes.

I nearly shit.

"You know the best part of it?" BeBe says. "He's exactly the same as he was fifteen years ago."

"I still hang out with my same friends," Mike says. "Same guys I grew up with."

"He is really, *really* good to people," BeBe says. "He's very generous. He would've been like that before, but he didn't have the money."

Mike is getting embarrassed. "Come on, let's show him the house."

I follow him into a room off the den, a dark-wood-paneled room modeled after Don Corleone's office in *The Godfather,*

Mike North's favorite movie. We prowl along the walls, passing framed autographed photographs of Mike North with arms around the Who's Who of Sports. I stop at a picture of North with Mickey Mantle, my all-time favorite athlete.

"The Mick," I say.

"Yep. Mickey Mantle. There's me and Jordan. Gale Sayers. He's a dear friend of mine. Bobby De Niro."

Mike stops at a picture of Mike and a group of goofballs draped all over each other on a golf course. Mike grins.

"These are my core buddies. The guys I grew up with. We went to a golf outing dressed as immigrants."

He points to a picture of himself, headset on, next to a serious-looking African-American man behind a WSCR microphone.

"This is me and Jiggetts. That's Dan. We won the Sports Show of the Year. Let's see, what else? Oh, yeah, I won these."

We cruise a series of plaques and pictures proclaiming him Man of the Year for several different Chicago charities.

"I take back one thing," BeBe says, returning after taking a phone call. "Mike is shy about all the awards he's won. He's won two Emmys, a Broadcaster of the Decade award. It goes on and on. He is truly respected in town."

"Yeah, I've been lucky. This one . . . this is the one I'm proudest of. I got the award for Best Midday Talent. Not just sports talk. All talk. Out of forty-five shows. Best *Talk* Show. I beat everybody. Limbaugh. *Everybody.* I'm proud of this. I really am."

He replaces the award. I notice a nick on the side. I pass my thumb over the chipped area.

"I broke it in a bar," Mike shrugs, and BeBe laughs. "Come on downstairs."

Downstairs is heaven above for sports fans.

The walls are filled with framed autographed pictures,

signed sports memorabilia, and jerseys belonging to Bobby Hull, Jim Brown, Pete Rose, Ryne Sandberg, Deion Sanders, more Sayers, more Jordan.

The basement itself is an actual sports bar, horseshoe-shaped and fully stocked. A dozen barstools. Six TVs. Couches, armchairs, pool table, poker table, and arcade games.

I have a VCR and a Game Boy. I wipe the drool from the corner of my mouth.

Mike walks over to a framed University of North Carolina basketball jersey. "This is my pride and joy. This just went for sixty-three thousand at an auction. Michael signed it for me. I went to his camp. Cost me fifteen thousand. It was a thirty-five and over. He busted my balls all week because I busted his balls on the air. We had a lot of fun."

"Do you have people over to hang out and watch the games?"

"Every week. I have ten, fifteen people over, we watch the games, eat. It's the best. If you were in town during football season, I'd have you over. Now, let's go upstairs."

Mike bounces up a back staircase. I linger, cover the basement like a camera.

"If my wife reports me missing, check down here," I say to Mike's back. A laugh echoes from somewhere I can't see.

"This is where I do most of my . . ."

I scamper up the stairs and practically run up North's back. He's standing in his bedroom. A mammoth bed, not king-size, *emperor*-size, dominates the room. Along one wall is a huge TV.

"I lay here. Got a table here. Fridge right there, stocked with everything I need. We spend a lot of time in here. I got TVs in every room. 'Cause ya never know what's gonna happen. Like here."

He darts out of the room. I chase him.

Turn a corner and we're in the bathroom. TV in here, too.

"I got a total of seventeen televisions."

Ladies and gentlemen, we have a winner.

Back upstairs in the den, plastered into the folds of his leather couch, Mike North and I gaze at a videotape flickering on fast-forward. Mike speaks in a hush.

"My father *drives* me. He thought I was a complete fuckin' bum. He thought when I dropped out of high school that it was all over for me. The end. The last five years, though, we reconciled. He saw my success and he forgave me. I'll never forget this though. He'd had a stroke. I was at his bedside. It was three days before he died. He's slurring and he says, 'I gotta ask you something. I gotta find out, Mike. How much money do you make?'

"I said, 'Dad, I can't tell you how much I make. But I'll tell you this. For what you did for us, for your family, you deserved to make more than I ever will.'"

Mike nods and swallows.

"Yeah," he says. "My dad drives me."

May 24, 1997.

Pat Riley's been through the ringer. His Miami Heat have just lost a home game in the NBA conference finals to the Michael Jordan–led Chicago Bulls, and they're about to lose the series. Riley's tie is askew and looks clawed at. His eyes are grim, watery, and hard. His forehead is furrowed with long, thin parallel valleys, looking like they've been carved out with a chisel.

But that *hair* . . .

Perfect.

Every wave in place, not a stray strand in sight. Lacquered straight back, mostly black, flecks of gray here and there adding a dash of maturity and style.

Riley's shirt is soaked with the sweat of defeat, his throat raw from two hours of screaming and imploring, his heart heavy with the impending thud associated with second place.

But that *do . . .*

Let's face it. When you think Riles, you don't think rings. You think *coif.*

It is the postgame press conference and Riley is fielding questions from the media. The pressroom is swarming and sweltering. There's a question about defense, another about rebounding, back to the same question, worded differently, about defense. Suddenly, Riley's ears perk up beneath his magnificent hair as a thin voice with an obvious Chicago inflection curls toward him from the back of the room.

"What?"

"I said . . . *If God came down tomorrow and said you will win the NBA championship, but you gotta shave your head, would you do it?"*

Every eye in the room turns toward the voice.

Mike North stares at Riley. Riley stares back and blinks first, then says nothing for what seems like an hour. Mike, eyes locked into Riley's, grips the microphone like a comic between jokes.

It's a simple question, thinks Mike. *A legitimate question.*

Would you trade your most valuable possession for an NBA Championship?

Mike North, high school dropout, standing tall in the center of a barrage of mundane sports questions and well-worn clichéd answers, has dared ask Pat Riley a question inspired by, of all things, *literature.* The question is right out of O'Henry's classic story "The Gift of the Magi": If you had two loves in your life, would you give up one for the other?

Would you shave your head for an NBA Championship?

Mike North waits.

At the podium, Pat Riley clears his throat. "That's a very nice question, sir. Who do you work for?"

"I work for the Score in Chicago. The name's Mike North."

Two hefty security guards spring out from behind a curtain and pin back Mike's arms.

Mike grins.

He has Riley right where he wants him.

VI.

genius at work

REMOTE

Some listeners may think that talk show hosts are high-profile guys. I think my audience realizes that I'm not; I'm just like them. I have thirty-seven dollars in my checking account. I argue with my wife about what I'm going to eat and taking out the trash and cleaning the car. That is really who I am. It's the same on the air as at home. Except maybe with a few louder decibels.

I drive.

Up the 101 freeway into the guts of the San Fernando Valley, heading toward Santa Barbara. The smoggy patchwork of places like Van Nuys and Reseda lay in a brown clump behind me. Forty-five minutes pass, then an hour, and the landscape changes into a rolling countryside the color of a decent chardonnay. I slip off the freeway and pass through a contemporary adobe suburbia made up of SuperGaps, Super-Staples, SuperBlockbusters, and Super Supermarkets all in Super-sandblasted beige, spread like butter on either side of the road. Malls in the style of seventeenth-century Spanish missions built yesterday. We are in Thousand Oaks, California, where there is no moderation. The name of the game here is *scope*. After all, this is not Dozen Oaks or Hundred Oaks. It's *Thousand* Oaks.

An hour and a half from, in my mind, civilization, I pull into a development surrounded by a white stucco wall. At a guard shack resembling a tollbooth, I punch in a secret code, and a part of the wall opens like the entrance to a castle. I drive in, turn left, and look for the house, which is difficult because all of the streets have the same names and all the houses are clones. I find it, park, and walk toward the home of the Stinkin' Genius. It's a Tuesday, 9 A.M., about a month after our meeting at Mort's Deli.

Beth Spanier, her two-year-old son, Shea, clasped to her hip, and Knicky, their rambunctious golden retriever, greet me. Shea shouts happily and points off into the house while Knicky shoves a toy into my crotch. I grunt and limp inside.

The Spanier home is wide and spacious and has more toys than FAO Schwarz. We walk past a yellow plastic kitchen, an orange plastic car, and a miniature rainbow-colored Legoland. We enter a large family room, adjacent to the real kitchen where two real plumbers, dressed like they're about to wade into a flood, are filling out paperwork and grimacing. One shakes his head ruefully. This can't be good.

Arnie arrives, a yellow legal pad tucked under his arm, a cell phone pasted to his ear.

"He's always on the phone," Beth explains. "Shea, let's go put a video on."

I sink into an L-shaped leather couch that faces a huge-screen TV. It smells of morning here, coffee and Apple Jacks. Home. The opposite of sports.

"How's it going for Arnie?" I ask Beth. My instinct is that she *knows*.

"Better than he thought it would. Shea, where are your socks? Get your socks."

"We'll do that. Call me later," Arnie says into the phone.

I nod at the two plumbers, who huddle near the refrigerator.

"What's up with your plumbing?"

"Everything in this house is a wreck," Beth says. "Arnie wanted a swivel showerhead. He put it on and we've got water going everywhere."

Beth hands Shea over to Arnie. He picks up his son and allows him to drop maybe an inch. "Timberrr!" Arnie howls, and Shea giggles.

"He's so cute," I say.

"Thanks," Arnie says. "He's a handful."

Beth, hands on hips, muscles for inside position between the two plumbers.

"So you know what's wrong? What's the estimate?"

Rico, the first plumber, larger, older, in charge, crinkles his forehead. He squints at his paperwork.

"Hey, Shea, buddy, you want some apple juice?"

Not comprehending or maybe not thirsty, Shea stares at his father, then bolts out of the room.

"So I'm guessing you named him after Shea Stadium," I say.

"Oh, yeah," says Arnie. "And if we have another kid, a girl, I'm pushing for Madison."

I'm picking up the code. "After Madison Square Garden."

"Madison Fran Spanier." Beth tosses this over her shoulder, still between the two plumbers, the one in charge grappling with the estimate.

"If it's a boy, we'll go with Mookie."

"*What?*" says Beth. News to her.

Arnie grins. "Just kidding, baby."

The plumbers realize they have to go back upstairs. They slip plastic Baggies over their boots and tromp through the playroom. Beth crashes down next to me.

"Always something," she sighs.

"I better prepare my show," Arnie says. "Hey, Beth, where's today's sports section?"

"You had all the papers. I don't know."

Arnie finds it, tunes in One-on-One. He begins writing on the yellow pad, Jay Mariotti declaiming in the background. Shea streaks in from the playroom, towing a Teletubby. Knicky yawns, makes a circle at my feet, flops onto the carpet. Beth closes her eyes, takes what appears to be a short meditative breath, and begins massaging her temples.

"When you talk about Phil Jackson, you gotta realize this. He has *six* championships. He understands what it takes to win. There are certain things you have to do. Or when it comes crunch time, you will lose the game and the championship."

Rico the plumber is talking.

He has been staring at "Spanier" on the estimate and has finally placed the name. Now Rico wants to talk sports and the Stinkin' Genius does not.

"I'll tell you this, I don't know why they keep Derek Fisher," Rico adds.

Arnie can't help himself. He looks up from his legal pad. "The guy can't shoot to save his life. What was he yesterday? He has got to go. Look at this. Three out of nine. That's good for him."

Rico wags his head. "Thirty-three percent," he pronounces proudly.

His partner squishes in, holding the old showerhead. He stops and glares at Rico. His eyes say, "What the fuck are you doing? I'm up to my ass in water trying to fix this goddamn showerhead and you're down here doing a *talk show?*"

"Excuse me," says Rico the sports talk plumber, apparently going to commercial.

• • •

My parents used to ask me all the time, "What are you going to do with your life?" I really had no answers. If I couldn't do this, if they prohibited sports talk of any kind, I don't know what I'd do. I don't know what would become of me.

"You know what your voice would be great for?" I ask.

"Yeah," Arnie says. "Krusty the Clown."

"No, I'm serious. I think your voice would be great for voice-overs, cartoons, that kind of thing."

"As a matter of fact, I just hired a manager," Arnie says. "And he's trying to find me stuff."

He looks around, makes sure the plumbers are out of earshot. "There's a talking dog on NBC, but I think they might want somebody more recognizable. They wanted to hire me on *Malcolm in the Middle,* but I wasn't available. *Third Rock from the Sun,* too, they want to meet with me."

Jeez. The Stinkin' Genius goes Hollywood.

The plumbers are gone. Beth, Shea, and Knicky are out on a walk.

"Mike wants to sit down with me over lunch, go over a few things," Arnie says.

"Like what?"

"Well, to be honest, he had five pages of notes."

"Whoa."

"Yeah, but it's mostly little things. Like he doesn't want me to yell so much. And be so hard on the Lakers. He doesn't want me to be known as this screaming Lakers basher all the time. There's so much more to me than that, and he wants the other stuff to come out. He wants more of my life. More personal stuff. He wants me to talk about my wife, my kid. The other day he wanted me to have a doctor on to talk about my cold."

"What do you want to do?"

A worried look.

"I just want to talk about sports."

"Beth, am I going left or straight?"

"To the freeway. Straight."

Arnie is at the wheel of his SUV. I'm riding shotgun. Beth and Shea are in the back. We're going to lunch and we're talking money.

"So what is a good contract?"

"A good contract . . ." Arnie hesitates.

"Put it this way," Beth says. "At One-on-One, for that overnight shift, they'd pay someone like Arnie about ninety thousand dollars."

"Typically a good talk show host with ratings can make between a buck fifty and two fifty. With incentives," Arnie says.

"Such as?"

"Top twenty, top fifteen. You get free insurance—"

"Arnie's getting a free car," Beth adds.

"And the top guys?"

"Close to a mil easy."

We pull into the restaurant parking lot. I decide to ask a delicate question.

"Arnie, when you came to L.A., did you consider this a step down from the network?"

"Beth didn't think so. I did."

"Absolutely not," Beth says.

"In some ways, I wanted to continue doing national."

"Arnie likes the national because it's not tiring, in the sense that for six months you're going to talk Lakers. Whereas national you can talk about anything."

"Do you feel pressure to succeed?"

"So far I really haven't felt it. I haven't seen the ratings yet.

We'll see what happens when the first ratings come out. I know I'm under the microscope."

"Do you think there's pressure on Thompson, too?"

"Yeah. I would say there's pressure on him."

"This is a tough market, too," I say.

"No doubt about it," Arnie says. "No doubt about it."

Inside an adobe deli. Shea staring at four tiers of desserts revolving inside a split-level dessert case. He shrieks happily, presses his hand against a dense yellow New York cheesecake. Good choice. Kid's got potential.

"Three and a high chair." Arnie's voice does command you to listen.

"It's an awful business," Beth says.

At the table, Shea makes a structure out of sugar packets. We've been seated for maybe ten seconds and we've already ordered. A fruit salad for the Stinkin' Genius.

"I want respect," Arnie says solemnly.

"From your peers," I assume.

"Yeah, but—"

"His family," Beth says, one eye on Arnie. Is this okay to reveal? Arnie reaches over, helps Shea construct a sugar tower, working on a Sweet'n Low turret.

"Especially his mother."

A wound opening. Arnie clears his throat. Beth wants to get this out. Intimacy with strangers. My job description.

"His mom was like, 'Oh, that's not a profession. That's like an *actor.*'"

"What did she want you to do?"

"Lawyer," Arnie says, piling sugar packets perilously high.

"So she doesn't get what you do?"

"She doesn't get it. She still doesn't get it."

The din of the deli. A clatter of forks against plates. Shea howling happily. Then, at our table, silence, allowing the din to cover us like a blanket. Arnie, finally, swallows.

"I just want Shea to know that his dad was successful in radio," he says softly.

The sugar packets come tumbling down.

We're back in the Spanier living room. A loud knock on the door. Beth glances at her watch, nods her head.

"This is the neighbor," she says. "Like clockwork."

She doesn't get the door. A beefy guy with oily black hair, sunglasses on inside, a T-shirt rolled up revealing bulging biceps, bounces in.

"Hey, I'm Gary. I live next door." He throws himself into the leather couch, pumps his leg. "Where's the Stinkin' Genius?"

"Getting ready for his show."

"Yeah? Good. I wanna hear what's on for today."

Deep voice. Thick New York accent.

"Wait a minute," I say. "You're from New York and you live next *door?*"

"Yep. And what's really funny is that he named his son, Shea, after Shea Stadium, and I named *my* son, Shea, after Shea Stadium."

"No way," I say.

Gary backs off. "Well, my wife wouldn't let me name him *exactly* Shea, so we named him Shane and I call him Shea."

"This is nuts." I look at Beth. She shrugs.

"Unbelievable how things worked out. He's the perfect neighbor for me."

I look at Beth again. She shrugs again.

"So, Gary, what do you do?"

"I make glasses. I see your frames aren't my design."

I self-consciously slide my glasses onto my nose.

"No. Sorry."

"What are they, Calvins?"

"I'm not sure—"

"They look like Calvins. I could've given you a deal."

Another glance at Beth. Another shrug.

"What are you doing home from work?"

"I own my own company," he sniffs.

"Gary always comes over at this time, right before Arnie leaves," Beth explains. "Gary and Arnie have to have their power chat."

I'm confused. "Are you a consultant?"

"No. I just give him stuff to talk about."

"You know how Jay Leno tries out material the night before like at the Comedy Store?" Beth says. "Arnie tries out his stuff on Gary. If Gary hates it, Arnie knows it'll fly."

I look from Beth to Gary, then back to Beth. "Are you serious?"

"Yeah," Gary says. "I come here every morning."

"Does Arnie like the fact that you're here every morning?"

"I don't care."

We all laugh.

"Can I tell you something?" Beth says. "Arnie loves this. He really loves to have people around him all the time. He loves the guy thing."

"The truth is, I need it, too," says Gary. "Especially since my best friend moved back to New York."

"Yeah," Beth says. "It's a marriage made in heaven."

Beth Spanier cannot control her smile. She's trying to remain serious, dignified, but she's talking about Arnie and how they first met, and she's grinning, revealing a slight over-bite. Her face is *aglow*. There is no other word. After nearly five years of marriage, mention the Stinkin' Genius's name and she actually starts to blush.

"I used to date these guys who were so into themselves.

Whether it was working out or their careers or whatever. Everything was always about *them.*"

That smile again. You could read by it.

"Then I met Arnie. He was the sweetest, *sweetest* man. He would always tell me that I look pretty, or I love you. He made me feel like I was on top of the world. No one ever made me feel like that. No one."

"How did you meet?"

"When we were in Arizona, my sister told me she had someone she wanted to fix me up with. Arnie Spanier. I said, 'The guy on the radio? That loudmouthed New Yorker?' I told my mom and she said, 'Oh, I know Arnie. He's really funny!'"

"And Arnie was into it?"

"Yeah. You know why? We had met at a party a few years ago and he thought I was my friend Mindy who has huge boobs."

"A man with standards. Low standards but standards."

"He was in his bimbo-of-the-week stage."

The door bursts open. Gary.

"We need a *trade,*" he says. "A.C. Green for Elden Campbell, Glen Rice for Eddie Jones, and Derek Fisher for Nick Van Exel. Trade everybody *back.* Then we'll have a team."

"Gary, he left," Beth says.

"He *left?*"

"Call him in the car."

"I gotta reach him."

Gary sprints out the door.

"I was in Phoenix," Arnie remembers. "We had this idea. Blind date of the week. I'd take a date out to dinner at one of the local restaurants. The restaurants gave us a free meal and bought advertising. I told everybody on the air where I was going so they could check out what my date looked like. I said, 'Hey, if you're fat or ugly, don't come. Because I'm fat and ugly enough for both of us.'"

A sly smile on Arnie's face. A touch of crimson enters his cheeks. "I was going out with, uh, how shall we say . . . adult-entertainment dancers. Aerobics instructors. Girls named Treasure. Finally, Beth's sister called and told me that her sister had tickets to the Suns game. I'll go out with anybody who has tickets to the Suns. I don't like using media passes because I really don't consider myself part of the media. I pay for my tickets. I remembered Beth from U of A. We had hooked up, me and a friend and her and a friend."

"What did you remember about her?"

"I remembered trying to get some action that night. And since I didn't, I never called her back."

Big Stinkin' Genius tornado laugh. He gets sober quick but his eyes still twinkle.

"We had a great time on that date, but I told her, 'Look, Beth, I don't want to get tied down. It's not like we're gonna get married or anything.'"

The next thing you know they were engaged.

And the *next* thing you know, five months after they were married, they were on *The Newlywed Game.*

Arnie was sweating. He couldn't tell if it was the lights or the pressure, but it felt like a stinkin' sauna in here. This was worse than that stinkin' bungee jump. He'd lived through that. How, he didn't know. But this? Answering these stupid questions to win a trip to *Micronesia,* for godsake. Where the hell *is* Micronesia? *Somewhere near Guam,* he thought. *Now that's a fabulous place for a vacation. Guam. They got flies there the size of Jettas.*

The first round was an embarrassment. Beth pounded that buzzer like she was doing Tae Bo. She must've answered ten questions. Every one of them wrong. *The only thing keeping us in this game is that the two other couples are dumber than we are.*

Arnie mopped his forehead behind the flimsy plywood desk. The studio was a lot smaller and a lot cheesier than it looked on TV. The host, Bill or Bob, some guy who had spent five minutes on *Saturday Night Live,* cracked a lame joke. Nobody laughed. No biggie. They'd crank in some hysterical canned laughter later.

This was Beth's idea. A little pub for the show. Something different to talk about. How many sports talk show hosts have appeared on *The Newlywed Game?* Exactly none. *Can't imagine Mike and the Mad Dog doing this,* Arnie thought. *Truth is, Beth has a great head for business, and you know what, bottom line? All she has to do is get the final question right and we win. Hurry up already, I'm dyin' here.*

"Okay, Beth."

The host puckered his lips as if he were about to kiss the camera. "For the trip to Micronesia, what did Arnie say he was in bed? A Sex Speed Racer or Sex in the Slow Lane?"

She better get this, thought Arnie. *It's so obvious.* Speed Racer *is my favorite cartoon. She knows that.*

Beth flipped over her card. She'd written *Speed Racer.* They'd won. Somewhere they pumped in canned applause and fake delirious cheering, and Beth jumped up and down in her seat and kissed Arnie like they'd instructed them to back-stage. It was silly, but what the hell? They'd won the trip plus a year's supply of Turtle Wax. Shit. Now they'd have to buy a car.

But as Beth pressed her lips into his on national television and the two other clueless couples looked on wondering if they should clap or leave or what, Arnie was overcome with a feeling of sheer true love. No. Better than love. Bliss. Beth gave him bliss.

Man, if someone gives you stinkin' *bliss,* you gotta go with that.

It's drizzling.

I'm circling Westwood, looking for a place to park. I find a spot just up the street from the Union 76 gas station where Arnie Spanier is broadcasting live. As payment for this remote, Arnie is receiving a free tune-up, overseen by Dave in promotions. I park and walk a block to the gas station, where I find Arnie, arms folded, sitting out a commercial under a plastic tarp. This is his studio for today. Sitting next to him, producing, engineering, and looking equally miserable, is Steve "Phone Slap" Carbone. A portable hoop is set up next to them and a couple of mechanics play H-O-R-S-E. A former all-state guard, Steve looks over at them longingly, knowing he can take them both in that game or any other. Only a few people are here, a handful from the radio station and a couple of lookey-loos on their way to UCLA.

Arnie, arms still folded, glares at Carbone, who shrugs. I know what they're both thinking.

Other hosts hold their remotes in sports bars and draw five hundred people. They set me up in a fucking gas station during rush hour and I draw nine people, who are here for one stinkin' reason. Because they need gas!

The drizzle picks up. The sky turns ugly. Someone swears. In the background, Arnie's voice roars over the PA system as he takes a call. A guy and his daughter, coming out of Hollywood Video, wander over to check out the scene. They hear Arnie holler. The guy shakes his head. That's enough. They move on, nearly colliding with a figure wearing flesh-colored Superman tights, a black Superman mask, a red cape, and a top announcing XTRA-SPORTS 1150. A couple of the mechanics see Super Guy, point, and laugh.

"Arnie, I don't know if they're gonna get to your car," says Dave in promotions.

"What do you mean?"

"That's what they said. They're backed up."

"Backed *up?* There's three people here."

"Let me go talk to them again."

I say good-bye to Arnie, shake hands with Carbone, who's now playing H-O-R-S-E with a heavyset Mexican mechanic and the guy in the tights. Carbone sets up way outside, past the pumps, shoots. *Swish.* He winks at me.

I head up the street, ducking raindrops, past a movie theater where they're showing, appropriately, *Scream.*

VII.

afternoon drive

MIKE AND THE MAD DOG:
BOMBS FROM EVERY DIRECTION

the yellow cab rumbles over the lower level of the Fifty-ninth Street Bridge and I hear voices.

Simon and Garfunkel singing "Feeling Groovy." Bee Gees harmonizing "Stayin' Alive." Mel Allen's sweet Southern comfort going going *gone*. Phil Rizzuto's high-pitched vocal plunk like a ukulele left out in the rain.

The cab cuts in and out of traffic on the bridge, closed in by steel girders, a giant cage, until we're dumped off in Astoria, Queens, a bridge-length, but a million miles, from Manhattan. I can't tell if the neighborhood is seamy or safe, beaten down or on the way back. I could've taken a buck-fifty subway ride from my hotel, but I opted for the aboveground excursion. Get my bearings. Recover from a horrific cross-country airline nightmare that got me to the city at seven this morning instead of eleven-thirty last night, the result of the traditional mechanical difficulty.

But here I am, body ragged, eyes bloodshot, fingers cling-ing to the flimsy door handle of the cab as it zips past car sal-vage yards protected by rottweilers and razor wire, bars with peeling paint alongside freshly painted coffeehouses, and warehouses that house floors of fabric and warehouses con-verted into entertainment centers.

Like the Kaufman-Astoria Studios, home of *Cosby, Spin City,* Lifetime, and WFAN. The cab deposits me in front, and I dance through the revolving doors into the lobby.

To get to WFAN, just as to Oz, you need to follow the bro-ken yellow line. I walk up a short flight of stairs, across a car-peted lobby, enter an elevator, and press DOWN. The directions I've received and the map I'm consulting seem mysterious and diversionary as if I'm about to penetrate the inner sanctum of the CIA. The elevator doors burst open and I walk, head bent, eyes trained on the broken yellow line, which is flanked by a broken red line and a broken blue line. I turn a corner and I'm jolted by a tall, smiling, motionless African-American in a golf hat. I blink and realize it's a life-size cardboard cutout of Cosby. I keep going, past a set of glass doors inviting me into the Lifetime Channel. The blue line disappears. I whip around, hit an upgrade, then wind past the commissary. The corridor constricts now, providing barely enough room for one, and I notice the red line has vanished. I take a hairpin turn, an easy bank, and there it is.

WFAN.

A smudged glass door. A tricky step down, an ankle twister, the final challenge, and I'm in. A suspicious receptionist wear-ing a Madonna headset sits behind a minuscule desk. She wants to know my business. I tell her I'm here to see Chris Russo. She looks dubious. Mutters something into the head-set. Nods as if she can be seen. Tells me to have a seat. Another test. There are no chairs. I study the wall, which offers a collage of photographs. Guys at golf tournaments, unfamiliar faces flanking sports celebs. Everyone looking giddy. I glance into the control room and studio. The morning guys bookend Vincent Pastore, the chunky actor who plays Big Pussy on *The Sopranos.* Everyone's laughing now. But a few months later Big Pussy will be gunned down and the two morning guys will be axed.

I hear my name. Chris Carlin, twenty-seven, nicknamed Continent because of his resemblance to a landmass, greets me. He is ruddy-faced and serious and slightly put-upon, no doubt the result of nearly three years of serving as both Mike and the Mad Dog's producer and punching bag. Carlin steers me up three quick steps into an office in the far corner of WFAN. The room is furnished with three metal desks buckling under a mountain range of books, magazines, and newspapers.

"You can leave your stuff in here," Carlin offers. The question is *where?*

"That's okay, I'm good," I say.

"Sit down, relax. We'll get you fixed up. Today you're set for lunch with Chris, tomorrow you're good to go with Mike."

"Great. Thanks."

I nod and smile, meaning, truly, this *is* great and I am thankful. Suddenly I am out of this scene, outside of this reality, watching myself and Carlin from a different angle, as if we're characters on a TV show. I relive the journey I took to get here—the dozens of phone calls made, all answered amid a muffled concert of phones ringing, voices booming, things clacking and clattering, each call ending with "I don't know, call me next week," followed by a thousand miles spent pacing in front of my computer, literal hand-wringing and doubt, wondering honestly if I would ever get here, if I would ever experience this, the center of the sports talk radio universe.

Back to earth, I blink at Carlin. "Did you say something?"

"Nope." Carlin shrugs.

In the distance we hear a chant.

"Hadeedada hadeedada . . ."

Then louder: *"HADEEDADA . . ."*

—then roaring, *"HADEEDADA-HADEEDADA . . ."*

It's him. I stand, dry my palms on my pants. Damn. I'm nervous. Let's face it, in the sports talk radio world, Mike and the Mad Dog are *it*. I feel like I'm about to meet—I don't know—Letterman? Springsteen? Alan Greenspan?

"HADEEDADA-DIEEEEEEEEEEEEEEE!"

Carlin shakes his head and says, "Hello, Chris," five seconds before Mad Dog rockets into the room. He is forty-something, tall and trim, wearing street-corner cool like a suit. He's got a large, craggy nose, black hair slicked back, and a boyish grin that takes you in and warms you up. Carlin introduces us and Chris pumps my hand like I'm an investor.

"How ya doin'?" Chris asks.

"Listen," Carlin says to me gravely. "Would you wait outside a minute? I've gotta talk to Chris about today's show."

"Not a problem," I say.

"Mike's not coming in."

Chris Russo and I are walking in single file, on our way to the commissary. Chris moves like a blur, toes pointed *in*.

"Mike's got some personal business to take care of," he explains.

I nod, trying to keep up with him.

"You're gonna write a book on sports talk radio, you *have* to come to F-A-N," Chris says, veering off the subject. "We were the first station to do it."

The first thing that strikes you about Mad Dog is his voice. He has a clean and melodic tenor. But the words tumble out of his mouth in a strange stew; the *l*'s and *r*'s smoosh into *w*'s, particularly when he's talking fast, which is most of the time. It is the voice of a crooner with a speech impediment.

We tear into the commissary. It's just after noon. Lots of suits, men in shirtsleeves, ties undone, committed publicly now to the fresh fruit salad, sneaking Doritos out of their desk drawers by three. Don Imus, fit, thin, urban-outfitted in a blue dress shirt, jeans, and cowboy boots, thumbs his tray down a food line offering salad. Chris says hello. Imus nods. Above him oldies are piped in through a bass-heavy sound system. Percy Sledge wailing, "When a Man Loves a Woman."

I know this place. It is a smaller version of studio cafeterias I frequented in my television-writing days, wolfing down lunch while holding my nose. The light is dim on purpose, hiding the day's specials in shadows. The faint odor of cleaning detergent wafts over the sandwich line.

This commissary offers separate food stations with men in white, slouching, attempting to balance oversize toques on their heads. Food stations? Specials? This must be the new new thing—haughty cuisine. I browse the pasta station, am a bit concerned about the little log things bubbling on the surface of the tomato sauce, and move on to the Chinese station. I opt for wok-grilled vegetables over rice. I'm curious how they can screw that up.

"I don't always come in here," Chris says.

That's a good sign.

"Sometimes I bring my lunch in. Other days I have breakfast late, about eleven o'clock. I don't like to eat on the air. I try to avoid that. A one-o'clock start's a pain in the neck. You gotta get yourself together pretty quickly."

"You do a long show."

"Five hours."

Chris makes contact with the toque-head at the pasta station. Catches him in midyawn.

"Hi, buddy. Pasta for me. To stay. No garlic."

The order confuses the guy. Chris repeats it. The guy says something completely different. Chris repeats it *again,* patiently. The guy gets it, we think, tips his toque and teeters off to prepare Mad Dog's lunch. My togue-head tosses the veggies and rice at me. Smells like a combination of soy sauce and Murphy's oil soap. Chris's pasta does a one-hopper onto his tray. We find a table, sit down. Chris digs into his pasta.

"I'm from Long Island. Went to Rollins College in Winter Park, Florida. Worked in Orlando for three years, Jacksonville for a year or two, Philly off and on, worked at WMCA in New York and worked here. That's it. Fired four times. Actually *fired* is not fair. It was change of format, things like that. I was always solo. That was the biggest adjustment I had to make. Tomorrow you'll see a different show, that's for sure."

A guy in a suit walks by.

"No Mike today," Chris tells the suit. The suit smirks. Moves on.

"This common?"

"What?"

"Mike missing a show."

"No. He does it once in a while. He's got some personal business."

"Are you guys friends?"

"Umm."

Sneak attack so early in our relationship? Screw it. I got an hour of sleep last night crunched into a question mark in United coach.

"Well, you know, we've gone up and down with that. At times we have been. Other times we haven't been. We used to socialize more than we have in the last four or five years. Mike got divorced. That was a factor."

"I talked to Eddie Andelman," I say. "When I told him I was going to see you guys, he said, 'See them separately.'"

"Ahh."

What am I doing? Stick to the easy stuff. What are your hobbies? What is your day like? How big is your TV? That sort of thing.

"We get along pretty well. But like anything else—marriage, long-term partnerships—you're gonna have your ups and downs. The bottom line is, when you do a good show, whether you're solo or with your partner, you get a good buzz off it. It goes both ways. You just deal with it. Day by day."

His eyes start to scan the room. Mary Wells warbles, "Well, I've got twooo lovers and I ain't ashamed," and I think I'd better change direction.

"What about radio, Chris? Were you into radio as a kid?"

"I listened to it a lot. Absolutely. I loved John Sterling. Sterling used to do a talk show between '70 and '78 on WMCA. And then, of course, Marv doing the Knicks. You talk to anyone who grew up in New York, Marv's the guy he's gonna give you. I wanted to be a play-by-play guy. I got a job in Jacksonville in '83 and to make a long story short, I ended up doing sports talk. With the boss's son, who was twenty-three years of age and loved pro wrestling."

I nod at Chris's lunch. "You must've prepared your show at home this morning."

"Well, I'm always thinking about it, always thinking about sports. For example, I went to Washington, D.C., this weekend, and when I got back, the first thing I did when I walked in the door was turn on the Knick game. Fortunately I caught the last six minutes. I make sure I read all the papers. Make sure I keep an eye on all the games, all the teams."

"Do you write your show out?"

"No. Absolutely not. Never write it down."

"How did 'Mad Dog' come about?"

"Bob Raissman of the *New York Daily News* gave me the nickname back in 1988 when I was at WMCA. Before FAN was even around. I think he called me that because I'm an excitable personality."

"You are a pretty high energy guy."

Through a mouthful of pasta: "Oh, *yeah.*"

I check the wall. Since Chris has to be on the air at one, we're on the clock.

"You married?"

"I'm forty-one years old. I got married in 1995. She's seven years younger than me. Met her on a plane. We just had our first kid. He's fourteen months old. We live in New Canaan, Connecticut. My parents live in Santa Fe, New Mexico. I'm an only child. My wife's not a sports fan. She'll come to the Super Bowl with me, but that's about it. She doesn't have any real interest in sports. More now that she's with me, but she's not going to turn on the Knicks tonight. Not gonna happen. Right now she's just into a being a mother."

"What do you do outside of sports?"

"A lot of interests. I love to read. Mostly fiction. This year I'm going to try to read thirty-six books, three a month. This is March one and I've read six so far. Kind of a wide range. A Jack Dempsey biography by Roger Kahn. *Blood Work,* which is a '98 mystery novel by Michael Connelly. He's a good author."

"Yeah, I like him, too. L.A. guy."

"L.A. guy, right. Former reporter. Read *The Poet,* if you haven't."

"I have."

"What an ending. You weren't expecting *that.*"

How great is this? I'm sitting here talking *books* with Mad Dog. *Mysteries,* too.

"Did you read *The Alienist?*"

"Yes. Caleb Carr. Very good book. Solid book . . ."

For the next ten minutes we swap book titles, ones that

thrilled us, ones that fell flat. Lately, for some reason, Chris is into police procedurals, especially those that chase down serial killers. Okay, it's a choice.

"I have to tell you," I say, "most sports talk hosts are not big readers. Or if they are, they tend to read biographies."

Chris shrugs. "I read those, too, but I prefer fiction. Oh. *Snow Falling on Cedars*. Tremendous book. His second one wasn't as good."

We're off and running again. We talk writers—Richard Ford, Stephen King, Robert Crais, Dennis Lehane. We confess to each other that we both keep lists. I've done it for years; he's just started. I do it because I'm anal compulsive; Chris does it so he won't repeat himself. I think we're both nuts.

"I also play a lot of tennis," he says. "Good tennis player. Love to play. Try to play three days a week."

Mad Dog talks in staccato phrases, like a hard-boiled dick out of Spillane or Hammett. Most sports talk radio guys talk in nonstop volcanic bursts. Chris, in contrast, talks in quick, sharp jabs.

"I went to boarding school in upstate New York. My father went there. Darrow School. Named after Clarence Darrow. Went there for four years. 'Seventy-four to '78. A hundred forty kids. Coed. Loved the place. Really helped me. I needed to be there. I was struggling in seventh and eighth grade. Best thing I ever did was go there."

"When you're a kid, sometimes school gets in the way of your life."

"Yeah, well, my mother's English. She's into the arts and music and languages. And I'm a sports kid. So talk about friction, especially with my mom. Now it's different. Rollins was great for me, too. Very ritzy liberal-arts college. I was a history major. Great education."

"Were you a good student?"

"Yes. I wasn't a *great* student. I was a good worker. I had about a 2.3, 2.4 average after my freshman year. I made a goal that I wanted to end up with a 3.0. I took the toughest courses and I ended up with a 3.1."

"I'm getting that you're very goal-oriented."

"Exactly. No question about it."

"So as a sports talk radio host, you have goals?"

"I take my show on a day-to-day basis. I want to do a good show *today*. I'll worry about tomorrow, tomorrow. Things could happen overnight that could change the focus of tomorrow's show. I just worry about today. Think about what I'm gonna start the show with. Do a good hour. Do a good second hour. I've decided this year to keep it simple. I've done a lot of different things. Did some TV. I did forty shows on Sundays in the mornings and at night in and around the Jets. I've done *Letterman*. Been on with him a lot. But I decided this year just to do the radio."

He sips his soda. Coughs.

"Look. I've got the best piece of real estate there is. One to six on WFAN is a better piece of real estate than any *New York Times* columnist, than any *Daily News* columnist, a better piece of real estate than Warner Wolf. More people listen to this show than read anything else. There is *one* sports talk station."

Chris checks his watch.

"We're all right," he assures me.

"Well," I say. "You've made it. You have hit a home run—"

He brushes away the thought as if it's a fly. "Yeah, yeah, I try not to . . . hey, listen. My first job in radio in Jacksonville, Florida, at WEXI? I was making a hundred bucks a week. I lived in somebody's house, paid a hundred twenty a month. No TV, no kitchen utensils, nothin'. That first year I think I made five thousand dollars. I had some help from my parents. They'd give me a hundred bucks here and there when I needed it. When I moved to Orlando, I needed some money. I went to my church in Jacksonville where I was confirmed. I wasn't confirmed as a young kid. They lent me three or four hundred bucks to get myself started in Orlando. I tried not to use my parents too much, from a financial situation. They paid for me to go to college. Darrow was expensive, I know that. They gave me a car. My dad gave me his AMC Gremlin with ninety-two thousand miles on it to go to Jacksonville. Then, in '84, when I got that job in Orlando, he bought me a Honda Civic."

"You mentioned the church . . ."

"Yeah. Pretty religious. I'm Episcopalian. I try to go to church three Sundays a month. I was very active in my church when I lived in Manhattan. Worked on programs for the homeless. Taught Sunday school. Since we moved to Connecticut, I haven't gotten involved the way I did then."

He pushes his plate off to the side. Rests his elbows on the table.

"Gotta say, moving to New Canaan? An adjustment. I love it, but my wife? I don't know. Women need to be comfortable where they live. Not the same for men. Me? I could live any-where. That place in Jacksonville? I mean, it was a tiny little place. *Tiny.* A hundred and twenty a month."

"That's the part that *we* like."

"Oh, yeah. I can deal with that. And I was getting paid about the same. But I loved the radio."

"Yeah."

"See, I love the radio. I love to be on that radio. That's the thing with me. I *love* doing a talk show."

"Well," I say feebly, "you have a good radio voice."

"I know," Chris croons. "I have a good voice. But that aside, I love being on that radio, making that radio *sing.*"

• • •

A minute to air. Scrambling breathlessly down the corridor. Chris is silent for a beat. He snaps his fingers.

"There you go."

A click of the tongue.

"I just figured out what I'm gonna do. See? It comes to me. I'm gonna tie everything in with going to D.C. People like to hear that. They like that personal stuff. To know something about you. So I'm gonna tie what I did this weekend into sports in the first segment. Take a break. Then come to D.C. in the second segment. Get to one-twenty. Do some calls at two. And see where it takes me."

"Sounds good," I say.

Hell do I know? Some guys have their show written out segment by segment. The yellow legal pad is their net. Today Mad Dog's flying without a pad or a partner.

Thirty seconds to air. We hit the glass door to WFAN and rocket through the newsroom, called the bull pen, an area of six cubicles lined up three on three, all occupied with men on phones. Facing us on the wall above is a TV screen tuned mutely to CNBC displaying the stock ticker. I follow Chris into the studio. Ten seconds to air.

"Have a seat." Chris motions me to the chair next to his. Mike's. Mad Dog slams on a headset and the music is *up*, ladies voices in harmony, blaring:

Sports radio sixty-six W-F-A-N!

Then a soulful male voice wails:

They're talking sports, going at it as hard as they cannnn!

Music bridge. Horns.

Mike and the Mad Dog . . . on the FAANNN!

Horns holler and crescendo. And the ladies jump in for the big finish:

Mike and the Mad Dog . . . W-F-A-N!

Carlin, above us, through a wall of glass, like he's standing on an observation deck and we're in here operating, hatchets down his arm toward Chris, who kisses the mike and, for the next improbable eleven seconds exactly, imitates a plane taking off:

"AaaaaaaaaaaaaaaaaaaaaAHHHHHHHHHHHHHHHHHHH HHHHHHHHHHHHHHHAHHHHHHHHHHHHHHHHHHHH-HAHHHHHHHHHHHHHHHHHHHHHHHHHHHHHHHAHHHHH-HHHHHGOODAFTERNOONEVERYYYBODDY!!!"

Barely catches his breath, gushes, "How are you *today?* The Mike and the Mad Dog radio program on this Monday. Nice to have you with us. Talking about the world of *sports.* Mike's off today. But I'll be taking you all the way until six o'clock. I saw two things this weekend. Just two things. The first thing I saw was the second half of St. John's and Duke. I gotta say, boy oh boy, games get any better than that, I gotta see 'em. What a great basketball game that was. All the made shots down the stretch . . ."

And then Chris Russo, without benefit of a box score, notes, or newspaper, re-creates, from memory, in exquisite detail, the last five minutes of the game. He describes a rainbow three by Nate James, a dunk by Postel, a bank shot by Glover. As he does, he twists his body into a variety of positions previously known only to Olympic gymnasts and practitioners of the Kama Sutra. His movements are herky-jerky, sometimes cool like hip-hop hand motions, sometimes spastic and out of control.

"Bootsie makes the big basket with twenty-one seconds left. Carrawell misses. Ball caroms off the rim, goes to the far end of the court. St. John's grabs it and holds on for an unbelievable win. Eighty-three, eighty-two for the Johnnies. A great college game."

As Chris Russo describes the St. John's win, one thing is clear: this guy is blissfully in love with sports. Most hosts I hear analyze, criticize, and pontificate. Not Mad Dog. He is thorough, detailed, and febrile. But he is first and foremost an unabashed *fan*. I have to smile as Chris spouts on about the St. John's game, wishing now, damn it, that I had seen it.

He segues into the last six minutes of the Knicks-Sixers game. With a second left, Eric Snow, the Philly point guard, got a step on Allan Houston and put up a ten-foot banker to win it. The ball sliced off the rim and the Knicks pulled out the win.

"An NBA point guard has got to make that shot," Chris hollers. "He's got to. The Knicks escaped with one yesterday. *Escaped*. One-eleven on the FAN."

Music up. A commercial about a local Chevy dealer. Chris tosses the mike aside and begins to whip through the *New York Post* and the *Daily News* laid out in front of him.

He shakes his head. "Not a lot happening."

"The Dead Zone, huh?"

"Yeah. A little bit. There's nothing really juicy to start the show with. St. Johns, Duke? Eh. The Knicks? You know. Um. Right now I'll do a little D.C. for a bit. Get me to one-twenty. I didn't see De La Hoya this weekend. Did you?"

"No."

Chris slides his chair to the door, flings it open, and shouts into the bull pen, "Anybody see De La Hoya this weekend?"

"Stand by, Dog," roars Carlin.

"*Weeeer'e* back," howls Mad Dog. For the next eight minutes, Chris gives a blow-by-blow account of his trip to Washington, D.C. He lists the attractions he and his wife visited—Vietnam Veterans Memorial, Holocaust Museum, minitour of the White House. In the middle of his White House rant, a short, quiet, balding man slips into the studio. This is John Minko, the Update announcer and resident of the FAN since its inception. Minko takes a chair opposite me, puts on a headset, and faces Chris.

"The other thing that's interesting was Amtrak. What a kick I got getting on that train in Stamford, in business class, decent seat, lotta room, with a *New York Times,* a *New York Post,* a *Daily News,* a *Stamford Advocate,* a *USA Today, Baseball Weekly, Sports Illustrated,* and a book. And, believe it or not, by the time I got off that train yesterday at five o'clock in Stamford, everything was read. Jeannie and I had a perfect weekend. We didn't talk."

Minko laughs, a half-grunt, half-cough singsong.

"Not one word to her. Hi, Jeannie. How are ya?"

He waves, as if she's standing in the control room next to Carlin.

"It was absolutely perfect. I got a weekend away and now I can watch all the basketball I want for the next three months. Did my fatherly duty. D.C. for three days and now I can watch sports through the baseball season. *Hoooo, babyyy!*"

Chris rubs his hands together as if he's about to crack a safe.

"How about that, Mink?"

"So Jeannie didn't want to talk to you at all?"

"Not particularly."

"And you got away from her cooking."

"Which is always a pleas—which is always a . . . *pipe down, Mink!*"

"Ha *haaa,*" grunts Minko.

"Mink's got the latest scores and sports news. One-twenty on the FAN," Chris announces.

He bolts from the room as Minko launches into the Update. I follow into the bull pen.

"Okay," Chris says. "Bottom line is, get this show on the tracks. See, I can't do that when I'm with Mike. It's a different feel. I wouldn't be able to do five minutes at one-twelve on Washington, D.C. I have to pick my spot. Somewhere else in the five hours. Get Mike in a good place. I can throw it on in."

He sips a soda from Minko's cubicle table. We head back into the studio. Mink finishes the Update, squeezes by us, nothing said.

A minute to air. Chris presses a button in front of him. The producer hot line.

"Continent? We got some calls? Or nobody's callin'?"

A beat.

"Really? I'm surprised. . . . What? I don't hear you."

"Sorry," Chris Carlin's voice rains down through overhead speakers. "Hit the phone number."

"See, it's quiet," Russo says to me. "No calls."

The empty-phone-bank nightmare. It's happening.

"This is very surprising." Chris blinks. "What do I do— *Strawberry?*—to get something going? I hate to even get into that."

Carlin mumbles something only Chris can hear.

"What? Tell me. Don't worry about Alan."

"No, no, I'm not worried about Alan," Carlin's voice booms into the studio. "I don't care about that."

"Well, obviously, nobody cares about the Knicks or St. John's either."

"I'm just . . . Strawberry, for Pete's sake. Just hit the numbers and we'll see where they go. Do five minutes on something else and—"

"That's what I mean."

"I wouldn't do Strawberry though."

"Let me hear your suggestion on five minutes on something else."

A pause. A test. Continent staring at an exam question he hasn't studied for. Mad Dog switches off the producer's button and leans over to me.

"Let's see if he's thinking. As a producer."

"Well."

Carlin's voice is back. A catch in the rumble. "Can't do Washington, D.C.—"

Chris Russo nods in agreement. "Can't be Washington. Can't be the Knicks, and it can't be St. John's. Give me something else now. Go ahead."

Chris folds his arms across his chest. It *is* a test.

"You could do something about Porter."

"*Nooo*. Nobody cares about Chris Porter at Auburn. Nobody knows who he *is*. What else?"

"Stand *byyy!*" Another voice crackling from the control room.

"I gotta do something on Strawberry."

"I guess," Carlin says. "I just . . . do we really need to hear from nine billion more addicts?"

"I can do Knicks-Heat tonight," Chris suggests over the intro music.

He winks at me. A saver. He's had it in his back pocket all along.

"Let's try to do *that.*" Sheer relief from Carlin. I can't see him but I know he's mopping up a puddle of sweat from his forehead.

We're back. Dog spends the next five minutes pumping the Knicks-Heat tonight and Lakers-Portland tomorrow night. He hits on the Nets and their pathetic run at the playoffs and breaks down the Big East. He insists Seton Hall deserves a NCAA tournament bid even though other so-called experts claim they're on the bubble. The segment ends and Dog still hasn't taken a call.

"Here's a little secret. He's a young producer. He does not want to go through five hours solo with me with no guests. He's a little nervous. So he's gonna throw me a lot of ideas. Some of which, you know, eh, I'm not interested in. Producers do not feel like they're contributing to a talk show unless they get guests. Just putting calls up and listening to me talk? He feels like he's not doing anything."

Maybe it's the vibe off of Mike's chair, but I suddenly feel the need to contribute.

"I'm trying to think of what happened over the weekend," I say, stretching my memory.

Dog scans the paper. "Anything in golf?" he wonders. Sounds like he's pulling at straws. "St. John's. The Knick game. Golf."

"The fight." I shrug.

"I did not see the fight," Dog says, rustling through the *Post.* "We're down on boxing anyway."

"Yeah," I say as if I knew that already.

The studio door flies open and Carlin crushes in. "Got Gammons today." He's winded. Hands on hips.

Chris looks at me.

"You know, that's not a bad idea. Do a little round table with the baseball."

"Yeah," I say, Carlin thinking, *When did he become a partner?*

"Maybe Bill Pulsipher and his nutrition situation again," Carlin blurts out, then chugs off, looking to hook up Mad Dog and Gammons or Pulsipher and quick.

"See, he'll put a couple of guys up that he knows I like to talk to that Mike doesn't love so much. He's got a tricky job in there. He's got to deal with two talk show hosts who are a bit of a pain in the ass. Plus he's got four or five guys over him who are gonna drive him crazy. He's in a tough spot. The last time I did a solo show, a couple of weeks ago, he got me a great spot. I'm close to him anyway, but he got me John McEnroe. I said, 'Continent, you wanna put a smile on my face? John McEnroe, before the end of the show. Five-twenty. There he is. A good spot."

"Thirty seconds, Dog."

"Look at the screen, Al. We're all over the map."

I check the computer monitor in front of me. All four lines

are flashing. Mad Dog is beaming. Callers had nothing to say about Washington, D.C. Mention the Knicks and the phones are ablaze.

"Let's start it off with Mark. Hey, Mark!"

Mark calls with a complaint. On Saturday, prior to the St. John's–Duke game, the local CBS station aired the Indiana–Michigan State game, an important Big Ten contest. The game went into overtime. Realizing the overtime period would conflict with the start of the St. John's game, CBS decided to switch from Indiana–Michigan State to show the St. John's game from the beginning.

Bingo.

After an hour of treading water, Mad Dog now has a *topic,* a cause, somewhere to place his energy. He has found a road on which to drive his talk show.

"Continent!" he screams into his mike. "Get me somebody on from Channel 2 in New York! That is a disgrace! What was their reasoning?"

"I called 'em," moans Mark. "They had a machine on. I gave them my complaint—"

"I didn't know *that!*" Chris hollers. "I would've led with that if I knew that was the issue! That is a *terrible* job! *Awful!* They blow off an overtime to give you the beginning of St. John's–Duke? That's an absolute disgrace! I'll try to track that down for you, Mark. That is a terrible job."

Mark is gone. Clicked into oblivion by a press of a thumb.

"I did not even *know* that was the case. Nor did I read about it. Was it in any of the papers? I'm surprised nobody picked that up. That's a *terrribbllle* job. If that's local Channel 2, they're lost. I'll be honest with you . . . they are *lost!*"

During the next call, Mink tiptoes to his chair. On the air, Chris calmly discusses North Carolina's chances in the tournament, then roars back on track.

"Mink, I did not realize this whole situation about how

Channel 2 in New York got off the Indiana–Michigan State game."

"Yes, they did. I was not pleased with that."

"That is a terrible . . . how can . . . did anybody write about it? Mushnick? Raissman? Come on! You're killing everybody else! Write that! That is a terrible job! Continent! Get somebody on! There's your spot! Put Bill Pulsipher on hold. We'll talk about his nutrition another day."

"Ho *cough* ho," laughs Minko.

Chris grins, chokes down a laugh. Got a live one and he knows it. He's home now. The phone bank's blinking like a pinball machine.

Breathing hard but happy, a pop in his step, Carlin pushes into the studio, a minute to air. "They're giving us the head of college sports programming. Mike Orosco. You gotta give him a little time to speak—"

"Yeah, sure—"

"Yeah, but, Chris, our friend at CBS said, quote, 'He can't thrash him like any other guest.'" Carlin laughs. Alone.

"I'll give him time," Chris promises.

"I'll put him up at two."

"Do it right now, Continent."

Why wait? Why lose the heat?

"All right." Carlin shoves his shoulder into the studio door and bulls toward the nearest phone.

"I won't thrash him, but I'm not gonna let him off the hook. You can't explain that one. You miss the first ten minutes of St. John's, so be it. You can't do that."

Arms across his chest. A small breath, maybe a tiny sigh of relief. Chris licks the tips of his fingers and grabs the *Post*.

"Here. Look what's in the paper. That's how you do this."

He flies through the sports section, ticking off each article with a stab of his finger.

"You got Knicks. Forget all this stuff. Knicks, Knicks, a little

Tiger, more Knicks. *More* Knicks. Baseball. This town loves baseball. *Baseball.*" He slaps the paper with his palm. "So the whole damn late edition of the *Post* . . . one, two, three . . . *nine.* You got nine of the first twelve pages on baseball and the NBA. See? That's what people are reading, and that's what we're gonna talk about."

Carlin's voice shoots through the overheads. "He's on, Chris."

"Here we go. Mike Orosco. This is a good spot. Get a little somethin' going with this. My goal is to get him off by fifty. Six minutes."

Music up. The finger point and—

"Hi, Mike is off today, we'll take you to six. Mike Orosco is the vice president of programming for CBS sports and he joins us . . ."

Orosco is deep-voiced, articulate, nervous, and defensive: "Look, Chris it was a tough decision, a very tough decision . . ."

This is the epitome of sports talk radio. A caller to the Mike and the Mad Dog show complains about a decision made about a basketball game. Less than five minutes later, the man who made the decision is on the air explaining himself to Chris Russo.

Less than five minutes later.

That's respect. And power.

The spot changes Chris. He bolts into the bull pen.

"Good spot," he says, massaging my neck. The bull pen is buzzing. Chris introduces me to the guy in the last cubicle, Eric Spitz, assistant program director at WFAN. Chris Carlin bounds down the stairs outside the control room. He's beaming. The guys in the newsroom debate whether Orosco did the right thing. Half agree with switching to St. John's. The other half are with Chris.

"Second-guessing," Spitz says. "That's what this is all about."

"You got it," Chris laughs.

Dog barrels back into the studio. I follow. He studies the computer screen.

"See? Got 'em lit up. Little topic gets me through the first hour. But to do a good sports talk show you need baseball and football. The problem with football is it's Monday and Friday. Baseball is every day. You can always come up with something in baseball to get you through a show."

Calls come in. The second caller, Rob on a car phone, drops another log on the fire.

"I totally agree with you. I had over two hours invested in that game. They kept giving scores at the bottom of the screen. One follow-up point. With fourteen seconds left in the overtime, they went to commercial instead of going back to the Michigan State game. They didn't even show you the last shot. It was outrageous."

Chris grits his teeth, shakes his head. Glares at me. "I wish I knew that. I didn't know that."

"Fourteen seconds left. Tied. And they don't show the final shot," moans Rob on a car phone.

"And how much time was gone in the St. John's game? About four minutes?"

"Yeah."

"Okay, Rob, thanks. Two o'clock. We'll come back."

Music.

Back to the bull pen, hanging out. Feels like Saturday night in a frat house. Chris rubbing necks, pounding backs, the frat president. Carlin, full of confidence now, brushes by Spitz.

"CBS called," Carlin says, a sly smile on his face. "They did show the end of the game."

Chris looks up, his hands enclosed around the neck of Eddie Scozzare, the middle-cubicle occupant. "Hold on now. They may be wrong. This guy said . . . he gave the time . . . call them back. Did they show the last shot in New York? I want that confirmed. You just had a guy who's a pretty good sports fan, two hours invested in the game, give you a good rundown. I'm gonna believe Rob before I'm gonna believe CBS."

"You're lost," Carlin says.

"I'm not going by some CBS PR guy. You think he knows?"

"Chris, they're in the *studio*. They *have* to watch the games. You're lost. You're so lost."

Chris shakes his head as everyone around him laughs. "The guy calls *up*," Chris yells. "I got two hours invested—"

"How do you know he's not watching in a sports bar or somethin' like that? Or on the dish? Why would you trust a *caller?*"

Chris turns to me. "Did you trust that caller?"

"Absolutely," I say. Can't sell out my partner.

"Why?" asks Carlin.

"He was very credible. He called on a *car* phone."

Carlin throws up his hands. Chris snickers, whacks my back. Minko emerges from the studio, tries to tiptoe into his cubicle.

"Hey, Mink, you saw the game. Did they go to the last fourteen seconds of the overtime?"

"I don't know."

"How can you not know?"

"Maybe I left the room or something."

"There you go," Chris says.

I'm dubious. "Fourteen seconds left and you leave the room?"

Chris catches my eye, gives the jerk-off sign.

"He didn't leave the room," I say.

"There you go," Chris sings. *"There you goooo!"*

Eric skips down the stairs. Chris changes the song.

"Hi Spitzy, Hi Spitzy, Hi Spitzy, Hiiiiiiiiiii-eye!"

"Can you believe it?" Spitz grins. "We're all buying new houses based on this chucklehead."

Big laugh.

At that moment, I can't imagine a better place to be than hanging with Mad Dog in the bull pen at WFAN.

The next half hour passes. With the exception of a six-minute conversation with Mike from Montclair, who calls about the upcoming Veterans' Committee decision to vote Gil Hodges into the Hall of Fame and is treated more like a guest than a caller, everyone wants to talk about the CBS decision. The final caller, a gruff truck-driver type, adamantly agrees with Chris.

"Then lemme ask you something," Chris says. "Why didn't you call CBS and complain?"

"I, uh, couldn't," the caller grunts.

"Whatdya *mean?* Why couldn't you?"

"Well, I was at my sister's wedding."

"Jeez," Chris laughs. "You shouldn't even have been *watching the game.* Two thirty-two. We're coming back."

We shoot out of the studio. Chris skips by the bank of cubicles, slapping high fives with each guy like he's in the starting lineup. Carlin, a smug look on his face, fills up the doorframe of the control room.

"I just spoke to CBS. They went to a highlight less than a minute after the break."

"Bottom line is, they didn't go to it *live,"* Chris says.

"It was *virtually* live."

"Continent, stop backing up CBS. Take it easy, willya, please? What's the matter with you?"

"I don't have any *problem*—"

"Then why are you kissing CBS's ass? What, do you think you're gonna get a *job?*"

"No, I'm actually thinking about getting guests for you from CBS for the next millennium."

"CBS likes me, you know that. Down deep they do. See, he gives me grief about how I piss off all the guests, nobody wants to come on. We get everybody we want."

"What are you killing me for?" Carlin groans. "All I do is look out for you."

Chris puts an arm around my shoulder. "Come on, let me show you a picture of my kid."

We head back into the studio. Carlin shakes his head and lumbers into the control booth.

Chris Russo is right.

Tough job pleasing everybody.

I spend a few minutes with Mark Chernoff, program director of WFAN, a top player, the guy who tried to hire Mike North. Mark is an impeccably neat man who rocks nervously behind a cherrywood desk. Cherny, as Chris calls him, wears a leather jacket and glasses, the frames of which match the color of the desk. His speech is punctuated by a continuous and pronounced nasal sniff.

"WFAN is not only the most successful sports talk radio station in the country, it was also the first. It began back in July of 1987. Before we went to all-talk, we were actually a country-music station. We struggled for a while, then we got Imus in the mornings and the station started to take off. After we put on Mike and the Mad Dog in the afternoons, we really zoomed."

A woman pokes her head in.

"Oh, Kristen, it's . . . just . . . give me a few . . ."

I got the message. I pick my ass up out of my cheery cherry chair and head back to the bull pen.

• • •

"What are you talking about? Bonds had thirty-four home runs *last* year. He's gonna have a big year."

During a commercial, Chris Russo stands center stage in the bullpen. If you want to get Mad Dog to blow up, all you have to do is mention his beloved San Francisco Giants.

"What about pitching?" Spitz goads.

"The pitching's okay. You start with Russ Ortiz."

"You're not really gonna pin your hopes on that guy."

"*What?* Last year, eighteen and nine. Three eight one ERA. On an eighty-six-win team. What else you want the guy to do?"

"He fell apart during the stretch."

"He was *good* down the stretch. I'll give you every start he made the last month and a half. Mets. On a Friday night. Seven innings, six hits, two runs. Start after that, against the Phillies. Got the win. Seven innings, four hits. The start after that. Wrigley Field. I was *there*. Got the win. First game of a doubleheader. Then the Expos. Ninth inning. Got the win. Giants won five, four. A little trouble in Milwaukee and Chicago. Then he beat the Phillies."

"You're witnessing an *idiot savant,*" Spitz says.

"Very impressive," I say. "And just a little scary."

"You should see him do this when there's nobody in the newsroom. That's really scary."

"Spitzy, how about the fact that the Giants will be sold out for every game this year?"

"You won't be able to go," Spitz says.

"I have to work with these guys every day," Chris says. "I don't know how I do it."

He shakes his head and disappears into the studio.

The Darryl Strawberry decision comes down.

Commissioner of Major League Baseball, Bud Selig, announces that he has suspended the Yankees' designated hitter for one year for his latest cocaine abuse. The calls immediately shift from St. John's–Duke to Darryl's drug problem.

One caller, a woman postal worker, complains, "If I got caught using coke at my job, I'd be fired on the spot, no questions asked, and no second chances."

"Me, too," Chris says. "The difference is, we can't hit a baseball five hundred feet. Appreciate the call. Back in five."

"This is a good show," Chris says, flipping his headset, aside. "Not a classic. But a good, solid show."

"Seems like it's going fast."

"Oh, yeah. When it's going good, it flies by." He taps his fingers on the side of the microphone. "What do you think? You think I'd play in L.A.?"

"I think you'd *kill* in L.A."

"Yeah?"

A young woman swings into the studio and hands Chris an envelope.

"Ahhh. My paycheck."

He holds the envelope up to the light and squints at it.

"You know where you'd really play?" I say. "San Francisco."

"I do love those Giants."

"He's not going anywhere," the woman says, darting out the door.

Chris fidgets, rubs his eyes, allows himself a cavernous yawn.

"Tired?"

"Little bit. I'm surprised. I ran seven miles today. I run every day. Except when I play tennis. I run three, four times a week, easy. I average about five miles a day."

Three more people come into the studio: a tall brunette in a cashmere coat, a husky guy balancing a video camera on his shoulder, and a wiry young kid schlepping a light stand. The Channel 2 news crew shooting Mad Dog for the local eleven-o'clock news.

"Set up anywhere you need," Chris says. A wave of his hand. He's been through this before. Like a million times.

I start to get up. "Am I in the way?"

"No, you're fine," Chris says. "They want to get some calls." Then into the mike: "Awright, four before five. Nice to have you with us. Bob is in Merrick. How are you?"

The brunette flings the cashmere coat over Minko's chair and folds her arms like a schoolteacher. Chris continues with calls past the hour, mostly about Strawberry, a spotlight baking him head-on, a video camera a foot in front of his face. He is totally focused, completely undistracted.

The callers, as a group, are intelligent, well-informed, and articulate. No one calls with a take or a comedy routine. There are no crazy characters with whacked-out ramblings. Few mangle the English language. I mention this to Chris during the break.

"Yeah, I'd say we have fifteen core callers who are exceptional. But this is New York. Very intelligent sports fans. Passionate. Opinionated."

He sips from a bottle of water, then indicates with a flick of his head that we should go into the bull pen, away from the TV crew.

The newsroom guys are winding down. It's like the party is over and people are cleaning up.

"This is the toughest hour of the show," Chris says. "The five-o'clock hour. You know why? More people are listening at this time, yet it's your fifth hour on the air. But you have to treat every hour the same. You can't try to turn it on at five."

"It's like running your seven miles," I say.

"That's right. After your first six, if you're not in position to win the race, what's the point? You know that, right, Continent?"

Carlin, who's been hovering by the cubicles, laughs and comes over.

"Now, Continent, what did you show Alan today as far as your ability to book guests?"

"Oh, I, uh—"

"Mike Orosco? For a minute?"

"I'm a big fan of his, by the way," I say.

"I believe I told Alan before, the Dog is the *best* at making something out of nothing."

Russo roars, applauds.

"And I think Dog said, that's because Continent always gets me nothing."

Mad Dog slams me on the back, sucking down deep gasps of laughter. It's okay. Carlin is laughing, too.

Bob Gelb has seen it all.

"I've been here since the beginning, July of 1987. I produced the very first show at this radio station. I saw us lose five or six million dollars our first two years. But I knew this concept would work."

"Why?"

"Passion. Passion from the fans. New York has nine professional sports teams and people just . . . I'll give you an example. I was at the Garden when the Rangers won the Stanley Cup. I'm sitting next to this guy and he holds up a sign: 'Now I can die.' A lot of towns have front-runners. New York has deeply passionate fans, fans no matter what. I knew it was gonna work."

"But you never thought it would turn out to be this."

"No. I never thought it would be the number one billing station in the world. Has been for the last three years."

"Imus had something to do with it."

"He saved the radio station. I pray for his health every night."

"And Mike and the Mad Dog?"

"The show debuted September fifth, 1989. Mark Mason is

the genius who's credited with putting them together. I was the guy on the phone every night lying to both of them about what they were saying about each other. Finally, even though they despised each other, they realized that, hey, this is a good gig. Let's make it happen."

Bob Gelb stares at the ceiling of Mike and Chris's office. He sits on Continent's desk and scratches his chin for a second. Gelb is bald and built like a linebacker. He has warm, intelligent brown eyes that occasionally twinkle. He is now an account executive. Translated, a salesman, which explains the blue suit.

"So you were their producer for . . . ?"

"Seven years."

"Long time."

"*Long* time."

"What's the secret of their success?"

"Passion, knowledge, and chemistry. They *mesh.* Two guys. One, very intelligent, on a barstool. Talking to Dog, the fan's fan. Sometimes people have the perception that Dog's not the smartest guy in the world. That is complete and utter BS. The guy's got a photographic memory."

"I've noticed that."

"And talk about *passion?* He has more passion for this job than any person I've ever worked with."

"Was there a time that you thought they were either gonna kill each other or kill you?"

"Oh, yeah. Every day. It still happens."

"They kind of sound like my parents."

"No. Your parents love each other. It's a business, okay? They're partners in a business. You don't have to be friends to be partners in a business. They spend five hours a day talking with each other. You're gonna get sick of each other. They don't need to be best buddies. That, for sure, they're not. And they'll both admit that."

Gelb pauses, sorts his thoughts.

"They know that down deep . . . and they might not admit this to you . . . but they work well together. Hey, look. They've been first in 'men twenty-five to fifty-four' in the ratings probably twenty-five times. Which is incredible. In the toughest radio market in the world. They're not *schmucks.*"

"Sounds like the Siskel and Ebert of sports."

"Yeah. Two guys, very passionate, who actually need each other. The difference is the *energy.*"

"What was your role?"

"My role was referee, diet Coke getter, breaking stories, screening calls, getting guests, and being a friend to both of them. Look, between Philly and here, I produced radio sports talk for seventeen years. I've seen a billion guys come and go, and I will tell you this: nobody's got it going the way those two guys do."

"Here's my take," I say. "I think what makes them tick is that they're competing with each other."

"Boom. Bull's-eye."

"And how long can they keep it going?"

Bob Gelb shrugs. "As long as they want."

Night is falling. The CBS television crew is gone, replaced by a news crew from ABC. Two people this time. A camera operator in his fifties and what could be the same brunette, standing in the back, arms folded. The camera guy, whose name is Calvin J., circles behind me to get a tracking shot of Dog. Nice touch. A bit of style. Throw in a little Scorsese for the news.

Dog is bouncing in his chair, ready to take us home. I can almost feel him getting ready to howl at the moon.

"John in Point Pleasant. John, bring it."

"I just heard about the Strawberry thing. I am not happy. In fact, I am quite upset about it. This is a disease—"

"Not a disease the first time you do it, John."

"Chris, he can't help it—"

"Not the first time."

"He, he—"

Chris's voice rises. "When he walked into some room and saw cocaine, it wasn't a disease then!"

"But, Chris, he's addicted to it—"

"He wasn't addicted to it before he ever did it!"

"But, Chris, the second he does it, everybody tries it—"

"What happened, John, before he did it? Why did he do it? Huh? Why did he do it?"

"I don't know—"

"That's the problem I have with this disease stuff! When he first saw lines of cocaine in his early twenties, he knew the difference between right and wrong, he was not addicted! And he did it! What do you want him to do?"

"I want them to help him—"

Chris, weary, "John, it's been five times. Come *onn.*"

"He's human. Don't you have any compassion for this guy?"

Chris rubs the bridge of his nose. "A little bit. Of course I do. But I'm not gonna go crazy over it, no. But this weakness or disease stuff? To me, it's a bit of cop-out. On the FAN. Back after this."

Chris winks at me. "Trying to rally here. Take us home."

The camera off, Calvin J. approaches tentatively. "Comin' from a man who never got high."

"That's not true either," Chris says.

"Strawberry? Bottom line? He doesn't like himself," the cameraman says.

"That's probably true," Chris admits.

"I know about that shit. The difference is, I like me. I'm fifty-three now. I know why I did it. I don't do it anymore. I got a next-door neighbor. He still smokes pot and he's older than me. I ask him, 'What are you doing that for?' I couldn't do that anymore. That stuff leads to something else."

"I don't know about that. Does one drink lead to ten drinks? I don't know."

"Well, I know with Strawberry, he doesn't like himself to get that blasted."

One more segment. Chris dances through three more Strawberry calls, thanks "Radio" Ray Martel, the engineer, and Chris Carlin, announces that Springsteen is playing Penn State, rocking and rolling for three hours, drug-free, and closes it out by saying simply, "Adios."

Calvin J. lays down his camera and rushes over to Chris. He offers his hand.

"This was a pleasure. I listen to you all the time."

"Well, thank you." Chris smiles.

"I thought you were a little fat bald guy."

"Did you? A lot of people think that."

Calvin laughs, heads back for his camera.

Mad Dog bolts from the studio, rubs Continent's neck, slaps Spitzy's back, a reliever after striking out the side, a rock star after the final bow, ducking out of sight behind the curtain.

"Nobody is knocking at our door. No one's getting ready to take our place. Our competition now is ourselves."

Mike Francesa thumbs his gold metal frames back onto the bridge of his nose. Behind the glasses, his eyes are sky blue and he squeezes them shut when he laughs. His teeth are two rows of small white picket fences, so white they glisten. His face is round, the color of cookie dough. Francesa gels his rust-colored hair straight back. His voice is deep, full, and ripe, and he speaks in a *rumble*. The sound is New York, born and bred. Mike is a man of bulk, thick and solid as a castle door. He waddles when he walks, listing to one side, giving the impression he's about to tip over. He has had six knee operations, and the last one, several years ago, didn't take. He's scheduled for a seventh surgery in the next few weeks.

We sit in the commissary at a table out of the way. Mike is eating a turkey sandwich. He has poured himself two gigantic diet Cokes, one he'll drink now, the other he'll carry back to the studio for later. I've steered away from today's special and gone with plain pasta. He has bought me lunch. The food tastes better today.

"So, what are you planning for today's show?"

"Welp," Mike says, caught in between bites of his sandwich, "the events of the day pretty much plan the show. The way it happens is, by the time I go to bed at night, I know where the next show's going. I get on the phone with Continent between nine-thirty and ten every morning. Like I said to him this morning, here's where the show's going today. Three things. The Knick loss to the Heat. Strawberry repercussions. Preview the Portland-L.A. game tonight. Those will be the stories that will drive our show today. We'll work our guests around those three topics. Dog'll talk to Continent, too. He doesn't really have to talk to me. If he wants someone badly, he'll put him up. I might disagree, we'll talk about it. Doesn't happen too much. Driving the show editorially is a little more my job. It's just always been recognized that way."

"What's your background?" I play around with my pasta. Not exactly Rao's.

"Went to St. John's. Got out and went to work for ESPN. ESPN was in its infancy. Then I went to CBS in 1981. Went to work for *NFL Today* and the NCAA basketball tournament. Became an editorial consultant with the network. Worked very closely with Brent Musberger, Jimmy the Greek, then Jim Nantz when he jumped aboard in 1984. Stayed there for a long time. Did some writing, too. *Inside Sports* magazine. Sports radio started and I took a shot at it. CBS put me on the air and everything took off from there. That was 1987."

"And you and Chris started in '89?"

"Yeh."

"How was that?"

"It was terrible in the beginning. We had a rough start. We didn't get along. The problem was that we both had a different idea of what we wanted to do. We're both very demonstrative, very talkative. We had to develop teamwork and chemistry. Once we got past that initial stage, we discovered that we did have a kind of extraordinary chemistry. But it took a few months to get there."

"Could you tell? Or did people have to tell you?"

He blinks, holds his sandwich in midair for a beat.

"*Uhh*. I think I recognized it, but I fought it for a while in the beginning. Because I didn't know if that's what I wanted to do. I wasn't sure if I wanted to go off and do a show by myself. In that first year, I really wasn't married to the show. It took me a while. I think we still fight it sometimes. You have to make concessions. There are days you're not happy with. There are days that are real good. There are days you'd rather be by yourself. We've both always kept our own shows. He does a Saturday show, I do a Sunday show."

"You each have to bring something different to the table."

"Exactly. He brings outrageousness and a quick-trigger, impulsive view of things. He'll make up his mind in twenty seconds. He brings a lot of what the regular fan feels. I don't do that. I'm too entrenched in who I deal with and who I know. A lot of my best friends are coaches and TV executives, and big in business. The circles I travel in are different than the ones a normal guy travels in. I don't think most sports radio guys in this country deal with the kind of people I do, day to day."

"People like . . . ?"

"Bill Parcells is probably my closest friend in the world. I'm close to a lot of coaches. Van Gundy, Calipari, Jimmy Johnson. I've just kind of grown up with them. I knew a lot of them when they were assistants and I was at CBS. I developed relationships with them that I've kept all these years. I knew Jimmy Johnson when he was an assistant coach at Pittsburgh. I knew John Calipari when he was a grad assistant. Guys like that. So my view is a little different. I think, more than anything else, we're just very different people."

"Tell me about you growing up."

"Welp. I was a sports guy. I wanted to be a player. I was a pretty good baseball player, good athlete. Had a lot of knee problems by the time I was seventeen. Grew up in Long Beach, Long Island. Watched everything. Huge Yankee fan. Grew up on Mel Allen, Phil Rizzuto. Obviously, Marv Albert. Marv Albert was a cult hero. There is no one in this business, in New York, between the ages of thirty and fifty, who was not affected by Marv Albert. Remember in those days, the games were only on the radio. There was no TV, no cable yet. You wanted to follow the Knicks, you turned on the radio and there was Marv giving you a virtuoso performance. And it was those great Knick teams that have spawned so many interesting people like Bill Bradley and Phil Jackson. I was a typical New York kid who loved sports. But I always knew my life would be in sports, somehow, some way."

Mike Francesa dabs his chin with his napkin. I consider his size, his voice, his confidence, combined with his look of a well-heeled businessman nattily attired in a smart brown sports jacket and contrasting but perfectly chosen maroon tie. His presence fills up the room.

That's what it is.

Mike Francesa is *presence;* Chris Russo is *energy.*

The two products are combustible. Stand too close and you will get scorched.

I wonder about his family.

"Two brothers. Older one raised me. I didn't have a father after I was eight."

"Did he pass away?"

"No, he took off. He left. I was eight years old. My older brother was fourteen, my younger brother was six."

Then he drops a bomb.

"Probably the worst year of my life was 1990 when my younger brother committed suicide."

"Wow, I'm, I didn't know," I stammer.

"That's okay. It's all right." Mike is calm, soothing. "I talked about it on the air."

"How did that change you?"

"Interesting. I'm sure it changed me profoundly, but I don't know how to tell you exactly. I went through a real wild streak in my life after that. I think that's over with."

"So you sort of acted out—"

"I dunno," he says quickly. "I dunno. It's hard to say. A lot of people who know me pretty well seem to think that. Uh, I don't know."

"How long did the wild streak go on?"

"Four or five years. Marriage broke up. Girl I was married to for a long time. We're still good friends but, you know, things got a little crazy. I got a little crazy. Not drugs. Not doing anything illegal or anything like that. Just doing things I shouldn't have done. Now I've settled down again. I'm an old man of forty-five. I'd say it happened about two years after he was gone. It definitely had an impact on me. How exactly? I can't really put it into words."

"I guess people deal with that kind of thing in different ways. Some people go inside, others take it outside. Sounds like you went outside—"

"Hard to say. Whatever it was, it took a while to justify it. That's wrong. You never really justify it. You have to just learn to live with it comfortably. No one's gonna go through life and not be hit with tragedy. I've never been one to use excuses. Instead, I've used those things in my life to motivate me. I grew up without a father. That motivates me. You can either go that way or use it as an excuse."

"It's been a powerful motivator."

"Very. In 1988, I asked them to give me afternoon drive. I saw Pete Franklin wasn't getting it done. I *really* wanted to do afternoon drive. I *knew* I could be successful at it. I said—this is a true story— 'You give me afternoon drive, I'll be there for fifteen years.' That's what I told Mark Mason, the program director at the time. He came in the next summer and said, 'You're getting afternoon drive. But you're not getting it by yourself.' I was resistant. I said, 'Just give me a year by myself.' It's all based on getting the ratings, right?"

"Yep."

"I mean, that's what it comes down to. Whoever finishes first is right. That's all there is to it. See, in our business, if you're first, you're right. That's what it's all about. It's about finishing first. Now, we've always done it differently. We do a classy show. We don't do garbage. We're not a scatological show, we're not a sex show. We do *sports*. Now we get pretty insulting sometimes. We come down hard on people. But we're not degrading and we don't make it personal. We don't get into someone's appearance or their family or their ethnicity. We might knock 'em for the job they're doing and we will be very candid about what's right and what's wrong. We are very outspoken."

"No guy talk."

"We do not do guy talk. We do sports talk."

Mike folds his hands in front of him. His fingers are pink and stubby. A catcher's hands.

"What are your interests outside of the show?"

"Business. I'm a businessman. Investments. Stock market. Real estate. Thoroughbred racehorses. I'm involved in a lot of different things."

Sip of the Coke.

"I'm also very well versed. I could do a show about business on the air tomorrow. I could do a *political* show on the air tomorrow. *Tomorrow.* I could do a show on the Academy Awards tomorrow for three hours. I am very well versed on what's going on in the world. *Very* well versed. You can't do these shows without being *current.* You have to stay current. I don't wanna just attract the sports guy. I know the die-hard sports guy, he's there for us. He's not going anywhere. He *loves* us. Because we really are a hard-core sports show. That doesn't mean we can't do different stuff."

He coughs, holds a fist to his mouth like a microphone.

"Give me a typical Mike day."

Mike nods. Something's stuck in his throat. He takes another sip of Coke, clears his throat.

"Hi, Dog."

Chris has come into the commissary. He's wearing a blue suit.

"Hello, baby," Mad Dog says with a wave. He heads to the pasta station, stops to chat with Imus, who slaps a lunch tray against his thigh.

"I get up about seven," Mike says. "I have a live-in girl-friend. I might spend some time with her in the morning. First thing I do in the morning is watch *SportsCenter.* That's required. You don't have to do anything else. Then, honestly, I spend a couple of hours doing investment work. Trade some stocks, do some different things. Then it's my time to talk on the phone. The phone rings constantly. *Constantly.* I talk to Continent. Do what we have to do with him. Beat him up a lit-tle. And he gets his ass *kicked.* Because we're tough. We're both very temperamental. We're not easy to work for. We're good bosses in that we're good payers, and we share the wealth. But we're hard on him. We beat the hell out of him. That's a hard job to do. Plus we get *mad*. Sometimes we get mad at each other, too. Okay, then, I leave for work about eleven-thirty. About a half-hour drive in. I listen to stuff in the car. Sometimes I listen to Rush Limbaugh. It depends. I bounce around. Whatever interests me. I like listening to talk. Bob Grant, sometimes, on the way home. I try to listen to different things."

"You ever check out other sports talk?"

"No." He sounds annoyed. "I never listen to sports talk. I'll listen to other kinds of talk because I think I might grab something from that. I'm not gonna grab something from sports talk. Okay?"

Mike stands, walks over to the soda machine and fills up his giant Styrofoam cup with ice. No soda. This must be my cue. Juggling my coat, tray, notepad, and tape recorder, I follow. Like Jimmy fucking Olson.

"When I come in, I'm ready to go."

He sits back down. I read that cue wrong. I join him, lay all my crap on the seat next to me.

Francesa barrels forward. "Then I'll go through the papers. But I don't need to see the papers. See, a lot of paper guys will say, 'Oh, those guys can't do a show unless they read the papers.' Around the country, that's true of a lotta guys. That's not true of me. The paper guys tune in to me because I got better sources than they do. And they know it. They can't get to Parcells. I talk to him every morning. My relationship with him has created tremendous controversy. Nothing I can do about it. We've been very close for fifteen years. I'm not gonna change that."

"Lot of conflict between journalists and sports talk radio hosts—"

"Very adversarial. They're terribly jealous. A couple of reasons why. One, sports radio has been the worst thing that could ever have happened to the newspaper guys. If a story breaks at eight o'clock, it's on the radio at eight oh one. They can't get it into the paper until the next *day*. That's a terrible, *terrible* hardship for them. It would drive me out of the business. Think about it. I have immediate impact. I've broken stories at two in the morning. They gotta sit on a story for twenty-three hours. Newspapers are dead from that standpoint. *Dead*. Number two, they're jealous because of the money. Paper guys don't get *paid*. The lowest guy at our station who's doing a regular shift makes more than almost anybody who works at a newspaper. Forget what the top guys at the radio station make. It's a different world. But if they thought they could do it, they'd be over here in a second. Every one of 'em has tried. They've all begged for jobs. Tremendous jealousy. But here's the difference and I'll say this straight out. These guys on TV, the talking heads? They come in and do their three minutes? A lot of 'em don't know anything. You can't come in and do my show and not know anything. How you gonna do it? Five hours. You're gonna get *exposed*. You know how many guys, TV guys, writers, who have walked into talk radio and said, 'Holy *shit?*' It's like bombs from every direction. You don't know where the calls are coming from. Every *direction*. It's eight different topics. It's free-form."

"It sounds like you love it."

"I do love it. It's very challenging. Plus I know I'm good at it. I not only think I'm good at it, I think I'm the *best* at it. I don't think anybody's ever been better at it. I really, truly believe that. It sounds cocky, it sounds arrogant. It's my belief. I think I have the right kind of mind for it. And I think I've taken it to a higher level. I really do."

He suddenly smiles.

"Funny. I thought at first that I didn't have a good enough voice to be on the air. Matter of fact, if you based it on the old days, where voice was a big issue, Dog and I wouldn't have gotten *hired*. Dog's got a terrible voice. Unique but terrible. I have a terrible voice. But it's amazing. People *like* our voices. I think it's my worst quality. There comes a point where you can't separate the voice and the personality. You can't divide them. My personality is entwined in that voice. The people in this town hear my voice now and they immediately know the personality attached to it. Our show has been covered like a team. We get so much publicity and so much criticism. We were the darlings of this town. I told Dog, I said, America loves success stories, but they hate success. They want to knock you off the same pedestal they helped put you on. In the beginning, everyone was complimentary. Now everyone takes shots. What fun is it to be complimentary to the guys who are now on top? We have to maintain. Work hard to stay there. Sports is what I am. It's my being."

Mike Francesa stops himself for a nanosecond. He repeats what he has just said as though he has made a discovery.

"That's what it is," he says. "Sports is my *being.*"

A flick of his glasses.

"You know why we're so good? You know why? We bring this inner, kind of, *arrogance.* We both think we're good alone. That we don't need each other. Here is this really good top team that actually doesn't need each other. I'm better without him, he's better without me, that sorta thing. You put it together and it can be tremendously volatile. Some days it can be as cohesive as a violin concerto, and some days it's like scratching glass. Some days it's like taking two cars and ramming them together. We won't agree about the weather. From Jump Street, we're at each other's throats. Some people relish those days. We don't plan those days. We don't say, 'Let's have a fight today.' We can be going along smoothly and all of a sudden we'll get into a brawl. Just the way we are."

Mike stares ahead, almost as if he's putting himself into a trance.

"A lot of days, I really like to close out the world. Sometimes I go in my house—I got a nice house—and I have my girlfriend there, and we just watch TV and just close out the world. No phone, no nothing. And that's about as good as it can get sometimes."

"I can tell by your face—"

"Shut the world out." He closes his eyes. His head sways ever so slightly. "I need that. I have to do that at least once a week. I gotta shut the world out. No one else there."

"Think you'll be doing this in five years, Mike?"

"Maybe. *Maybe*. It's funny. I'll tell you this. I'll never work with another partner. I'm not saying I wouldn't do another show. But I will never work with a partner again. I will never do another two-man show. Mike and the Mad Dog is it for me. Because I don't think you can ever duplicate it. It's been too successful. It's been too good. I can understand Jordan not wanting to play on another team. When you achieve success like that, it's so hard to do again. There was definitely a time when I considered running out on it. That time has passed. I have to say, I think he's bent more than I have. Whatever the reason. He's been more pliable. You have to give him credit for that. We are both very protective of what Mike and the Mad Dog is. Look, we're not dumb. We know what we are. We know how we're looked at across the country. We know we're kind of like the IBM—I think that's what *Sports Illustrated* called us—the IBM of sports talk. Whatever, we know we're the gold standard."

He stands. The signal for us to squeeze back down the corridor and head into the studio for the show.

"The best part of a two-man show is you're not ever reliant

on anything else to do the show. We always have each other. We don't have to rely on guests or calls. You do a one-man show, you can't do monologues for five hours. You have to go to the calls. You have to go to the interviews. Here we can do five hours, just us. The other thing is, when one of us is down or distracted, the other one can always carry the load. Or provide the energy. There are days when you don't feel well, or things aren't going right. The other guy can always *sense* that. And he'll just take the lead and go. You know that. Nothing is ever spoken about it either."

Mike Francesa lurches down the corridor. Breathing hard, he motors, *fast* for a big guy with a bum knee.

And then, seemingly as part of his breathing, he exhales softly, "You just *know* it."

As promised, Mike starts with the Knick loss to the Heat, a game in which the Knicks raced to a twenty-point advantage, watched Alonzo Mourning crumple to the court with a knee injury, and then sleepwalked through the second half as such household names as Clarence Weatherspoon and P.J. Brown powered the Heat to victory. Mad Dog believes this was a game the Knicks needed to win; Mike shrugs it off. He claims that Heat coach Pat Riley burns his team out during the regular season while Knick coach Jeff Van Gundy doesn't get his team up until the playoffs.

"The Heat won't get past the second round," Mike asserts.

Two more segments, exactly as Mike has planned: a heated discussion of Strawberry and a breakdown of the Portland-Laker game.

During the break, I ask if they dressed for me.

Chris snickers. "We're going to a charity event tonight."

"We gonna be back for that Portland-Laker game? I wanna see that," Mike says.

"I think so. I think we'll make it," Chris says.

Continent muscles through the door. "Got Ainge. I figure between Stockton, Hubie, and Ainge, you'd want Ainge."

"What is that, three guys in the booth for a regular-season game?" Mike asks.

"Yeah."

"Put Ainge up early. The show's slowin' down," Chris says. A look from Mike? I can't quite see. But Chris backs off: "Well, maybe not. Maybe not."

First segment of calls. Chris mans the phones. He chooses the calls and cuts off the callers when he feels it's time. The calls, five of them, go Knicks, Strawberry, Knicks, Strawberry, Knicks. Mike and Chris ease in and out of each call smoothly. They are like a sports-talk dance team, dipping and sliding effortlessly, Chris at the trigger, controlling the flow of the phone calls, Mike controlling the flow of the conversation. At this break, taking us to the end of hour one, Mike and Chris bolt out of the studio. They go in opposite directions. Chris takes a seat in Minko's cubicle and fires through the *Post* on Mink's desk, wetting the tips of his fingers as he flips the pages. Mike heads toward Chernoff's office. Continent lumbers into the bull pen.

"Typical show?" I ask Continent.

"Yeah. I would've thought though that we'd have more Knicks and less Strawberry. Whenever the Knicks lose a game like that, after being ahead by twenty, it always makes for a better show. That's not to say we're rooting for that, because we're not. The better they do, the better we do. But for that show, you know people are gonna call in, ticked off, wanting to talk about it."

Mike comes back into the bull pen. "Don't take any information from him," he advises me. "He knows nothing."

Carlin chuckles, then rolls his eyes and leaves. Mike sits in Spitzy's chair.

"We're gonna have a bad month. I can feel it. The ratings are gonna be terrible."

"Why?"

"Instinct. It's just been flat. Not a lot going on. We can usually tell. There hasn't been a lot of sizzle. We didn't have much football to go on. The local teams were out of it. We've been talking about it for a coupla weeks now, it's not any surprise. You can kinda feel when it's been slow. Yeh, the ratings are gonna suck."

Mike and Chris devote the entire next segment to an interview with Danny Ainge, former Boston Celtic player, ex–Phoenix Suns coach, current NBA announcer. Mike and Mad Dog alternate questions. The questions are smart and pointed; Ainge's answers are sharp and direct. To my ears, it is a strong interview, the perfect setup to tonight's big Portland-Lakers game. The only concern going in is that Ainge is calling on a cell phone.

"He was okay," Chris says. He presses the button into the control room and says, "Line was okay, Continent, no problem."

Mike, suddenly quiet, begins to go through his mail.

"Needed that," says Chris, biting a fingernail. "Needed that spot."

"Now, to me, that was a good interview," I offer.

"It was good, solid, no problem with that spot. That was a good Mike and the Mad Dog spot. Would you agree, Mike?"

"Yeh it was fine," Mike says, not looking up from his mail. The sentence comes out of his mouth machine-gun fast, almost as one word: "Yehitwasfine." When Mike talks this fast, it's a message: he's telling you he really doesn't want to talk at all. It's not exactly dismissive, but, well, almost. No one speaks until the next segment. During the segment, Mike flips through his mail and Chris gnaws at his nails.

The program director, Mark Chernoff, comes in, places a sheet of paper in front of Mike. Chris catapults out of his chair, darts into the bull pen.

"Not a fax you have to read on the air," Chernoff says to Mike.

Close your eyes, it's Woody Allen talking.

"I'm just showing it to you," Mark says. "You wanna address it, fine, if not . . ."

"What is this?"

"From a listener. Her husband used to listen to the station all the time. He passed away. You don't have to address it—"

"What do you want me to do with it? What are you giving it to me for?"

"I'm just showing . . . sometimes there's an appropriate moment. If not, you don't have to, I'm not—"

"It's the new warm and feeling good, is that it basically?"

"Well, yes, that's—"

"Until the ratings come out tomorrow?" Mike nods toward me. "Have you talked to this man?"

"Yes, we're going to talk again later," Mark promises.

"Talk to him," Mike says to me. "He knows what's going on. He's actually a good program director. Excellent dealing with talent. Which is not easy. Especially guys like me."

From the bull pen, a roar of laughter, Chris's high-pitched peal in the lead. He reenters the studio, a grin stitched on his face. He whacks Cherny on the back. The program director winces and escapes into the newsroom, otherwise unscathed.

In the next ten minutes, I see the best of Mike and the Mad Dog. In their headsets, from Continent, they receive the announcement of the Veterans' Committee's electees into the Baseball Hall of Fame: a Negro League player, a player from the nineteenth century, and Sparky Anderson.

"That's it?" Mike asks. "Those three? So the Gil Hodges people can get up and scream for another year."

"Didn't make it," says Chris.

"Didn't make it," Mike confirms. "You know, I'm not one who romanticizes about Gil Hodges getting in, but they've let guys in with worse stats."

"Mike, he's got the same stats as Tony Perez."

"Yeah, listen, I know they don't wanna let in too many guys from that team. I know that's what it is. Basically, half that team's in the Hall of Fame."

Chris wags his head and reaches over for a hefty volume with a faded red cover: *The 1992 Baseball Encyclopedia.* You'd think the number one radio station in the world could afford a more current edition but . . .

Dog leafs through the pages, an ear cocked to the conversation.

"You can make a case," Mike says. "The guy hit over thirty home runs six times. He hit over twenty home runs eight times. He knocked in over a hundred runs seven times. He was a slick fielder."

"Mike, I agree." Dog reads out of the *Encyclopedia,* "Perez, lifetime .279; Hodges, .273. Perez, 379 home runs; Hodges had 370. Perez, lifetime, had 1,600 RBIs; Hodges had 1137, but—"

"That's a big difference."

"*But.* Perez played seven hundred games more than Hodges did."

"Oh, no question."

"*And* Hodges was a much better defensive first baseman. At least that's what everybody tells you."

"Oh, yes. Hodges was a slick fielder."

"Plus he managed the '69 Mets—"

"I think that really helps him—"

"He's a Hall of Famer in my book."

"I'm now a proponent of putting Joe Torre in the Hall of Fame," Mike adds. "When you couple his Yankee managing career with his baseball career, which was superb, borderline Hall of Fame to begin with, that puts Joe over the top. Same thing for Hodges. The problem is, Dog, how many Brooklyn Dodgers from that team are in?"

"Well, you got Reese in there. You got Robinson. Snider's in there. Campanella, that's four. Anybody else? No pitchers—"

"Newcombe's in the Hall of Fame."

"Oh, Newcombe. Five. That it?" Chris's face clouds. "Is Newcombe in the Hall of Fame?"

"I think he is, yes."

"Okay. That's five off of one *team*. I think you're right about Newcombe. Let me just double-check him. I *think* Newcombe's in the Hall of Fame. Ahhh. I think Hodges should be in the . . . *huh*. Newcombe is not in the Hall of Fame."

"I thought he was. How many games did he win?"

"One forty-nine."

"We might be missing one."

"Well, let's see, Reese.

"Definitely."

"Robinson."

"Definitely."

"Snider."

"Definitely."

"And Campanella."

"Definitely."

"Pick a Dodger team, Mike."

"I'm trying to think if we're missing a pitcher."

"Junior Gilliam's not in the Hall of Fame."

"Noo."

"I'll pick . . . 1950."

Mike, fingers splayed, shakes his head. "I guess it's four."

Chris, pointing at the page, reads, "Preacher Roe, Cox, didn't make it. Four. Four guys made it. You know what? You can put Hodges in the Hall of Fame. You think that's too many?"

Mike shrugs seriously. This *matters*. "That's a lot off one team. What team's got more?"

"I'm sure the Yankees do—"

"Yeah, but what *team*? You gotta pick a team. You wanna pick the '36 Yankees?"

"I wouldn't go that. Because that's a *great* team."

"That might be the best team *ever.*"

"Let's take the '41 Yankees? How's that? Is that fair? Because that was the first year of Rizzuto. You gotta give me Rizzuto—"

Mike smiles. "Okay."

"Joe Gordon in the Hall of Fame?"

"No," Mike says, making a face like there's a bad smell in here.

"Rizzuto is."

"Yeah."

"DiMaggio is."

"Yeah." Mike checks them off on his fingers.

"Bill Dickey is."

"Yeah. Any of their pitchers? Is Red Ruffing in the Hall of Fame?"

"Yes."

"Four. Lefty Gomez is. Five. Is Tommy Henrich in?"

"Yes. I think so."

"I don't know. Let's check . . ."

This segment is not at all what I expected from Mike and the Mad Dog. I expected heat, confrontation, fireworks.

Instead, right before my eyes, Mike Francesa and Chris Russo, feared and famous kingpins of New York sports talk radio, become two twelve-year-old boys sitting on a stoop on a hot summer's day, tossing a ball back and forth, smacking it occasionally into the well-oiled pockets of their gloves, talking *baseball,* the most important topic in their lives. The conversation about Gil Hodges being worthy of the Hall of Fame is riveting radio. Riveting because it is so simple, so gentle, and so genuine. And so passionate that the conversation continues off the air. Mike walks behind Chris and peers over his shoulder as Dog looks up Carl Furillo of the Dodgers. They look up Joe Gordon, Red Ruffing, Lefty Gomez, and Duke Snider. The break is over before they know it, before they're ready, and Mike limps back to his seat.

"That was great," I say.

"Well, talking baseball, trying to jog your memory, it was a long time ago," Mike says.

"Yeah," Chris says. "That was a good spot."

Then, with a thump, he closes the *Baseball Encyclopedia.*

Joe Torre has turned Chris Carlin down.

"Torre won't come on," Continent reports over the speakers in the studio. "Quote, 'I'm done talking about Strawberry.'"

"What about Leyritz?" suggests Chris. "Let's talk about the DH, do a baseball spot."

"I'll call and ask him," Continent says.

"See, you can tell he's getting antsy," Chris says. "Only the one spot yesterday. Only Ainge today. Two spots in ten hours. No Sparky, now no Torre. He wants to get somebody on the air."

Mr. Update, John Minko, tries to sneak to his seat.

"Hey, Continent, who's our update guy Thursday for the Radio-Thon?" Mike asks, back on the air. "You know, the Radio-Thon's our biggest charity event of the year. Whatdya say, Mink?"

Chris roars. "Hey, Mink, get you all dressed up."

"Mink," Mike says, "we decided we want you. Are you in town?"

Mink, on the spot, on the *air,* fidgets in his chair. "Am I in *town?* Well, no—"

"Are you off Thursday?"

"Yes."

"Not anymore. You're gonna be with us," Mike announces. "Dust your wedding suit off."

"Oh, *man.*" Chris laughs. "Mink is looking at me—"

"Continent, change the schedule, Mink has decided to join us Thursday. Mink, get down there bright and early for the nine-o'clock 'cast. We'll join you about one."

Mike, Dog, and Mink erupt with laughter. But Mink's forehead has flushed a scary shade of pink.

"To make him feel better, Mike, tell him Butler is gonna make the tournament."

"They have to win their league," Mike says.

"Jeez, they've won twelve in a row," Mink complains.

"I know you have a blind spot for Butler, but they still have to win their league. Who's their best player, Mink?"

"I don't know. I'll tell you who's been playing well, Dave Robisch's son."

"Really?" Mike says. "Is he a lefty, too, this kid?"

"I don't know. I've never seen him play."

"You've never seen Butler *play?*"

"No. Not this year."

"Don't you watch 'em on the dish sometimes?"

Minko laughs. "What dish? I'll have to come to your house."

"The only way you're coming to my house is if you're picking me up for work."

Chris is really laughing now.

"Hey, Dog, are we gonna do that Hofstra game?"

"I believe so, Mike."

"That's coming up soon, Dog. And you're doing the play-by-play. You've got some work to do. I'm doing the color, but you have to know all the players from both teams. I can do the color whether I know the players or not. But you gotta know their names, their backgrounds, where they're from, the whole thing—"

"Oh, Mike, take a look at the screen."

"Continent?" Mike howls. "You wanna do three in the booth that day? You wanna let Continent do the play-by-play?"

"You know what? I've always done the play-by-play," Chris says. "How about it?"

"Continent? The whole game?"

"He's always telling me how good he is—"

"Okay," Mike decides. "Three in the booth. He can do the play-by-play."

"How's that, Continent? You're in. Now you have a lot of work to do. Gotta learn all these players. Wait a minute. When are you going on vacation to Bermuda?"

"Saturday," Carlin says over the speakers, "but I'll, I'll, get the information faxed to me down there—"

"Oh, man," Mike says, "he's stuttering."

"The Maine Black Bears against the Hofstra Dutchmen. He'll have no clue."

"Can you see him on the beach? *Hi, honey, I'm the Hofstra play-by-play man.* That'll go over big in Bermuda. Continent in his white shorts and straw hat."

Mink laughs so loudly he actually begins to shake.

While Minko finally does the Update, Mike, Chris, and I gather in the bull pen and surround Carlin.

"You just got a huge break, Continent," Chris says.

"I know. I'm really, thanks, I don't—"

"Let me just confirm it with Cherny."

Chris rushes into Mark Chernoff's office. Mike plants himself beneath the television monitor in the room. He watches the stock ticker flashing by. I join him.

"What do you like?"

A different tone of voice, all business, as he rattles off five or six stocks, companies *and* symbols. I scribble the symbols down in my notepad. Chris returns, whacks me on the back as he races past, heads into the studio to read a commercial. A second later, Chernoff, looking dazed, appears.

"So Continent's doing the play-by-play?"

"Well, yeah," Carlin says, a hopeful look at Mike.

"And Eddie's gonna be a runner," Mike announces.

"Eddie," Chernoff says.

"Yeah. If Continent's in the booth doing play-by-play, who's gonna get us our diet Cokes?"

"Well, okay, we'll talk about the Hofstra game on Monday," Chernoff says.

Head down, knees nearly clanking together, he speed-walks back to his office.

"As a program director, I try to listen as a fan," Mark Chernoff says.

"So if you didn't have this job, you'd listen to Mike and the Mad Dog?"

"Oh, *absolutely*. Listen, Mike and Chris are so good. The way they converse with each other, the way they converse with callers. There is both a likability and a tension factor because they don't always agree on stuff. Their manner and their knowledge . . . they are so special and so different from any other sports show I've ever heard. And I've listened to all of them when I'm looking for other talent. It's hard to pick other talent because you want to compare everything to them—"

"Chern."

Mike's presence first fills the doorframe, then the room.

"Yes, sir," Chernoff says.

Mike hobbles toward his program director. Like an awning collapsing, he leans his barrel chest over Chernoff and circles his arms around him. It is a fatherly gesture, both a hug and a wrestling hold.

"Come on now," Mike says, his voice a hoarse whisper.

"Yes, Mike."

The little man, dwarfed by Mike, trapped in his embrace, embarrassed in front of the stranger, blushes.

"You need a pep talk," Mike says. He lowers his voice even further, presses his mouth to Chernoff's ear. "Don't you worry so much about these ratings. If you're down in the dumps, it shows. You're always worried about the ratings book. Your head is always in the book."

Mike sways him back and forth. In Francesa's powerful grip, Chernoff can do nothing but go with him, back and forth, back and forth, and laugh, a high-pitched, falsetto giggle.

"Mike, what's my job?" he manages, a plea for release.

Mike holds him tight, ignores him. "You're translating the wrong message to the whole place." The statement comes out in a wheeze. Francesa goes from father figure to Mafia don.

"You're down right now," Mike says.

"I only had this discussion with you and Dog," Chernoff protests.

"You're walking around with the brook-trout face on—"

"Do I look like I'm walking around like that?" Chernoff asks me.

"No, I—"

"You're worried about it," Mike says. "I told you this was gonna happen. We discussed it. You knew we were gonna have a soft winter. We're having a soft winter. Okay?"

"But what's my *job?*" A tiny, barely audible whine.

"I understand that. It was a tough winter. You could tell it was coming. No question about it. But we're moving into March. We'll be okay. I'll be back in one piece before the spring book. The bottom line is, I will come back here and get you a one in the spring like always."

"Okay."

"Guarantee it."

"But March . . ."

"That's gonna be tough. But I'm guaranteeing a one in the spring. So let's go. Let's pick it up."

"Okay."

Mike releases Chernoff and claps his hands. A football coach now. "I wanna see more enthusiasm."

"Awright," says Chernoff.

"We have a big Radio-Thon. Okay? It's your big day."

Chernoff sighs.

"He plans this whole thing," Mike tells me. "*Huge* charity event. Twenty-eight and a half hours. He's the man. He does everything. *Everything*. He either whispers in my ear or hands me a card the whole day. That's all I do. It's the only day all year I listen to him."

I laugh and Mike staggers out of the office.

Chernoff needs a moment. I bring up Mike's surgery. We talk offhandedly about it, when it's scheduled, what it entails. Mark gains his composure rapidly, in about twenty seconds. I can feel a shield go up between us like the dividing glass in a taxicab.

I nod at the doorframe so recently vacated by Francesa. "That was nice."

Mark sniffs.

"It seems like he genuinely cares about you."

Chernoff's voice goes up an octave. "Oh, he does. He does. No, I think we have a long-standing, excellent relationship."

"Do you take the ratings personally?"

"As a program director, you constantly worry. You get ratings every month. I have friends who are program directors who literally throw up every month. I don't do that. I don't take it that much to heart. The way I look at it, when the ratings are good, they're never good enough. And when they're bad, I take it personally. My job is, I have to be number one in my target demographic. I'm not the host. But I'm still the director. I don't tell Mike and Chris what to say and what to do. Do they *need* a program director? I'd like to think they do. For the moral support, for help, scheduling, to help them when *they're* down in the dumps. I'm the one responsible. They look at my report card."

He abruptly stands. "I'm done for the day."

Five oh five. Continent puts up Johnny Bench to talk about Sparky Anderson. Mike and Chris alternate the questions. Bench launches into stories about Sparky, the 1976 World Series sweep of the Yankees with Thurman Munson, Pete Rose's gambling, and his relationship with Tony Perez ("I cried when Tony got traded and I cried when he got into the Hall of Fame. I don't know of a finer man"). The interview ends at five twenty-five. Twenty minutes. Twenty minutes of terrific radio.

"You know what? He helped," Chris says. "We needed that."

"Itwasagoodspot." Mike shrugs.

"That's a spot maybe we don't normally do, but it's slow, five oh five, and he turned out to be good."

"Well, it's John Bench, I mean, that's not a bad spot," Mike says.

One segment left.

"So how was Washington?" Mike asks Chris. "Awright, let's go through your trip. Friday?"

"Capitol Hill," Chris says.

"Awright, next?"

Mike's voice is hoarse. But they're in the home stretch and he doesn't hold back. I wonder how he'll get through the charity auction tonight, after the show. Well, there's Chris. He can carry the ball for the team. Just like Chris will carry it when Mike's recovering from knee surgery.

There are no gimmicks here. Hard-core sports only. Check your guy talk shtick at the door. Because (a) they don't like it and (b) they don't need it. They begin segments with phone calls, announcing simply, "Mike and the Mad Dog," then instantly, "Bill on a car phone." No intro, no setup, no frills. Just the ID. Mike and the Mad Dog. This is usually a sports talk radio no-no. But Mike and Chris do it this way because they *can*.

"Adios," Chris says.

The segment is done. Another show in the books.

They're gone, done for the day, blowing out of the studio like two separate twin tornadoes.

VIII.

line two

PAPA JOE CHEVALIER:
BITE ME

armand Joseph "Papa Joe" Chevalier is fifty-two years old, six feet tall, and chubby. He has a soft round face partially hidden behind large gold wire-rimmed glasses. He reveals two perfect rows of gleaming white teeth when he smiles and small brown eyes, one of which veers slightly off center.

"I began as a caller. Made my first call when I was in Vegas, working as an 'eye in the sky.' Great job. Better than dealing dice. Besides your pay, you could sign for your meals, which was incredibly attractive to me."

"What's an eye in the sky?"

"Your job is to detect cheating. You sit in a room above the casino. One entire wall is TV monitors, and another whole wall is VCRs. Everything is being taped. There are about two hundred VCRs going all the time. You can pan, zoom, tilt, everything. The camera's capability was incredible. I could read the time on your watch."

Toward the end of his twelve-year run as an "eye," Papa Joe phoned a local all-night sports call-in show. The call led to guest appearances in-studio with Rod Stowell and Rick Rosen, the cohosts, and eventually resulted in his own show.

"Knock wood, the phones lit up the first half hour I sat down, and they've been lit now for eleven years."

Papa laughs, thankfully it seems. His voice is a mellifluous tenor dipped in a barrel of western-Pennsylvania brine.

"You know how I got the name *Papa*? You know what bumper music is, right? It's the music you use to rejoin a segment. I play oldies rock 'n' roll. In Vegas, I used Dixieland. One of my favorite kinds of music. A caller from Boulder City, Nevada, sent me a tape with a note: 'This would be perfect for your bumper music.' It was 'Down at Papa Joe's,' sung by the Dixie Belles. The song was about the famous bar in the French Quarter, Papa Joe's. I started using it as part of my regular bumper music. One day a guy calls and says, 'Hey, Papa Joe.' The next day another guy did it. A few days later, other people started doing it. Within a few months, I was Papa Joe. No plan. Just happened. It all came from this caller's tape."

"You seem to have an unusually close relationship with your callers."

"You might be right about that." He shrugs and scratches his head. "I once had a caller say to me, 'I turn on the radio, and if you're there, I know everything is going to be all right.'"

Valentine's Day, 2000. Chicago.

From the studios at One-on-One Sports, Papa Joe begins his 6–10 P.M. national show. He launches into his theme for the day. He mentions a book titled *Taboo*, which poses the argument that when it comes to playing sports, black people are genetically superior to white people.

"This is always dangerous ground, to be treaded upon

lightly. But. It's also worth talking about. Since one turns on the television and sees the predominance of African-Americans playing these games, one *has* to ask the question, and it doesn't have to be whispered at the water cooler. It can be addressed over a microphone to millions of you. And we expect intelligent discussion."

The topic clearly touches a nerve. The four lines light up and remain aglow throughout the show. The callers include angry validated blacks, dismissive whites, scientists who debate both sides of the research, and talk show regulars ranging from the articulate to the tongue-tied. Joe is jazzed, animated; his arms flail out and up, his fingers clench in a repertoire of jabs, punches, and prayers, four hours of sports talk aerobics.

"My work is my life," Joe says during a break. "My day is all about my work. And when I'm finished at night, I don't have anything left. I'm dead. When I get home at nine-thirty, I have trouble keeping my eyes open. I stay up until midnight, read, watch TV until I crash. I'm single. Always have been. Close to getting married about three different times. Once there was a woman in L.A. But she wasn't willing to relocate to Vegas and I wouldn't move to L.A. I guess if it was love, one of us would've moved. I don't know. Maybe it was love. Now I'm so set in my ways. And getting cantankerous. Growing into a curmudgeon. I'm not sure anyone would have me or would want me. This is not an easy lifestyle to subject anyone to. I haven't ruled it out, though. I'm only fifty-two. There's still hope. There's still a chance."

At nine forty-five, the show winding down, Papa Joe takes a moment to massage his forehead and allow himself a yawn. It has been, from start to finish, a show worthy of the archives. The discussion of *Taboo* has been a masterstroke, better even than a "Bite Me Wednesday," Joe's signature, his weekly show in which callers complain about people in the world of sports, then scream, *"Bite meeee!"* at the top of their lungs into the radio.

"Please," Joe says. "I want to be known for more than 'Bite Me.'"

Joe begins stuffing newspaper clippings and a yellow legal pad into his briefcase. I glance toward my monitor at the calls that await. One catches my eye. Elise from Madison, Wisconsin. Below her name, Joe's producer has typed: "Wants to wish Joe Happy Valentine's Day." I see, also, that she has been on hold for over an hour.

Back on the air, Joe chooses a call. Not Elise from Madison, Wisconsin. Some guy hollering that the book is hogwash. Refers to a previous book, *The Bell Curve,* which covered similar ground with less scientific data. Joe, pissed, waves his arms in a defiant shrug and knocks over his mouse. Joe rolls his eyes, reaches to the floor, and nearly strangles himself with his headset cord. Red-faced, he cuts the caller off. I figure now it's Elise in Madison, but no, he pops in someone else. I know he sees her name. And I know he sees her message. He stares straight ahead, past me, into the control room. I look over my shoulder. His producer's on the phone, both arms wrapped around the receiver, his eyes squeezed shut.

One call to go. Two choices. Papa Joe presses line one.

"Elise from Madison, Wisconsin. Welcome."

"My God. Papa Joe. I don't believe it. I've been waiting over an *hour.*" A sexy voice. A mature sexy voice. "I always listen to you. But this is the first time I've ever called. My kids actually made me. Normally, I would never do anything like this but, well, it's Valentine's Day—"

"Yes?"

"And I know you're unattached. And I'm unattached. And listening to you, I've always thought, actually *fantasized* . . . this is so embarrassing . . . I can't believe I'm doing this . . ."

Joe looks over at me. He circles his index finger next to his head. I shrug. I think Elise from Madison sounds sort of great.

"Elise, we don't have much time," Joe says, ice in his voice. "What is it that you want to say?"

"Well, okay. First I want to say that I'm a college biology professor. I am one of the few white graduates of Howard University. As a scientist I have to say that cultural differences *dwarf* physical differences."

"Do you discount this theory?"

"I would have to read the book, which I will, and take a look at his research. But I will say that you never know, scientifically, what DNA will develop into. Statistical findings are meaningless when you're not applying them to individuals, to humans."

"Huh," says Papa Joe.

Then, incredibly sexy, Elise says, "Now. About us."

"What about us," Joe says, winking at me.

I look at the clock: 8:55.

"I really think that . . . *I don't believe this,*" says Elise. A little-girl giggle.

"Whatever it is you don't believe, you better say because you've only got thirty seconds."

Elise from Madison sighs. A big, breathy genuine sigh. "Joe, I've listened to you for so long and I really feel I know who you are. I think you and I would really get along. We're about the same age. We have the same politics, sensibilities. I'm attractive. I'm a scientist but I just have this feeling that you and I would click. I would love to meet you. For Valentine's Day, will you give me your number so I can call you off the air? I'm really serious."

I look at Joe. He pushes his thick, gold glasses up against his nose, squirms in his chair, his slightly oval body trying to find a comfort level. Joe Chevalier, former eye in the sky, denizen of Las Vegas for seventeen years, admitted gambler, aspiring to a gentleman's life of good food, good wine, and a condo on a Southern-California beach, pauses, blinks.

Do it, Joe.

On the first Valentine's Day of the millennium, take a shot on Elise from Madison, Wisconsin. In sports talk, as in life, you never know. Go for it.

He hangs up on her.

A few minutes later, we're in his office, bundling up to meet the Chicago night.

"That last call was pretty amazing."

"Yep. It was good radio."

"But, Joe, why didn't you give her your number? Why didn't you take the shot?"

He snaps the top button of his coat and looks at me as if I am without hope, without a clue.

"Good Lord," he says. "She's a *caller.*"

IX.

evening drive

LEE "HACKSAW" HAMILTON: CONTROL ROOM

i drive down the 405 toward San Diego to spend the day with Lee "Hacksaw" Hamilton, the venerable sports talk radio host, broadcasting, he claims, "From Baja to the Canadian Rockies." Hacksaw's station, XTRA Sports, the Mighty Six Ninety, is located in a long, flat, nondescript building on an industrial road between Balboa Island and Old Towne in San Diego. Next door to the building is a car repair shop; across the street are railroad tracks. I circle the small parking area in my new Jetta, looking for a safe space to park. I park next to a reconditioned hearse, think better of it, move to the other side next to a freshly detailed Civic. One big difference between television studios and radio stations: in radio, the glamour is all in your head.

I enter the lobby of XTRA Sports. Overwhelming earth tones, warm, woodsy, antiquey, and ornate. Picture a Spanish mission now talking sports twenty-four hours a day. I announce myself to a young woman behind a receptionist's desk. Large, oak, Spanish. The desk, not the woman. She calls Hacksaw. Shrugs into the phone. Tells me to have a seat, he'll be right out. I sink into a brown leather couch.

I consider Lee Hamilton. Hacksaw has held court in the same studio, in the same time slot, 4–8 P.M., for fifteen years. In my mind's eye, he is tall and dapper, handsome and authoritative. His voice is booming, filled with facts, a human sports ticker. I imagine Peter Jennings with white hair.

"Hey, man, sorry, it's just been *crazy.*"

Hacksaw. No doubt about it. The ear never lies.

I look up.

Wait a minute. Where is Peter Jennings?

In his place is a man in his early fifties, about five feet six, *maybe*, stocky, no, *pudgy*, a full figure camouflaged inside an oversize blue denim work shirt with "XTRA Sports 690" embossed over the breast pocket. He wears jeans and running shoes and a baseball cap. He has a big bushy mustache and gogglelike aviator glasses with an orange tint that almost completely obscure his face. He reaches out his hand.

"Lee Hamilton."

"Hey, Lee, thanks for taking the time—"

"No problem. Come on, I'll give you the grand tour."

We thread our way through a maze of hallways. Arrive at the control room. Small and empty except for a lone engineer, a tall, young guy in a plaid work shirt, who's operating the board. He nods as we come in. Hacksaw's lead-in, the Jim Rome show, is running now, on tape, and all the engineer has to do is pop in the proper commercial carts and station IDs. In other words, his entire job consists of staying awake and not screwing up. We move on, down another hallway, to Hacksaw's office, a tiny room cluttered with bookshelves sagging with books and tapes, and a desk stacked high with more of the same.

"Got to get to this someday, straighten it up. I do it every six months or so. Not much to see in here, really."

He steers me out, down yet another hallway toward the newsroom. Several computers are set up in an L, all on-line, connected to different Internet sports sites. Prominent as you walk in is the ticker machine. Hacksaw rubs an open palm along its side.

"I check the ticker at every break. I like to keep everything fresh, updated."

Again I nod, taking it in. What I don't see, what seems conspicuously absent, are *people.*

"That's pretty much it," Lee says. "You got your control room, my office, the newsroom. Everything really happens in the studio. Come on, we've got some time."

I follow him to his studio. Hacksaw settles into a chair in front of two computer monitors, one that indicates incoming calls, the other locked into yet another Internet sports site. Directly across from him, high in the corner, is a television set tuned to ESPN. Lee faces the control room, eye to eye across the glass from the engineer in the plaid shirt. Lee motions for me to sit opposite him, on the other side of a long metal console.

"Ask away. Just don't mind me if I do a coupla last-minute things."

I notice that he doesn't look me in the eye. Not then, and really, not ever.

"I'll give you a capsule of my background."

Hacksaw lowers his voice and speaks slowly and quietly. "My father was a baseball player in the Philadelphia Athletics farm system. My uncle was a sportswriter. He was the first president of the Baseball Writers' Association of America. He covered the old Brooklyn Dodgers. My whole life has been sports and journalism. I went to Ohio University, got undergraduate and graduate degrees in communications. I have been doing this since 1968."

Even though Hacksaw avoids my eyes, it feels as if he's confiding in me, telling me a family secret. His voice is soft and soothing; he is a born storyteller.

"I love what I'm doing, have a passion for it. I've moved from a small market in Appalachia, to midsized market in upstate New York, to major-market Cleveland, Phoenix, to San Diego. Been here fifteen years, really the exception to the rule. This is a volatile industry but I've been very stable. Was in Cleveland for seven years, Phoenix for seven, so I haven't bounced around a lot."

"To what do you attribute your longevity?" I ask. Jesus. Who talks like this? For some reason, Hacksaw has me back on my heels.

"Hard worker. Loyal. And *style.*"

Still speaking softly but giving a little spin to the last syllable. He puckers the word *loyal* as if he's blowing smoke rings.

"A lot of the things I was doing back in the 1970s in talk radio, everybody else is doing now. I think I was ahead of the curve. In terms of packaging. Who to interview, how to interview, what to do, how to change the scope of the show. I did all that twenty-odd years ago."

Hacksaw looks away, then down at something. I peer over the top of the console to see what it is. It's a small yellow legal pad. I read the word *Evidence* etched in the header at the top of the pad. He turns back, his voice resonant, clear, a tad above a whisper.

"I have a very broad range of interests. Anybody can talk about the three teams in town. But not everybody can talk about all the teams in all the leagues and all the other sports as well. I have a thirst for knowledge and information. I think that's what's made me successful and why I'm a little bit different."

I'm blocked from a direct view of him by a microphone and a bunch of other gadgets on this damn console. I close my eyes and listen, wrapped up in the melody of his voice.

"The upside to what I do? It's different day to day. It changes. Hour to hour. It *changes*. The downside? It never *ever* ends. It's like being on a treadmill every day of your life. You've got to keep up with it. You've got to pay attention to what's going on. You've got to watch the Bob Hope Classic on Sunday because somebody might call you on Monday and ask about it. You've got to pay attention to the opening of the Winston Cup NASCAR season because somebody's gonna call up and talk about Daytona. The damn thing never ends. I'm a victim of the monster that I created for myself."

Guy needs a vacation. Little trip to a spa. Or maybe go all out and steal a couple of weeks in the south of France. Get hammered on a good burgundy, hit a topless beach, stay away from sports for a while.

"I work twelve hours a day. I produce my own show. Which means I book my own guests. I network with everybody. I know everybody in every market. That's how I get a lot of information. I work a phenomenal amount of hours."

He looks at the little yellow legal pad. Writes something, crosses something out. He's a lefty. He touches the brim of his cap, leans back, arms locked behind his neck.

"The most important facet of the show is the information I present. Second most important is my opinion off that information. The third biggest item is to get you, the listener hyphen caller, to *react*. My philosophy is different than, say, Arnie Spanier's. What's fatal about talk radio is that every host is talking about the same subject, saying the same thing. We have been so successful here because we are so unique."

He leans forward, checks the ESPN feed as he continues. "I argue with management all the time that callers are important. We turn over so many calls. I take more calls in my four hours than everybody else on the station. If all you do is sit there and pontificate, after a while that gets old. I think that what you want to do is, boom, give the information, express an opinion off that information, and find out what Joe Six-Pack out there thinks. Interaction. That to me is good talk radio."

Hacksaw fidgets in his chair. The chair hisses.

"I love my job. I really do. But doing play-by-play is a great outlet for me. Because if all I did was talk, I think I'd burn out. I tell you, I never would have imagined sports talk radio becoming what it has. I would've said it's too narrow. How you gonna build an audience? It has just grown by leaps and bounds. But not everybody's succeeding at it. Not everybody's good at it. You've got to have a big signal, you need some play-by-play around it, and you better have the right people to put on the air. We've got all the combos you want. Monster signal, seventy-seven-thousand-watt Clear Channel station, very unique talk show hosts, and enough play-by-play to put around it."

"What do you think of guy talk?"

He shrugs. "It can work, it can be successful. I do sledge-hammer sports talk. Different strokes for different folks. In all honesty, I don't listen, except to sample what other guys are doing in other markets. It all sounds the same to me, even though it's not. When I go back to New York to visit my mother, I listen to WFAN all the time. I love Mike and the Mad Dog. We're good friends. But I can only take so much of that. That's just Yankee talk, Met talk, Knick talk. Ours is truly a national talk show."

Suddenly, Hacksaw removes his cap and I do a double take. Hacksaw's hair lays thick, black, and flat on top of his head like a carpet sample. He wrestles his cap back into place.

"The one thing that really bothers me is this whole negative spin on everything. I don't think that every call has to have a negative take or every call has to be a *shot*. There is so much cheap-shot stuff on the radio right now. I think that's what's wrong with sports talk radio."

He begins to tear paper. I can't see what he's ripping, but he's tearing small, even strips from another yellow pad.

"Some program directors will do anything just to get attention. If that includes somebody committing suicide in your studio on the air during drive time, okay. I don't buy that. But I do buy that everybody's got to come at it from a different sales pitch. There are some great guys doing talk radio. There are also some ying-yangs who aren't worth two nickels who are an embarrassment to what the rest of us are trying to do."

"Would you call yourself a journalist?"

"Journalist first, entertainer second. I get criticized for being too serious. Well, it's my *job*. I am serious. It's intriguing to me that radio-TV columnists sit there and critique what I do. But, man, they listen at four oh five every afternoon. And we break a story on them? They go *crazy*."

"Good afternoon, everybody, this is Lee Hamilton, and for the next couple of hours . . . I want to talk sports with you!"

Hacksaw sits six feet away from me. His mouth is a cavern of enunciation and expression. And he is *loud*. He has just begun his signature piece, "Hacksaw's Headlines," which he immodestly calls the "best fifteen minutes in radio." For the next quarter hour, Hacksaw puts a full plate of topics on the table: the NFL playoffs (he picks Jacksonville and St. Louis), Jets' coach Bill Belichick's breach-of-contract issue, the Canadian parliament's decision not to bail out six ailing NHL franchises, baseball free-agent signings, and NBA trade rumors. He delivers the goods at a decibel level just lower than that at a rap concert.

". . . when we come back, pick it up, pal! I want you to call, comment, and vote in the playoff mini-poll. Get these lines *lit* on a Friday!"

Hacksaw twirls his index finger above his head as if he's doing a bad disco dance. Music up. He turns to me. He voice is down, quiet.

"Awright. So that's how it works. Put the topics on the *table.* That's what I ad-lib the whole show off of."

He slides the little yellow pad over to me. On the pad, written in minute black script, is the list of topics I've just heard.

He nods at the pad. "I've spent all day combing the wires and putting all that down. I make one of these up for every day of the week." I glance through the pad. It is intact, no pages ripped out, the days before bound with a rubber band. Hacksaw's printing looks like it was done by a professional calligrapher.

"I get in here early and I write things down all day as I do my research. Compiling stacks of wire copy. Usually I do it at three o'clock."

I nod. And become aware of the silence.

We are alone.

No frat-house feel here. More like a law library. The only sounds are the rustle of newspaper pages and the creaking of our chairs. The monitor in front of Hacksaw shows ten phone lines, seven of which are lit. Someone's screening calls somewhere. Maybe Engineer Boy behind the glass. Lee points to the monitor. "Look at that. All different people wanting to talk about different things."

Hacksaw slips on his headset. He gives the call letters, the time, the name of the show, then: "Let's take our first call of the day. Let's talk some NFL football. James in the city, on a car phone, yak at me."

"Hey, Lee, question. Has any team done a three-game sweep?"

Hacksaw scrunches his face and searches his memory. He poses a couple of possibilities, then punches a question right back at the caller.

"Who do you like this Sunday?"

"Jacksonville." James on a car phone then struggles through twenty seconds of inarticulate nasally nothing. Hacksaw listens as if he's got Al Michaels on the phone, then *continues* the conversation. "What about St. Louis, Tampa Bay?"

"The Rams. There's not gonna be no contest neither."

"It's gonna be a fun Super Bowl. If indeed it becomes the Jaguars and the Rams, it's gonna be a fun, *fun* Super Bowl."

"It's gonna be exciting, yeah."

"Hey, thanks for the phone call, James, and you have yourself a fun sports weekend. Call me again Monday and we'll assess these games."

Call me *again?* Jesus.

The calls roll in. One guy asks about the Oakland Raiders; the next guy wants to know about a trade rumor in Green Bay. We hit the bottom of the hour. Another disco wave toward the control room.

"That's how we do it."

I ask about his hand signal.

"Oh, that's just to tell him to roll the music, make sure he stays on top of it."

No name, just a *him.* I think if Hacksaw could do without him, or anyone else, he would. We talk job security. Hacksaw has a contract that he negotiates himself, no agent. He's just signed a new deal. The entire negotiation, dollar amounts, length of time, and other deal points, took a grand total of eight minutes. We discuss ratings. He is unfazed by them. In his local market, he maintains a one share or better, which is fine for drive time, in fact, the highest rating at the station.

Hacksaw keeps his voice modulated during the breaks. He is friendly, courteous, answers all my questions graciously. But I can't help noticing that he is more connected to his callers. There is almost a bond between them. When a caller earns a "Hey, you call me anytime," it is the ultimate compliment. It's the equivalent of Hacksaw inviting the guy home for dinner.

The show moves ahead. Hockey questions, golf, NBA, a lot of NFL. Hacksaw plays an interview with track star Steve Scott that he taped earlier that morning. He leads into the five-minute spot as if it's on now, live.

"I'll tell you why I do that. I worked three months to get access to Arthur Ashe just before he died. Finally he agreed to the interview. The only time he could do it was noon on a Thursday. I wanted to put it on five-thirty at night in the middle of drive. So I said, let's tape it. A columnist took a shot at me. I said to him, 'You mean to tell me that I shouldn't interview Arthur Ashe dying of AIDS because I can't do it at five-thirty to suit *you*?' Let's face it. It doesn't matter when I did the interview. It matters that I got Arthur Ashe on the air."

Hacksaw looks away, checks out the computer screen.

"That's the worst thing about my show. The columnists' reactions. My response is, 'Did you get Arthur Ashe? Did you get a one-on-one with him three months before he died? No? Then shut up.'"

A break at the top of the hour. Hacksaw pushes himself away from his computer screen. The calls are still coming, a steady stream of five, six, seven calls. Hacksaw grabs the phone like a police reporter and slams it against his ear.

"XTRA Sports, hello, this is Lee. . . . Okay, hold on. XTRA, hello? . . . What do you want to ask him? . . . Okay, Bill, hold on."

And he screens the calls. Suddenly, he swivels in his chair, faces me, and takes a short beat.

"Well. I don't know what else to tell you."

"No, no, this is great. You've been great."

A long silence punctuated only by the periodic tapping of Hacksaw's pen onto his tiny yellow legal pad. I cannot get over the starkness of Hacksaw's show. No one has ventured near the studio. Not one time. Finally Lee breaks the silence.

"How strange am I? I work sixty hours a week, twelve hours a day, I listen to classical music on the way home and I watch *Masterpiece Theater.* I'm a simple guy. Is what I do important to society? No. Do I want to be respected? You better believe I do. And I want to be respected by my peers."

"Well, that you are."

"But *who* respects me?"

"Everyone I've talked to. Every talk show host."

A shrug.

Tap tap tap.

Through the studio speakers I'm jolted by a commercial for auto insurance for people who can't get auto insurance.

Tap tap.

I look over the questions I've prepared. I've gone through all of them. Nothing left but the dredges.

"Do you do commercials, voice-overs, anything like that?" I blurt out.

"I do some stuff for NFL films. I do some commercials here. That's about all."

Tap.

The silence is oppressive. And eerie.

"I'm gonna check the wire again."

He leaves. I'm alone. I know somewhere on the other side of the glass a guy in a plaid shirt is watching me.

Lee returns. No hot news.

"I spent a day with Arnie Spanier," I tell him. "His show is a lot different than yours. It was kind of like a frat party."

Hacksaw nods. "All over the place. Yeah. Mine's a lot more structured. But mine's a lot more caller-driven rather than just jackin' off."

Ouch.

"My show is more journalistic, that's all."

"You've got it under *control.*"

"Yeah."

Silence.

The lead-in music comes on. An announcer's voice booms, "Sound off right now! Let's talk sports with Lee Hacksaw Hamilton!" and we're back on the air.

In the next segment, Hacksaw gets worked up over a NASCAR call. Lee Hamilton knows NASCAR. He tosses off terms like Indy car schedule, target racing, and IRL package. He might as well be speaking Senegalese.

"Okay, David," Hacksaw says, wrapping it up. "Who's going to the Super Bowl?"

"It's gonna be an all-Florida Super Bowl, Lee."

"Tampa Bay, Jacksonville? You wanna bet on that?"

"You know it."

"You get your butt on down here Monday and bring cash because I don't accept your checks and I know they don't let you have plastic!"

"I *will* collect from you."

"David, you call me anytime!"

I look over at Hacksaw. He is beaming. We go to a break. Engineer Boy pokes his head in. "Lee, have you seen that Jeff George story?"

"What's the latest?"

"He's not coming back to Minnesota."

"Is that on the wire yet?"

"It's on ESPN. I haven't seen it on the wire."

"Okay."

Engineer Boy is dismissed. He slinks back behind the glass. Lee and I turn our attention to the television in the corner. The story flashes past on the bottom line.

"There it is," I say.

"Hmm. Due to what was it?"

"Financial considerations."

"Well, they have a huge salary-cap problem. Huh. They may still sign him."

We stare at ESPN looking for leads. We comment on every story that passes us—Michael Jordan and the Washington Wizards (Me: "Now there's a team in need of rebuilding." Hacksaw: "Bad attitude, that's their problem"), Kurt Warner and the St. Louis Rams (Me: "What a great story." Hacksaw: "It's the American Dream come true"), Bill Belichick and the New York Jets (Me: "I don't get this at all." Hacksaw: "Weird guy. Very weird guy"). For these few minutes, Hacksaw and I become a couple of guys bullshitting about sports. I can feel the energy shift in the room.

Hacksaw tallies the final votes in his informal playoff poll, declares St. Louis and Jacksonville the overwhelming choices of his callers, and wraps up the broadcast. He is done for the day, another week in the books, another little yellow legal pad filled and filed away. I am prepared to thank him and watch him shoot out of the studio, but instead he tips his cap and settles into his chair. For the first time since we met, he seems relaxed. He pushes his oversize glasses up onto his nose.

"I gotta tell you, I'm gone so much from my kids that when I'm off the air, my family is the only thing that matters."

He pinches his nose, sniffs. "I need to have downtime. I need to have time with my boys. They're twelve and ten."

I'm thrown. I didn't expect this intimacy. Lee takes a moment, then sighs. "I grew up without my father for a long time. I was scarred by that. Then he dropped dead on me and I never got to share any time with him at all."

Hacksaw's voice cracks. "I'll always regret how that whole thing went. He died at sixty. I was like thirty, whatever."

He coughs. I say nothing, wait for him to catch his breath.

"I made sure that I was going to be in a stable environment, that I was not going to move around the country, and I was going to take care of my kids. This is hard right now because I'm gone seven days a week during football. I don't know, maybe I should—"

He stops. His voice, always so full and robust, is suddenly thin and small.

"We've seriously talked about . . . we've got to do it differently. I don't want my kids to grow up without me. And I miss . . . I'm on the road so much . . . I miss . . . I almost get weepy sometimes on airplanes because I know my kid is playing ball and I want to be there. Or my kid's in a play and I'm missing it. I left Christmas afternoon to go on the road. I had to leave New Year's Eve. I love doing NFL football every Sunday. But the crappy thing is I'm gone all, the, time."

He clears his throat, lowers his head.

"I wish it was structured differently. I don't know how to change the structure without giving up one of the things. I don't know that I *want* to give up one of the things. My wife's very supportive of me. But that doesn't mean it's easy."

Hacksaw turns to me for the first time. He looks right at me. Stares, in fact, for a good three seconds. When he finally speaks, it is with a ferocity that freezes me.

"It's important to have a good job. It's important to make a lot of money. I decided I'm going to work my ass off so I can pay for my kids' education in cash. Have my house paid off. And then decide what I want to do. I don't want to drop dead like my dad."

It is not a statement; it is a plea.

"My dad enjoyed *nothing* of his retirement. It was *horrible.*"

He turns away, looks into the corner of the room.

"He was a great human being. But my mother raised four kids by herself. I've got to find a way so that I can be with those two . . . guys."

He croaks the last word.

Now the silence *hurts.*

"I have two kids almost the same ages," I tell him softly. "My daughter is eleven, my son is thirteen—"

"All right," Hacksaw barks. "That's enough. You've heard enough of me."

Lee Hamilton abruptly stands.

Then, head down, eyes concealed behind the orange tint of his huge aviator glasses, he shovels today's show into his briefcase.

Case closed.

X.

late night

JOHN RENSHAW: FREAKSHOW

nobody gets me," John Renshaw moans. "You know why? Because I am a pio-fucking-neer."

Renshaw, sports talk radio pioneer, is coming to you live from his basement, where he spends the bulk of his day. The basement has been gutted and rebuilt with dark oak paneling, soundproofing, and the kind of fluffy red wall-to-wall carpeting you'd find in an adult motel. Packed into this cavern alongside wooden milk crates crammed with pregnant-looking file folders are thousands of dollars' worth of state-of-the-art video, audio, and computer equipment. The cellar has been transformed into John's media womb. *Wayne's World* for the millennium.

Fingers flying across keyboards. Headset half off, half on. Pale green Dolphin cap worn rapper style. Guitars leaning drunkenly in corners. The air in here crackles with high voltage and stinks of Thai sticks.

Tomorrow is the launch. Renshaw will unleash to the World Wide Web a new Internet alternative combining rock 'n' roll and sports talk. He calls the site Freaksports.com. He will begin his first broadcast at 1 P.M. right here. After the show, at 4 P.M., you are encouraged to lie back, smoke a doobie, and absorb the Beatles' *White Album* in its entirety.

Fade up on John's high-pitched Dolphin scream set to music:

John Renshaw knows nothing about sports. He just talks les-biannns!

John Renshaw has been fired. Again.

"If you haven't been fired, you're nobody. Best advice I give young guys starting out in this business? Never buy a house."

At thirty-one, Renshaw is both a young man and a grizzled veteran of the sports talk radio wars. He's worked in California, Las Vegas, Atlanta, and for five years in Chicago, on the One-on-One Sports Network. I discover him one morning, driving back from my kids' school. Turned off by local sports talk, bored by Bob Edwards, and numbed by the endless parade of commercials on alternative rock leading up to the obligatory commercial-free ten-song set, I jab STATION SEEK until I hear Renshaw sharing sports opinions with George, a redneck garbage collector from somewhere in the Deep South.

"You the only one takes my calls, Johnnie."

"I don't know why that is, George. You got a lot of good things to say."

"I ain't got no phone in muh trailer neither. Got to call you from this here phone booth ouch here."

"What you got, George? Give me what you *got.*"

Renshaw's drawl amping up and moving in lockstep with George's.

"Wanna talk some a that there car racing, Johnnie."

And George goes off. Discoursing on lap speeds, horse-power, engine dimensions, model types, and a hundred guys named Jeff and Dale. He is an idiot savant, the Rain Man of NASCAR. Renshaw is right there with him, prompting him when he needs a little help, slicing him up when he drifts into total cartoon. It's a brilliant segment of radio, hilarious and strangely poignant. Made out of *nothing*. When Renshaw finally shoves George off the air, you can almost see the garbage man lurching back into his mobile home.

Renshaw turns now to college basketball. With the speed and intensity of Kobe flying toward the hoop, he gives you in-depth analysis of tonight's big games, rocks you with stats and rapid-fires you with opinions. He segues into "The Sports Flash," riding a guitar riff from some band called Rollover. I have to catch my breath. Renshaw is that *fast*.

I become hooked on The Freak. I drop my kids off at school, find excuses to stay in the car so I can listen. I'm buying bagels, keeping the gas tank filled, loading up on lattes and a lot of crap we don't need at the market. I'm a Renshaw junkie.

Then, after a few months of fast, funny, riveting sports talk, The Freak trips up. It happens in three stages.

Stage one is an increasingly undisguised disdain for his callers. The Freak does this in a weird passive-aggressive way. He first butt-kisses each caller, then stabs each one in the back. Example: Caller: "Hey, Freak, this is Lonnie from Boise!" Renshaw: "Lonnie Lonnie Bo Bonnie, what is up, my brother? I love you!" Lonnie, thrown by Renshaw's gush of affection, stumbles through his call, offers a fairly standard look at the Denver Broncos. Renshaw thanks Lonnie profusely for calling, hangs up on him, and proceeds to rip apart his opinion as if he were a babbling buffoon.

Stage two. Renshaw takes a ride on a daily on-the-air emotional roller coaster. He begins by ragging on the other One-on-One hosts. Especially Arnie. One time he calls Beth Spanier, Arnie's wife, and insists that Arnie is a lousy softball player and a worse talk show host. He tells Beth she'd be a better host than Arnie. The exchange is not funny or revealing, and if it's not in poor taste, it certainly shows poor judgment. Then Renshaw abruptly changes his mood. Over the next five days he becomes morose. He explains he has to find a new apartment because his girlfriend threw him out. His energy and pacing go from high voltage to underwater. The Freak sounds hungover, and frankly, I'm not that interested in his personal life. He's much more provocative breaking down a game than breaking up with his girlfriend.

Third and final stage. The Freak flies to Kansas City to do a remote broadcast. I miss the remote, but for the next week there is a substitute host. The Freak is gone. He slinks back on Monday, humbled. There was an incident during the remote. He refers to cursing on the air and mentions the dreaded F-word: fired.

After a while, he is indeed fired. I ask him what happened in Kansas City. Apparently, he showed up for his show either (a) drunk or (b) hungover (not the first time for either). Someone decided it would be hilarious to see John, in this state, interact with four strippers. The strippers arrived and John, doing a poor Howard Stern impression, asked, on the air, "What do you like more, eating pussy or having a guy eat your pussy?"

"Fuck it," The Freak sniffs from his basement. "I probably deserved it. I was getting high on the air, drinking on the air, doing my show hungover. But, man, it was like a fucking party at these remotes. All these people passing out beers, joints. What did they expect?"

In his basement studio, Renshaw remixes a tape for the upcoming Freaksports.com broadcast. Reflecting on his life, he calls himself "the luckiest guy in the world." He might actually mean it. Or he could simply be doing a wiseass reference to *Pride of the Yankees*. The Freak is a film buff; he loves to intercut snippets of movie dialogue into his "Bearded Lady" sports headlines segment.

Renshaw was born in Greensboro, North Carolina. Early on, his family moved to Baltimore, where his parents brainwashed him into falling in love with the University of Maryland basketball team, the Baltimore Orioles, and the Miami Dolphins. A big sports fan anyway, the brainwashing pushed him over the edge. Renshaw became an *insane* sports fan. He played all the major sports, especially basketball, and followed his teams fanatically. Taking the Dolphin thing a bit too far, he also grew up looking like Dan Marino. Really.

With a year of college left, Renshaw dropped out of West Virginia and headed to L.A. "I didn't know exactly what I wanted to do. I knew it had to have something to do with *words*. Maybe acting or writing lyrics or something with sports. I really didn't know. I just wanted to have an effect on people."

At first it was the old story. Dues to pay. Wait on tables, go on auditions, live in your friend's car. Seeing radio as a possibility, Renshaw registered for classes at Santa Monica College. Most of the time, though, he hawked pizza by the slice, hung with his new buddy Arnie Spanier, and shared an apartment with Bryan Singer, who would later direct *The Usual Suspects* and *X-Men*. Finally, Renshaw broke through and got a nonpaying sports gig on public-access TV. This resulted in doing remotes, for free, for the Lakers and Clippers and ultimately led to his first paying gig in Riverside, California.

"I was in Riverside, I think, or maybe Vegas, doing a show, and I got riffing one night. I started screaming, 'I always wanted to be a lesbian!' Some guy calls me and says, 'Man, you are a *freak.*' After that I just started calling myself The Freak."

Renshaw likes to riff. On his show, he will suddenly go off on a stunning rhyming rap. It can be about sports, music, movies, or all three. You expect maybe two or three neat verses, tops. Renshaw will reel off a *dozen,* no sweat, no problem, off the top of his head.

Conversely, The Freak spends three to four hours each day preparing his show. He claims to read the sports sections of fifty newspapers. I believe him. He is both a voracious reader and human sponge. Nasty, knowledgeable, and nuts. He also holds nothing back, wears his feelings on his sleeve. He is loud, laser sharp, and passionate. He will happily list his passions for you. They are listening to music, smoking pot, reading, watching TV, running, watching movies, playing ball.

"All of my passions are interconnected. I love smoking pot and listening to music together. I *love* smoking pot. More than drinking. I've, like, done every drug except shooting heroin. I get high every day. I mean, that's what I do. My show, hang out, listen to music. I am *so* lucky."

What does he listen to?

"Mostly sixties and seventies rock. My favorites are, in order, Grateful Dead, Beatles, Led Zeppelin, Jimi Hendrix, the Allman Brothers. For sports, it goes college basketball, college football, pro football, baseball, and the NHL playoffs."

Renshaw is off and running. He wants to know the origin of my last name. I tell him it's German. *Eisenstock.*

"What does it mean, brother?"

"I think it means 'iron stick.'"

He laughs. "Iron Stick. That's cool. But we're changing your name. From now on your name is Steel Cock."

I like it. Well, I mean, who wouldn't?

Renshaw expounds now on the power of the Internet. "Radio as we know it is dead. The Internet is like television in the 1950s. I'm telling you, Steel Cock, I am ahead of my time.

Fuck traditional radio. I will never work at a traditional sports talk radio station again. *Ever.* Look at the freedom I have. I can program whatever I want. I'm going to have music, interviews, sound bites, gonna have it *all.* No language restrictions, no FCC. I'm not gonna have a lot of cursing, shock for shock's sake. That gets old. But I think it'd be pretty cool to hear Bill Parcells say 'motherfucker.'"

I ask Renshaw how he ended up in Kansas City.

He shrugs. "A girl."

Ironically, he met her on one of his ill-fated, drunken remotes. After getting bounced out of One-on-One, he moved into her house in Kansas City. I ask if he's plowed his own money into Freaksports.com.

"Nah. Got a silent partner. Very cool guy. He sees the future. He emptied his 401(k) to finance me. He digs risk. It's that new cable channel, All Risk, All the Time!"

Suddenly he seems tired. Running on fumes. His engine slows.

"I was working in Atlanta. WCNN. I didn't get along with the program director. I couldn't even tell you his name. Some fat piece of shit. It was a Saturday. A dead summer day. I'm bored as fucking hell. Nobody's calling, I'm sure nobody's listening so I started drinking on the air. Jack Daniel's and Coke. The PD heard me. Got pissed. We got into a huge fight. He suspended me for three days. Told me to use the time to chill. So I went down to Florida for a couple of days. When I got back, he'd fired me."

Renshaw flicks a knob and brings up The Who singing "You Better, You Bet," and The Freak is tripping to Townshend.

"When you're in Chicago, man, we gotta spend some time together. Kansas City's maybe an hour flight, tops. Costs like twenty-eight dollars. Midway Air. Come on, Steel Cock, we'll hang."

I might have to rearrange some stuff, but, hell, it might be worth it. Anything for my, er, art. Then I realize I'll probably have to get high, something I haven't done in twenty-five years. Even when I did it back then, I did it badly. Still . . .

As it turns out, I never have to make the decision. John Renshaw's domination of the Internet ends up lasting exactly three weeks. Renshaw climbs out of the basement and resurfaces in prime time, drive time, on a small station in Miami, presenting the Freakshow, live.

On the radio.

Traditional radio.

Even The Freak's got his price.

XI.

overnight

JT THE BRICK:
BLIND IN THE MIDDLE
OF THE NIGHT

Without question, the craziest talk show host in America is JT the Brick.

JT does two shows a day, live, for a total of *eight hours a day. Live.*

I know because I spent the whole eight hours with him. Live. At least I was live for most of it.

The air in San Francisco is the color of smoke as I drive in from the airport. I've taken a Lincoln Town Car, same price as a cab. A mile from downtown the Town Car grinds to a halt in morning commuter gridlock. The driver fiddles with the radio, settles on some really grating easy-listening shit. He adjusts the side mirror, nothing else to do. He points off.

"The new stadium," he says. "Right downtown. Be some night*mare.*"

"You like sports?"

"Sports? Oh, yeah."

"Ever hear of a guy on the radio, JT the Brick?"

"JT? *JT.* Oh, *yeah.* I hear him sometimes."

"You like him?"

The driver studies me in the rearview mirror. I can read his eyes. *Should I like him? Could affect my tip.*

"Oh, yeah," he says finally. "He's pretty *good.*"

We both know he's never heard of him. The driver points to the radio.

"Maybe you like I change?"

"Please."

He finds some hip-hop. The car jerks forward.

Bet this guy also lied when he said he heard of my hotel.

He did. But we find it. A little European job a block up from Chinatown. Not splashy but clean. I check in, throw my stuff in the room, and head right back out the door. I grab a cup of strong coffee and a short stack at Café La Presse, a way cool coffee shop tucked under the Hotel Triton. I sit at a counter surrounded by newspapers, magazines, and Europeans. I could easily hang here all day, kick back, read, drown myself in espresso. JT has given me directions to the station, called The Ticket, but they're not very clear. I ask the counter guy for a map. He doesn't have one but points to a large map of the area sketched on the wall. He studies the wall, searches for the street address. I tell him it's right down the street from the most notorious strip club in the city. Doesn't ring a bell. He calls over a waitress. She's French but lives in the area, and the address sounds familiar. Near the new art center, she thinks. I go over to the wall and now the *chef* comes out to help. For an intense thirty seconds the three of us stare at the wall map in silence. The counter guy suddenly shouts, "There!" Big smiles, sighs of relief. Team effort. The counter guy grabs a napkin, draws a map, and writes down really precise, really small directions. I know one thing. I'm back here tomorrow.

Carbo-loaded on pancakes, collar up, I weave my way toward the station. The crisp air nibbles at my face as I jog by Niketown and cook past Williams-Sonoma. I find The Ticket in a contemporary, slate gray building down a seedy little street with old-fashioned gaslights in place of streetlamps. A security guard escorts me to the elevator, which lets me out in a hip chrome-and-glass lobby with sharp angles and high ceilings. A skylight drapes a blanket of emerald light over me as I check in with the receptionist. It's around 10:30 A.M. and JT is on his way in. I plop down into a large, deep leather couch so cushy it gives me a hug. Overhead, Tom Petty howls "Free Fallin'" through speakers so perfect he could be here live.

Tom Petty segues to the Pretenders as JT arrives. He's six one, chunky now, but you can see he was athletic once. How he moves. Weight forward, always ready to pounce. Thirty-five years old, high forehead, wispy hair the color of brown sugar combed back inside a Yankee cap. Light blue eyes set deep, taking it all in. His face is pale, coarse, and scarred on the right cheek. He wears a white T-shirt with "Brick" stenciled over the left pocket, blue jeans, running shoes.

"Hey."

Hand out. Mouth snakes into a smile. "Good directions?"

"Great."

No use pissing him off within the first five seconds.

"Lemme show you around." He burns through a back door. I chase him.

He points out the control room. I meet Jennifer, his afternoon-show producer. Young, short dark hair, wearing a plain gray sweater matching the outside of the building. She's new and I pick up that JT's not sure about her. She goes off and we head into what will be our home for the remainder of the day. And night.

The Studio. Total state-of-the-art. Start with an octagonal center island, bar height. Three flat black computer monitors side by side with three black gooseneck microphones. In the corner a TV, and next to that a large, red digital clock. Metal chairs on casters that allow you to swivel and slide all over the floor. Behind us a wall of glass with a breathtaking view of San Francisco. One look through that window and Tony Bennett never would've left.

JT sniffs. He's fighting the flu. He breaks open a package of cherry-flavored Cold-Eeze, pops one into his mouth. He peeks at the clock, nods to himself, leans against the center island.

"I do two different shows. The daytime show is more of a local show with interviews. The nighttime show is a looser, entertainment-based, wilder show. My shows are both caller-driven. I take more phone calls than any radio host of *any* kind in America. I take about one hundred and fifty calls a day."

I scribble the math. That's 150 divided by 8, take away interviews, commercials, Flashes, and putting topics on the table . . . *Eighteen callers an hour.* Whoa.

"I was a caller. This is my way of giving back to the callers who can't get their opinions heard on other shows. I think sports talk radio is heading in a really bad direction now. Most program directors are trying to get away from the calls. They say, 'JT, you're the star. We want to hear *you.*' I say no. I think I'm the only guy doing the calls the right way. There are no other callers like these in the country. They're professionals. A lot of hosts are very cocky. They're prima donnas. They'll see you've been on hold an hour and they'll laugh at you. I do the opposite. I respect their time."

JT turns his head away from me but somehow not his attention. Fingers flying across a keyboard, eyes focused on a computer screen.

"I was a New York stockbroker and I moved out to San

Diego in 1990. I never listened to much sports talk in New York. WFAN was kind of just starting. But out here? There were times when I would stay in my car. Changing dials. Listening to what callers were coming in. I went overboard."

He sniffs again, coughs. Types. Eyes on the screen. Attention on me. "My image out here was I was this New York guy. Hard-core Knick and Yankee fan. This guy's passionate. When I'd go to a sports bar, I had this persona. One day, out of the blue, I heard the Jim Rome show and I got hooked. I'd sit in my office at Merrill Lynch and listen. And I'd go, 'Wow, I know more than these guys.' Hell, I communicate for a living so I started calling. Pretty soon, I became one of his biggest callers. In the old days, he knew he had twelve to fifteen *brilliant* callers just foaming at the mouth, ready to get on the air. Now he hardly takes any calls."

"I know. His show has changed."

JT shakes his head, stops typing, looks me in the eye. "Well. And I'll even say this on the record. He's done everything for me. But he's done nothing for me. It took Jim a while to get successful. I'm only in my fourth year. I've got two syndicated shows and I'm in the number four market. His fourth year, he was reading traffic."

He goes back to the screen, back on track.

"Anyway. I really got the bug. I started going to bars and people would buy me beers. Then I went to Rome's very first tour stop. The original one. Jim Rome *live*. I was kinda the star because I won his first Smack-Off. You know, the contest for his best caller of the year. That tour stop is the reason I'm in sports talk radio—in fact, Rome gave me the name Brick. There was a line of at least fifty people waiting for me to sign autographs. All from calling a radio show. It was wild. I'm telling you, if I didn't win that Smack-Off, I wouldn't be here today."

In 1996, JT heard about a small station in Pasadena that had switched to an all-sports format. Turning his bedroom into a makeshift studio, he pieced together a ten-minute demo tape, the focus of which was his winning Smack-Off call. Armed with his new tape, JT met with the program director of the station and sold like he'd never sold before. He wanted a sports talk show of his own, any length, any time.

"Give me a shot," he pleaded.

The program director looked him over. Sitting in front of him was a twenty-something Merrill Lynch stockbroker whose only sports talk experience was as a caller. A damn good caller but . . .

JT closed him. The program director handed him a time slot two steps from the graveyard shift: Sunday night, 10 P.M. to midnight. Oh, and his salary? Zero. As in you'll be working for free.

No way in hell JT could turn this deal down.

Every Sunday for the next ten weeks, JT hopped in his car at 5 P.M., drove three hours to Pasadena, did his radio show, drove back to San Diego, hit the sack at 3 A.M., got two hours sleep max, then straggled bleary-eyed into Merrill Lynch at 6 A.M., ready to wrestle with the day's bulls and bears. It was sheer unadulterated heaven.

A couple of months later, JT was called into the program director's office. He had a pretty good idea what this was about. The show was taking off and it was time for the station to step up to the plate. They were going to start paying him.

"We're letting you go," the program director said.

"What?"

The program director explained that the station had just signed a deal with SportsFan radio to carry their network programming all weekend. JT's Sunday show was going to be bumped.

"This *bites*," JT moaned.

"What can I do?"

"Wait a second. Can I pay for my time?"

"You would do that?"

JT fixed his sea-blue eyes into the eyes of his boss. "Why the hell do you think I've been driving up here every Sunday from San Diego? This is my passion. It's what I live for. I can't lose this chance."

The program director nodded slowly. "It'll cost you four hundred dollars. Two hundred bucks an hour. In advance."

Talk about a tough business. You start out working for free. Then if you do well, you pay *them. If I do any better, I'll go broke.*

Then JT had an idea. "Can I get sponsors?"

The program director shrugged. "Sure."

JT sighed with relief, then repeated to himself the promise that had become his mantra:

Once I get on the air, I'm never getting off.

The next morning he went into his office at Merrill and began cold-calling. Only now, instead of selling stocks, he was selling himself. The first call he made was to Higgins Bricks, the largest brick maker in Los Angeles. JT offered to mention the company in and out of every break and promised to produce a Higgins Brick commercial. The cost? Two hundred fifty dollars a week. Within days JT received a check for $1,000, a commitment for four weeks.

The brick company in the bag, JT turned next to sports bars. He called ones he frequented and called others cold. He asked each one for $100. By Sunday, JT had collected $1,200 in sponsorships for the first week. All due to hustle and chutzpah. JT had an abundance of both.

Three months later, JT got a call from KFMB in San Diego. The station had an opening Sunday nights from 7–10 P.M. Same terrific deal. No salary, pay for your time. But JT would have three hours instead of two. And KFMB was a well-known talk station with a big signal. Here was the beauty part. *The station was five minutes from his house.* JT felt like he had struck gold.

At night, in his apartment, he began to study the sports talk radio business as if it were a company about to go public. He decided to create, in a way, a prospectus for a hot new IPO. The company name? JTBRICK. He bought oversize sheets of oak tag, different-colored marking pens, and wrote down the names of the most successful sports talk hosts in the country. Eddie Andelman. Lee Hamilton. Mike and the Mad Dog. He researched how they had got so successful, sketched their time lines, and examined what they had in common. He created, in effect, a business model for himself. Then he applied it.

His target was SportsFan radio itself, the radio network based in Las Vegas. Charlie Barker, program director of SportsFan, was the man JT put in his sights. The Brick hit Barker with a barrage of cold calls and a steady stream of tapes. *Bam.* Nothing. Okay, go to Plan B. Shit. There is no Plan B. Then Plan B fell into his lap.

The highest-rated show on the SportsFan network was *The Pete Rose Show.* JT learned that Pete was going to appear at a remote in Los Angeles to promote his show. The Brick took the day off and headed up to L.A. He guessed that where there was Rose there was Barker. He was right. JT cornered Barker and virtually shoved a tape into the program director's palm along with his handshake.

"Mr. Barker, I'm JT the Brick," JT began, and never finished.

"I know who you are. Great story. I like what you're doing." Barker stared at the tape. "Let me take this home and listen to it. I promise."

He was good for it. A few weeks later JT was in Vegas, flown in by SportsFan, subbing for a host ill with the flu. It was the weekend of a Mike Tyson fight from the MGM

Grand. JT's shift was Saturday and Sunday, midnight to 5 A.M. *Paid.*

The other guy never should've gotten sick. JT's charge through the night shift was fearsome; he was electric. The powers at SportsFan knew they could never let him go. They handed him the weekend shift permanently. He was now working seven days a week—Monday through Friday at Merrill Lynch in San Diego, Saturday and Sunday on SportsFan radio in Las Vegas. Finally, a few months later, SportsFan made JT the offer that would change his life.

"I called my dad," JT says. "He's my financial adviser. They offered me Monday through Friday, midnight until five. I had to give up working at Merrill, which meant my six-figure salary. The pay was twenty-five thousand dollars a year. I told my dad I'd do it for free."

"What'd he say?"

"He said it was a no-brainer, go for it."

"He's your financial adviser?"

JT grins. "He's also my best friend."

Two minutes to air. Jennifer, the new producer, trying to find her way, slinks into the studio. She has the look of a 1940s movie star but the vocal lilt of a Valley Girl. She runs down a list of possible interview candidates. She's waiting for callbacks. While she talks, JT reaches into his briefcase and pulls out a headset. He caresses it absently, then places it on the island.

"You've got to build that relationship, Jen," JT says gently. "I want him to feed us a Spur. Last night they beat the Lakers, we have to hit on a Spur the next day. We're on in San Antonio, it's important."

"Right."

She looks down, hiding her face in her list. It's a gentle chide but the point is made. She should've thought of it.

• • •

One minute to air. JT flicks an invisible speck of dust off his headset.

"In high school I was a competitive swimmer. But I was a jerk-off. Pretty smart guy, never applied myself. My dad, who is a genius, and I really mean it, he *is*, looked around and found me the best college he could. Geneseo State University in upstate New York. I went from being this hotshot in high school to not knowing anybody. I truly believe that the biggest thing that made me what I am today is I joined a fraternity. It was the perfect thing for me. I was a guy's guy and I found the place to be a guy's guy. My senior year I was president of my fraternity and captain of the rugby team. I had to talk in front of people and I had to be articulate. Changed my life."

Thirty seconds to air. JT slips on his headset.

"What I'm about to do right now, my opening, my monologue, is my pride and joy. This is the only time throughout the whole show where I get to give my opinion. To the callers, I say I'm going to let you talk and run the show. Then I'm gonna step aside. But give me my first twenty minutes."

JT stands, plants a foot on the rung of his metal swivel chair, and leans into his microphone.

"This show goes from here, out of my microphone, through Las Vegas, where it's produced. That's where the network is based. Then the calls get rerouted back here. It's very technical. At night it's really unique. I do the show completely blind. My producer, my call screener, everybody is in Vegas. I get everything through Instant Message. It's pretty wild. I'm in here totally alone, every night."

Old-fashioned marching band music up. Sounds like a pep rally. The pep rally music fades and a chorus of female voices wails, *"JT the Brick!"* then a deep male Isaac Hayes soundalike croons, *"It's JT the Brick,"* and we're off.

"Great to have you in the Brick House. JT the Brick from San Francisco, California! A big show today. Coming off the Super Bowl in Atlanta. People are asking me, 'Brick, what are you gonna remember about your trip to Atlanta?' I'm gonna remember the double murder that happened outside the Cobalt Lounge. I don't think you people have gotten this yet. Do you understand what's happening in society today? John Rocker is an outright racist. You got a guy like Ray Lewis and his posse flying around in a Lincoln Navigator stretch limousine shooting guns off. Two people are on the ground *dead*. This is what's happening in sports. I have nothing good to tell you today. We're talking about murder and racism. I never thought we'd be hitting on this coming off a Super Bowl. It's *offensive*. I want your opinion on this . . ."

A sound bite of Ray Lewis's attorney pops in. JT turns his head, sniffs, coughs. He stands up, squawks into his microphone, his body in constant motion.

In his monologue he moves from murder and mayhem in the NFL to Dick Vermeil's press conference. Late yesterday, the emotional coach of the Super Bowl–winning Rams announced his retirement.

"Go to the cry, go to the cry," JT says into his microphone. Not shouting, just insistent. Guy knows exactly what he wants. Physically JT is *elastic;* but there is nothing, absolutely *nothing* about this show that feels loose or random.

JT points off and Vermeil cries on cue.

"Now you *know* Dick Vermeil couldn't have a press conference without crying like a baby. This guy is an emotional roller coaster. When he talks, somebody's gotta get the box of tissues."

JT stalks, stops, leans into the mike for emphasis, turns up the volume.

Sniff, sniff. Can't tell who's sniffling. JT next to me or Dick Vermeil on tape.

"I know I'm gonna miss my *players.*"

Sniff. Vermeil.

"Now," JT says on the air, "I'm on in San Antonio with my new syndicated show and the Spurs kick the Lakers in the *mouth.* They whack the L.A. Snake Crew. San Antonio? I officially have no one on hold from San Antonio, Texas! I am going to run into a brick wall and split my head open if I don't have ten people calling from San Antonio today!"

Go to Duncan slamming in two of his twenty-nine. JT on the move, kicks his chair back to give him more room to prowl.

"Here I go, here I go. I got a big show lined up. I got a gentleman in studio today who's writing a book about sports talk radio. He wanted to check out what we're doing. He heard about the Brick House. Heard about this caller-driven radio. And we're gonna show him today. Pick up the phone and *dial* it."

Fade-up music. JT slides a hand across his lip.

"Wow," I say. "Gotta catch my breath."

JT laughs. "If nothing else, I've got energy."

Ray Lewis's attorney, Max Richardson, appears above us on the monitor. JT shakes his head, walks over to a glass of water.

I indicate the TV screen. "Is this good for sports talk?"

The Brick nods glumly, then speaks softly. "I would rather not talk about it, but as far as driving sports talk radio, they call this time of year, no pun intended, the Dead Zone. The time right after the Super Bowl, and the time before football starts, right after the baseball all-star game, there's nothing going on. Most guys go on vacation. But, yeah, this is the type of topic that will generate talk all week. Very unfortunate."

Another sip of water. He clears his throat. "I keep a journal. I write in it every night when I'm done. I've been doing it now for the last couple of years. I write what worked that night, and what didn't."

Now the twangy electric-guitar intro. On top of it Dick Vermeil bids good-bye. JT roars in, sounds off about Sean Elliott's inspirational return to the NBA after receiving a kidney transplant. Then the phones.

"Mike in San Antonio, welcome to the Brick House!"

Mike is off, blowing up about Tim Duncan's big night against the Lakers, he's the strongest man in San Antonio, Spurs to repeat, and JT points to the computer screen in front of him.

"See that? All nine lines are full." Mike from San Antonio still going on and on, babbling about the Spurs, JT now into his headset: "Go heavy on Spurs' highlights after these calls. Do we have more than just Duncan?"

A muffled voice from above: "That was the only thing I cut."

"We've got to cut it *all*. Okay?" JT borderline angry, clearly insistent and annoyed. Rubs his forehead. I get his message, loud and clear: *Why can't the rest of them work half as hard as I do?*

The muffled voice again, the engineer, I think, trying to redeem himself. "Shaq, postgame, 'Get it back on track'?"

JT doesn't answer. Shuffles some papers. Begins to type something on his keyboard.

And Mike from San Antonio rambles on, uninterrupted. I have no idea what he's talking about. Something about Robert Horry playing soft off the bench. Mike's been talking for, what, a minute? Two? He's still going. JT goes through some papers that are cluttering the top of the island. Speed-reads them, crumples them up, tosses them into the trash.

Then, finally: "Mike, I gotta jump in. Appreciate the phone call. That's the type of call I want. A guy who can break down the game. Guy watched the game. And he's right about one thing. The Laker bench was *disgusting* last night."

Now JT goes off, on fire, railing about the Lakers' bench play. He rages about Derek Fisher, the Lakers' point guard, who managed to get exactly no assists. I'm amazed he heard one word Mike from San Antonio said.

Another call, Moses from San Antonio, then we go to a break.

I point to his monitor. "What are you typing?"

"I'm just answering E-mails. People E-mail me during the show. The head of my company just E-mailed me. They want me to go to Hawaii for the Pro Bowl. Stay there a week. I do a lot of business during the show."

"They call this multitasking."

"Yeah. And nothing against the callers, but a lot of times you kinda know where they're going. You don't have to have both ears locked in. You can do a couple of things at once. Like what I'm doing with you. I'm doing the show, answering E-mails . . . it's easy."

He takes a sip of water, leans a foot against the rung of the chair. "I'm very blessed to have this job. Compared to a nine to five job in a suit. When I worked as a stockbroker, it was the most unbelievable work I've ever done as far as mental and physical strain."

A glance above us at the red digital clock. A peek at his monitor. A look back at me.

"I'm a little concerned, physically, with this job. The shift I'm doing is getting to me."

He quickly edits himself.

"Not *getting* to me. It's just rough. There are certain days, like Wednesday, Thursday, middle of the week. It really starts to cave in on you. There is no end in sight. But I wouldn't be able to make the money I'm making now if I was only doing one show."

JT scratches his head, adjusts his cap. "My night show is so important to me. I'm on more radio stations than anybody. It's only because of the time slot. It's not because I'm better, and I understand that. But when you're on at midnight on the East

Coast, there is no one local on. I'd rather be on in Boston on WEEI, which is a *huge* station, in the middle of the night than not be on at all. My bosses know they can count on me. Look. SportsFan radio runs my day show three hours live, then my night show five hours live, then they *replay* my night show for five hours. I'm doing *thirteen* hours a day for them, eight live. They pay me one chunk of change, and they don't gotta worry about me. They know that with me more than fifty percent of their day is covered."

I feel like I'm in the presence of a maniac. I mean that in a good way. JT has more drive than anyone I've ever met and more energy than any three people. But at the center of this drive and energy there is a calm, a stillness. It's almost as if he is a chess master, planning ten moves ahead, coiled, ready to strike.

The calm has a name.
Julie.
"My wife, man. Thank God for Julie. She does everything for me. She handles all my money, pays the bills, picks up the dry cleaning, everything. I couldn't do this gig without her."

Ladies and gentlemen . . . the Rolling Stones!
The haze of smoke and throbbing of strobe lights in the small concert hall made it all feel like a dream. But it was real. As real as Mick twirling the mike stand like a gunslinger and howling "Satisfaction" practically in her face. She had come here alone but now she was with this new and strange and, yes, incredible guy. Did she pick him up? Or did he pick her up? Neither. Both. *Pick up* sounds too cheap anyway. She *let* him pick her up. That's better. Whew. I don't know. A couple of gin and tonics. Mick live. It's too much. But here's the question. Am I drunk or am I falling in love?

From the moment she'd stepped into the Hard Rock she'd felt this night was orchestrated by fate. She'd never tell this guy that she believed in things like that. Not yet anyway. Things like fate. And destiny. And love at first sight. Don't want to scare him off after an hour. But you know what? I think he feels the same way I do. He tries to come across as rugged and tough. That New York *thang.* Trying to sound like he's from the streets of Brooklyn when he's really from the circular drives of Massapequa, Long Island. Not that you can't be from Massapequa and be really tough.

Yeah, right.

She laughs to herself. She's got his number. He's not what he appears. Not at all. He's very smart and very sweet and she feels like she's known him forever.

This night started with a miracle. A ten-thousand-to-one shot. Only in Las Vegas do people live by odds like that. It began with a stranger's manicured hand poking out of a black tuxedo jacket, reaching deep into a barrel of ticket stubs at a John Mellencamp concert. She'd never won anything in her life. Never even got a match doing a McDonald's scratch game. Nothing. But the moment the stranger's voice read off the first number on the winning ticket, she knew. She'd struck gold. A ticket to the Stones.

Not a free ticket, of course. That would've been too easy. She won the privilege of *buying* a ticket to see the Stones, the privilege costing a neat $300. And that was for the cheap seats, up in nosebleed country. It didn't matter anyway. It might as well have been three *thousand* dollars. Julie was an elementary-school teacher, sixth-grade technology. Three hundred dollars for a rock concert was more than an extravagance; it was an impossibility.

"You're going," her mother said.

"Mom, I can't—"

"You are."

Mom handed her a single ticket to the concert. End of discussion.

And so began her night of magic.

She arrived early at the Hard Rock, alone. She meandered over to the bar and ordered a drink. And there he was. Next to her. Shorter than she was. Built like a jock, for God's sake. Talks like a jock, too. But smiled like a dream. And those *eyes*. Swimming-pool blue. She could float away in them. They talked. No. They *clicked*. They finished each other's sentences. After five minutes, they spoke in a shorthand that only they could understand. She was from Illinois. He knew all about the Fighting Illini, had an encyclopedic knowledge of sports. He was a DJ or something on the radio. John was his name. But on the radio he was JT the Brick. She shrugged. Never heard of him.

The bar was crammed with people but they could've been the only two in there. Then they got the two-minute warning. Time to get to their seats. He had the front row; she had the balcony. Oh, well. It's been nice. He watched her make her way up the stairs, slowly.

I can't let her go.

He'd better come after me.

He couldn't and he did.

Six weeks later they were discussing marriage.

Destiny.

JT believes in it now.

The Big Break came in Vegas.

"I'm doing the late shift. Pete Rose is on our network. Turns out Pete is taking off every other day. Pete can't find time to do his own radio show. They're paying him three, four hundred *thousand* dollars to do a two-hour radio show. I see the opportunity there. I told the program director that I wanted to host *The Pete Rose Show* when he's out. So I started hosting Pete's show. Filling in for Pete. They liked it so much they made me Pete's cohost. And me and Pete hit it off. Without a doubt, no one did more for my radio career than Pete Rose. So I'm doing the overnights *and The Pete Rose Show.* It was my first taste of this double shift. I go on the road with Pete, and we're doing the show in front of five-hundred people. Pete's not even paying attention. He's just watching the races. You know Pete's story. I'm anchoring the show. I turn out to be Pete Rose's confidant."

JT keeps an eye on the clock above us, the control room next to us, the three monitors in front of him, the TV overhead, the phone lines blazing, and me. And he keeps going with his story.

"We're going on the air in two minutes, Pete's saying, 'Brick, what are we doing today?' I'm like, 'Pete, I got it. I'll handle it. You jump in.' We're getting Hank Aaron, Nolan Ryan on the show because they're all friends with Pete. It really did great for me. Then I got the opportunity to move to San Francisco, keep my night show out of Vegas, and do the midday show here. This all happened in *four* years."

Stand by.

The voice from above. JT snuggles into his headset like it's a helmet, bends the gooseneck mike toward him, and leans both hands on the island. He begins an interview with a soft-spoken, slow-talking British journalist who's written an article on the Web about violence in the NFL. It's a stark contrast of styles. The Britisher has the dubious ability to make this incendiary subject matter sound dull as shit. Finally, JT shuts down the interview, thanks the journalist. We go to commercial.

"That guy sure knows how to suck the energy out of a segment," I say.

"Yeah."

JT's thinking, planning, wondering if he can use any part of that interview to prop up the night show. Tricky. At midnight it could work as a sedative.

JT gets up every morning between nine and nine-thirty. He immediately goes on-line to Sportspages.com and reads the sports sections of the *Boston Globe, Miami Herald, Detroit Free Press, New York Daily News, Seattle Times, San Francisco Chronicle,* and *Los Angeles Times.* He then clicks over to the major sports Web sites—ESPN, CBS Sports, CNN—and scrolls through them for anything he's missed. He lives four blocks from the studio and usually walks to work, arriving an hour or so before the show. At three o'clock, the midday show in the bank, JT sometimes sneaks off to a movie with Julie, or if it's midweek and he's drained, he'll crash, grabbing a nap anywhere from 3:30 until 7 P.M. He wolfs down a quick dinner, heads back to the studio no later than eight-thirty, checks in with Bobby, his producer in Vegas, and gets ready to pump up the volume, five hours white-hot, solo flight, no cohost, until 2 A.M. Then it's straight home, suck on a medicated ice pop to soothe his throat, and in bed by two-thirty. JT puts it all out there for every show. He leaves nothing in the studio. He is never wired; he is totally wasted. Sleep comes easy.

"What drives you?" I ask.

"Money. I am one hundred percent driven by money. It's all about the Benjamins. My goal is to make more money than anybody else in this business."

"I'm the manager of the team and the talk show hosts are the players."

Lee Hammer, program director of The Ticket, offers me a seat in his office. Lee looks like a younger version of Skinner, the FBI chief on *The X-Files*. He pushes himself away from his desk and yanks a basket filled with audiotapes toward me. Must be a hundred tapes in there.

"I need to hire a new host. Someone to lead in to JT. I put a tape in, listen, and say, 'Is that gonna work?' People ask me all the time, 'What makes someone good?' I don't have an answer. I don't know what *it* is. But once I hear it, I know it's right."

He slides the basket back onto a bookshelf.

"It's someone you just want to listen to. You don't want him to stop talking. You can't turn him off. He's going to keep you listening through the commercial break. That's what radio is. Get someone to listen for fifteen minutes, then fifteen more. Then get him to come back tomorrow."

"Why do we listen to sports talk radio, Lee?"

He answers without hesitation. "Sports is our common denominator. You can be a blue-collar worker and you can talk sports on an equal level with the chairman of a Fortune 500 company. You can't talk business that way, or world politics that way, you can't talk about anything else that way. That's why we listen. Now here's why I love sports talk. You write something you don't like, or you make a mistake, you can change it or use your delete key. No one will ever know. But JT doesn't have a delete key. None of these guys do. Once somebody says something, it's out there. You can't bring it back."

Eight fifty-eight P.M. All quiet in the studio. And still. JT is sitting for this show. He is comfortable. Relaxed. He wears a beige sweater and slacks. No hat. Hair combed. The boss is in from New York, and he took Julie and JT out to dinner. No Chez Panisse for the Brick and his bride. They ate outside at a restaurant near the new ballpark. JT looks bright-eyed, energized, raring to go. I had a cup of coffee but I could've used a nap.

"How do you feel?" I ask.

"Good. Yeah. Tonight's a good night."

JT purses his lips into his mouthpiece. "Can you hear me? Are we cool? Okay. Let's start with the mayor of Atlanta."

Horns up. JT pushes himself back a few inches and blasts now, at full volume: *"Live from San Francisco, this is JT the BRICK . . ."*

JT goes into his monologue, referring only to a newspaper and a couple of pages printed off the Internet. There are no notes, nothing written down. The Brick busts loose with more news on the murders in Atlanta, reading a statement from the medical examiner that suggests this has the makings of a professional hit: "The killers knew what they were doing."

Nine-fifteen P.M. JT finishes the monologue. Feels like a stampede. Energy, energy, energy. I'm trying to get myself up. He's smiling, sitting. At home here. No sign of illness. The night show heals him.

"I want to understand these sound bites," I tell him. "I don't see how you cue your producer."

He grins. He loves this shit. The more technical the better.

"Every night before we go on the air, I get a sound sheet." He holds up a piece of paper. "All these are highlights and sound bites. I get this faxed to me. Tonight I decided that numbers four, seven, and nine were the highlights I wanted to do."

He shows me. The highlights he's chosen are circled in black. "I basically throw to the highlight I want. I'll say, 'Mike Martz is the new head coach of the Rams.' I pause. My producer knows, in order, what I'm doing. When I pause, he fires the bite."

"So you call him before the show—"

"Right. I get in at around eight, eight-thirty. All this has been faxed to me. He dials in the network. We set up the Internet. I review the sound and get a feel for what's best for the opening. The rest of the night, say I'm on the phone with a caller from Sacramento? Either my producer will think of it, or I'll type in 'Kings 80.' He'll type back or say in my ear, 'Got it.' Then to the caller I'll say, 'Yeah, you gotta like that Jason Williams behind-the-back pass.' And we'll throw to it."

"You and your producer really have to be in sync."

"Totally. The hardest thing that Bobby, my producer, and I have to do is to keep one step ahead of the callers. You see these calls? I have no idea what they want to talk about. And in one segment I'll go from Ray Lewis, to the Celtics, to the Detroit Tigers, to the Jacksonville Jaguars. Mike and the Mad Dog are only talking New York. With all these phone calls and no screener, I don't know what's behind door one, two, or three. It's exciting and it keeps you on the edge."

JT cracks his knuckles. Stretches his fingers. Grins again.

"Yeah, we're very aggressive with sound bites. We also take a lot of cuts from movies. It's all timing. Bobby and I've been together three years now. We got it down pretty good considering we're not even in the same building. Hell, we're doing it blind in the middle of the night."

Nine twenty-three P.M. The rumor is that he's a made man. It's said that he has watched people die and he knows where the bodies are buried. It's said that he is a bookmaker running legal gambling from his yacht somewhere off Cape Cod. He *sounds* like a bookie. Or a longshoreman. Or a bartender, as he verbally blasts away at every Boston sports team and sports star in his wildly intolerant yet poetic bazooka blather.

Last summer he invited JT and his dad for a day at the Cape. The exuberant talk show host, retired U.S. Department of Health and Human Services accountant, and the supposedly made bookmaker sipped Guinness beer and ate sandwiches as they trolled leisurely around the Cape. He is, according to JT, the greatest caller in the history of sports talk radio.

He is Butch from the Cape. And he's on the air.

"Oh, yeah, Ray Lewis is innocent, JT. So was O.J. It's like Tony Montana said in *Scarface:* 'Me, I always tell the troot. Even when I *liiiee.'* I just came back from walking my dogs. It's eighteen degrees. And wit the wind chill, it's five below. You could *walk* across the river tonight, that's how cold it is. But even the bleepin' river ain't as cold as the Celtics and Bruins, JT. I ain't no Johnny-come-lately. I tole you from the gitgo Pitino wouldn't do nothin' in the pros. This bum crapped out in New York and he's goin' belly-up in Boston. Slick Rick's been in Boston for tree years and the fraud is twenty-eight games under five hundred. *Twenty-eight games.* Nobody listens to Pitino . . . they see troo him. Everybody sees troo him but the Boston media. Pitino's gone from Lexington to Loserville in tree bleepin' years. Dose hicks wit green teeth that squeal like pigs down in Kanetuck bought into Little Ricky's BS. And now their counterparts up North are the most gullible bleepin' fans on the planet . . . the Boston bozos. Those yahoos are so grateful this sauce-peddlin' fraud's come to Boston, they wouldn't say crap if they had a mouthful . . ."

This is less than a third of Butch's call. He does another minute on Pitino, shreds the Bruins, rips the Patriots, and finishes his call with the following assessment of Pats quarterback Drew Bledsoe: "Drew Bledsoe's got a million-dollar arm, a ten-cent head, no heart, and he ain't got the balls he was born with. JT, I'll talk to you later."

Four minutes and twenty seconds. That is longer than most songs that are played on the radio. *Four minutes and twenty seconds.* I honestly don't think I could talk for four minutes straight. And what's even more amazing is that JT lets Butch go, uninterrupted, uncensored, for as long as he wants. For a moment I feel sorry for Pitino, Bledsoe, and everyone else Butch has brutalized. Then I get over it. It's after midnight in Boston; the kids and the media are safely out of earshot, asleep in their beds or passed out in their bars.

JT trumpets the last four minutes into his microphone. "I will put that call on my Web site so everybody can know what it's like to be a legendary caller like Butch from the Cape. That's why you listen to this show. The best callers in the country line up to get on this radio show. It's the Brick House."

"Awesome," I say.

"He's *it*. And he's such an expert that he knows that this hour is replayed at five tomorrow morning in Boston. I'll tell you, this hour that you're hearing, and it has nothing to do with me, I'll put this hour up against any hour you hear anywhere. Monologue, live interview with Bill Frieder, Butch, interview that we did with Gil Brandt, and into another good call or two. This is the kind of radio I like to do."

JT shakes his head.

"Lee Hammer and Mike Thompson have no clue what a Butch from the Cape can do for a radio station. It's like being in a rock band and having a great guitar player. Let him *play*. If you have a radio show, you get a guy like Butch? Let him go. Let the guy *go.* "

Nine fifty-six P.M. First hour in the books.

I notice a white box in front of JT.

"To me, it's a passion," JT says.

He fingers the white box absently.

"I have a vision. I actually want to be the biggest name in the history of sports talk. I'm gonna treat it like a business plan. My plan is to figure out how to be better and more successful than all of them. Because I'm just starting out, I can think that way now. I couldn't picture doing this job, in one market, on one station, making fifty grand a year. I'd lose my mind. The only thing that's driving me is to make more money and become more well-known than Mike and the Mad Dog."

He flicks the box with his finger.

"In this business there are a lot of people who are just *negative*. Not only on sports. They have nothing good going on in their lives. I want to paint a picture through the microphone for my listeners that, 'Hey, you can't go to the Super Bowl, but I'll go for you. I'll shake hands with the players and get them on the radio for *you.*' There are a lot of guys who don't appreciate how good they have it."

I can't stand it anymore. "JT, what is in that box?"

"Oh, you're gonna love this."

He flips open the lid. Lying in a row are six fat, flaky, cream-filled pastries, sugar-dusted crusts the color of a tan.

My mouth literally waters. "Oh, God."

"Yeah. The cleaning lady leaves them for me every week. They're from Rosita's Bakery. They're awesome. Have one."

"I just had dessert."

"So? Me, too. Try one. They're unbelievable."

"I'm sure."

"Around midnight you're gonna want one of these. We both are. Trust me."

I poke a finger into the box, scoop out some cream that's oozed up the side. I pop it into my mouth.

Oh *myyy.*

JT's in the box, too. He breaks off the tail of the fattest pastry. I stare at this stuff like it's cocaine.

"My midday show? The reason I'm so passionate about it is I don't get a lot of respect in the industry. Most people think I'm the overnight-piece-of-crap guy who can't make it. They don't get the big picture, that I'm the syndicated guy *making* it and could have *their* job. I could have their job *yesterday*. I don't get that respect."

"Yet," I say.

"Yet."

The door to the studio swings open. The engineer, a phantom in a faded blue T-shirt, stands in the shadows of the doorway. I haven't seen him before, doubt I'll see him again. He is in the control room, alone, operating the board. He comes in, holds for a beat.

"Brick, do you know a guy named Shave Joey?"

"*Shave* Joey?"

"I guess. Or." He shrugs and disappears.

"That's another thing in this business," JT says, wiping some cream off his lip. "A lot of prank calls."

Ten-seventeen P.M. Calls backed up. JT goes to Brandon. Guy sounds like he's tripping. Speech slurred, thoughts bouncing off each other. In the background, an intermittent *clanging*. Sounds like a road crew busting up concrete. JT on the keyboard, answering E-mail, finally says, "Hey, Brandon, where are you calling from, man? Sounds like you're in *jail.*"

Brandon, insulted, "No, man, I'm in my apartment."

"Appreciate the call. Rick in Quincy, Mass."

JT, off-mike, to me: "This guy loves my show. He's an old disabled guy. Lives through the show. I don't hang up on him. I let him talk. His calls are only about forty-five seconds. People hate his calls but this is how he lives."

Ten thirty-seven P.M. Fatigue check. Yep. I'm fatigued. JT is on the phone, on the keyboard, eyeing the TV screen above us, sports talk radio's version of a one-man band.

"This is not my job," he says. "This is my career. There's a big difference. When you're dealing with your career, you can make sacrifices. If it's your job, you tend to hate it. When I got into this, I had everything to lose. I actually gave up a career. I had to make it work. Because if it doesn't work, I'm going back to cold-calling people on high-yield bonds and stocks. And I never want to do that again."

Ten forty-nine P.M. JT clicks on his Web site, jtthebrick.com. Pictures pop up, including one of a guy who looks like a member of ZZ Top. This is Benny Jet of Detroit, a fortyish rocker, frequent caller to the Brick House, and one of JT's biggest fans. Benny calls now and JT threatens to do a set of songs with Benny and his band.

"You sing?" I ask JT at the break.

"Well, yeah, for fun. I started doing it at weddings and stuff."

"What kind of songs?"

"'Mustang Sally,' that sort of thing. I sound like Joe Cocker."

I ask him if I could listen to a tape. He laughs. Ignores me.

Ten fifty-three P.M. Fuck it. We break out the pastries. We need the sugar rush to get us through. JT tears one apart, slides the box over to me.

"Oh my God," I say again.

"This is stuff you die for. Just fabulous," JT says. "So where we at?"

"Let's see."

Neither of us really cares. JT takes a bite out of his pastry like it's an apple. I shove a little square of a flaky doughy cream dream into my mouth. *Ummm.* Now I can die.

"Here's a question that might sound weird," I say. JT moves onto his second piece of pastry. "What is inside there?"

"I don't know. A lot of 'em have cream filling. That one there looks really good. Go for it."

I do.

Mannnn.

We'll be back with JT the Brick after these pastries.

Ten fifty-eight P.M. "Now I bring in two brand-new audiences. Seattle and Miami haven't heard the first two hours. I automatically have to get up. That's what keeps the energy going. We're not even halfway home and we have new listeners. I do a whole new monologue."

JT stands, grips the console with both hands:

" . . . in the Brick House we play the hits. Whatever's hot, that's what I go with. So during this last break I updated my Internet Web site to look at some late scores . . ."

He whispers now, telling a secret.

"I didn't realize that the Chicago Bulls . . ."

Into a *roar.*

"Beat the Sonics! Ohhhwhooaaa! Tony Kukoc, the subject of trade talk, scored thirty-one points, as Chicago stunned your Sonics, eighty-eight to eighty-one. How the hell does this happen in the two oh six of the Nightriders of Seattle? And check this out, the Phoenix Suns beat the Clippers, one fourteen to sixty-eight. You know like when a horse is old and it can't go anymore, sometimes they shoot it? David Stern, the commissioner of the NBA, should fly to L.A., go into Donald Sterling's office, and say, 'Donald, give me the keys. You no longer can have this team. You need to go out of business!'"

Eleven twenty-seven P.M. JT is reflective. The glow from the TV douses us with a pale blue sheen.

"I don't know how long I can keep up this pace. To get where I want to be, it's gonna take everything I got. Eventually I want to settle into a nice life, have a couple of kids, and provide for them. I'm not gonna get greedy with this. I wanna go off on my own terms."

"Is it important for you to have a family?"

"It's the most important thing. I'd give up this radio show and *everything* for the opportunity to have children. That is my priority."

He goes to a call. "Mr. Hockey in Boston, next."

Caller starts rambling. JT turns to me. "He's a prison guard in a Boston jail. He's a hockey fanatic. He calls in and you can hear all the inmates yelling in the background. He just goes into his hockey rant. It's unreal."

Eleven thirty-eight P.M. We watch Leno's monologue. Nod at the jokes. Too tired to laugh. But JT keeps going. He's carrying me now.

"I couldn't tell you the names of the defensive linemen who play for the Minnesota Vikings. But I know what it's like to be a Vikings fan. I know their pain. And I try to plug into that. I want to tell you what the fans are thinking in the third deck, when they're walking out, pissed off. That's what I'm trying to tie into. I think that's missing."

I yawn. Leno does a lame John Rocker joke. JT switches to Charlie Rose. I sneak a peak into the pastry box. It's nearly *empty?* When did we eat all of those? No wonder most sports talk hosts are overweight. Pastries sneak into their bodies like burglars.

Eleven fifty-three P.M. I'm getting a second wind. JT's raging into the phone like it's nine o'clock.

"You're out of your mind! Appreciate the call. I like that phone call. How dare you say Grant Hill should be considered as MVP? Of *what* league? Shaq Daddy's your MVP. What the hell has Grant Hill done? Are you kidding me? Seven phone calls in one segment. That's fast-paced. Let's keep it up."

Two hours to go.

•   •   •

Twelve-seventeen A.M. "I know them all. I study them. I'm like a sponge. Because I want to get better. Remember I told you about that piece of oak tag I had? I wrote down all the big names in the business, the year they started, agent, style, where they are now. I noticed that when they had their downfall, it all came back to the same thing. They couldn't deal with their egos. They couldn't handle who they were. And they couldn't take direction. You think you're so big, you don't listen to anybody. They would go up against their program director and suddenly find themselves fired. You gotta be careful. If you do one stupid thing, you could screw up your whole career. I really think this business is a house of cards. You get caught with drugs, or a stripper, your whole career will come crashing down. Some of these guys get to a certain level and they think they can say or do anything, and they're wrong."

Twelve twenty-three A.M. "I went out to dinner tonight so I'm kind of dressed up. I don't usually do my night show like this. My wife got me these Nike slippers. And I wear pajama pants. All my callers know I wear these loose-fitting flannel pants. I wear sweatshirts and a baseball cap, like you saw me today. I dress . . . comfortable."

Translated, when he does his night show, he wears his *pajamas.*

Twelve forty-six A.M. JT reads an E-mail on the air from Iron in Boston, who won the Brick House "E-mailer of the Year Contest." Iron ends his E-mail: "P.S. Tonight is one of the best shows you've ever put together."

"Appreciate that, Iron," says JT. He smiles at me. "John in Atlanta on The Zone."

"We had nothing here in Atlanta in 1991," John says. "The

Falcons sucked, the Braves sucked. Everything sucked around here. Until we got sports talk radio. When we started calling and complaining and griping, *then* things started to happen. Because the people knew they had accountability now. There were people who had hourly wage jobs who knew more about football and baseball than the people in charge. We got some coaches fired. And we made it to the Super Bowl and the World Series. End of story. Sports talk radio is the way to go. Long live caller-driven sports talk radio!"

It's almost as if the guy's on JT's payroll.

And JT's not going to let this opportunity drop: "True story. The Mets were thinking about getting Mike Piazza. The GM of the Mets came on WFAN in New York, the biggest sports talk radio station in the world. He came on their big show there, Mike and the Mad Dog, and they opened up the phone lines. This shows you the power of sports talk radio. Every single call said, 'Get Piazza, you must get Piazza, please get Piazza.' *Every* phone call. For *hours*. Next day Mike Piazza was in a Mets uniform. Dead serious. These executives, managers, coaches, listen to me and they listen to you. They're out there. They think *you're* nuts. They think *I'm* crazy. They think we're a bunch of vampires. But they *listen.*"

Twelve fifty-five A.M. Kent from Kansas City, a younger, thinner- voiced Butch from the Cape wanna-be, weighs in with a high speed *whoosh* about the Chiefs. In the middle of his two-minute nonstop blast, Bobby the producer pipes in live from Vegas, "JT, gotta name him Best New Artist."

JT laughs. "Gotta run, Kent."

Music up. Kent dispatched into the night.

"This is a good show," I say.

"Yeah. I'm most proud that we don't let it tail off. We try to keep the energy going all night. I think Joe DiMaggio said,

'You never know when that kid's gonna see you for the first time ever.' I treat the show that way. You never know when some guy, a monster's gonna be driving his car home from the airport, going, 'Who is this guy?'"

One oh seven A.M. "Last hour of the show. What a long day. This day felt like it started four days ago. Now representing the two oh six of the Nightriders, Evil Ant."

JT's entire face breaks into a smile. "This guy's like a character on the show. The callers between one and two A.M. I call the Nightriders. It's like an exclusive hard-core club."

"That Tony Kukoc, man, he bust us up," Evil Ant moans.

"I like this guy," JT says. "He's really funny."

"And I seen that new Staples Center on TV, man," adds Evil Ant. "It looks like a KFC bucket."

JT and I break up.

One twenty-two A.M. "How you doing?" I ask JT.

"Good. A little under the weather. Get a good night sleep, I'll be fine. How you feeling?"

"I'm okay." I mean it. Surprisingly. Another question occurs to me. "Do you gamble?"

"I have never, ever, made a bet in my life on sports. I totally despise it. When I was in Vegas, I kinda got scared straight. I watched a lot of people and the problems they had. I never had an interest in gambling. I think there are a lot of phonies and fakes on the radio who claim they know what they're doing. People listen to them and throw their money away. It's sickening."

One forty-five A.M. Rick Rock, a caller from Boston, drones on. JT's fingers still flashing across the keys, phone to his ear, eyes flicking back and forth, monitor to monitor. He glances at me.

"You know how to get to your hotel? You know where it is?"

"I know where it is, yeah."

"I can give you a ride."

"Really?"

"Yeah. No problem."

"Great. Thanks."

I am relieved. I was wondering how I would negotiate the stretch from the station past the strip joint without getting hassled or hit on. I was actually going to call a cab from the studio, but JT is saving me the trouble. I feel a little guilty about disrupting his schedule, but screw it. I wouldn't mind the ride.

One fifty-three A.M. A caller with a Southern accent right out of *Deliverance* is punched in. JT and I both rub our eyes.

"I watch your show every night. I like the good caller-driven radio . . ."

JT squints at me. "Did he say he *watches* the show?"

"Every night," I confirm.

One fifty-eight A.M. Speed Brick. JT insists you call now with fast takes and tons of energy. The last call of the night comes from Green in Vancouver, who decides to sing the praises of Kordell Stewart of the Steelers.

"Green, *Green,*" JT interrupts. "Kordell Stewart *stinks* at quarterback. Can you admit that to me? No? Okay, have a good night."

Click.

"Admit it to me tomorrow."

A wrap-up, a good-night. Another eight hours in the books. JT tosses himself back into his chair.

"*Awrigghtt!*" He holds his palm up and we slap five. "Let's go."

"Appreciate the ride," I remind him.

"Not a problem. Let me just check out and we're history."

He shoots out of the studio. I pack up my tape recorder, tapes, notepad. Start to organize everything, then give up and sweep it all into my briefcase. It's 2 A. friggin' M. I stand, stretch. Whoa. Feels like there's a piano lashed to each of my legs.

JT reappears. "All set?"

"Yeah. Man, JT, I don't know how you do it every night."

"It is a grind."

He swivels toward the door. I take off after him.

Two-oh-seven A.M. Elevator down to the parking structure. JT's body rhythm is on fast-forward. He cracks his knuckles, drums his fingers against his thighs.

"See, my goal really is to have a three-hour midday show only. Get a niche like Mike and the Mad Dog. Pull down the kind of serious money they do and just enjoy life. Smell the roses."

Elevator opens into the parking structure. Harsh light bouncing off the cold concrete makes me squint. The smell of tires.

"I don't know how long I can keep this up. It's not so much the physical strain, it's the mental—"

He stops abruptly. We're standing in an empty parking space. He stares, confused, then blinks a couple of times.

"My car's gone," he says.

He looks left, right, to the other side, then back at the vacant space as if the car might magically reappear.

"Wait, I parked on level *three.*" He sighs, shakes his head. I'm as relieved as he is. He heads down a ramp.

"At least I think I did," he murmurs.

We practically jog down the cement ramp and arrive at level three. No cars here at all.

"Shit," says JT.

In the distance I hear a woman's high-pitched laugh. Just another night at the strip club. JT jerks his head up toward level four.

"That was my parking space," he says.

"No car there," I say.

"Fuck."

Then, ridiculously, we climb *back* to level four, just to be sure.

Two-fourteen A.M. We're standing in his parking space. JT scratches his head. "This is crazy."

"You think your car was stolen?"

"No, can't be. Lemme think. Julie and I went out to dinner with my boss. I told her I wanted to take you home. Did I drive? Yeah. No, wait a minute. She drove."

He looks at me triumphantly. "That's right. She dropped me off."

"In other words," I say, "you don't have a car."

"Not a problem." He whips out his cell phone. "I'll call Julie. She'll just pick us up."

"JT, it's two o'clock in the morning. Maybe she's asleep."

"No, no, she's up."

He dials the number and waits, ear to the cell phone.

"Damn, Julie, where are you?"

I'm thinking, in bed. Probably asleep. That's where my wife would be. And if I called her to pick me up now, because I forgot my car, she would, then when I got home, she'd kick my ass.

"I don't understand it. Why isn't she answering?"

You got me. All I know is that it's 2 A.M. and I'm stuck in an empty parking structure in San Francisco with JT the Brick.

"Maybe she's waiting for us outside," he says hopefully.

Sounds logical. I buy it. He bolts for the parking structure door and shoves his shoulder into it. I'm right there. We're like *Bad Boys* on a bust. We dash down a hallway, burst into the main lobby, and go outside the front door. No Julie. Up the street more laughter and squealing from the strip club. A bottle breaks. I flinch.

"She's probably at the back door." JT takes off. I'm right behind him.

Two twenty-three A.M. She's not at the back door. A scrawny alley cat crouches and hisses. JT dials the cell again.

"I can't figure this out. Why won't she answer?"

I'm at a loss. But we're in this together now.

"Maybe we should call a cab," I suggest.

"No, no, we had a plan."

"You just don't remember what it is."

"Bingo." But JT's smiling. Then the smile fades. "I'm dialing her *cell*. I should be dialing our house."

I nod. "Smart."

"Hi, honey," JT says into the phone. Contact. "Yeah, we're here." He covers the mouthpiece. "She was waiting for my call." Then back to her. "I was calling you on your cell. I don't know why." He clicks off. "She'll be here in five minutes."

He puts away his phone. Sighs. "I guess it's getting to me."

Two forty-three A.M. I'm in the back of the Tournours' SUV. John Tournour, alias JT the Brick, rides shotgun. His wife, Julie, tall, blond, more than his wife, a *gift*, drives. She picked us up smiling as if it were three in the afternoon. As we climb Lombard Street toward my hotel, JT fiddles with the radio, sliding past any music.

"I've got to ask," I say. "What happened there?"

"The dinner with my boss. It's that simple."

"It threw him off," Julie explains.

He tilts his head back to me and looks me right in the eye. "I lost my groove, man. I lost my groove."

JT concentrates on tuning the radio. Finds what he's looking for.

A replay of his show.

He settles back and closes his eyes.

Three-oh-three A.M. San Francisco.

Riding with JT the Brick, as he dozes off, falling asleep to the sound of his own voice.

XII.

line three

JOE THE WAITER

On a dark and cold February evening, I find myself in a cab, heading out to a quiet neighborhood in Queens, to have dinner with a man I have never met. He is Joseph Talaja, known to listeners of the Stinkin' Genius as Joe the Waiter. Not only have I never met Joe Talaja, I know him only from his phone calls to Arnie—hilarious, agonizing, and sometimes poignant pleas in which Joe begs Arnie to bail him out of debt to his bookmaker by giving him just a couple of guaranteed football winners. Poor Joe has to be the worst gambler in the world. Every week he's in trouble, in the hole to his bookie and in Dutch with his wife. Based on Joe's broken-English malapropisms couching his garbled cries for help, I don't know if he's ever won a single bet.

The world outside my window changes. We've left Manhattan far behind and entered a moonscape of small two-story houses, all-night convenience stores, quaint cemeteries, dilapidated elementary schools, and shadowy beauty parlors. A chill courses through my body.

The cab stops at a neat brick house in the middle of a tree-lined avenue.

"This is it," the driver says doubtfully.

I peer out my window, hesitating. The front door of the house swings open and a small man wearing a T-shirt and no shoes appears on his landing. This is already disconcerting. It's February, remember? He waves at the cab, a cigarette pinched between his lips.

"This is it," I say now, certain but unsure.

I climb out of the cab and approach Joe the Waiter, who smiles at me warmly.

"Come, come, I show you. First, *deener.*"

He waves me into his living room like a matador.

A haze of dim brown light hovers over Joe Talaja's living room like smog. The house smells of garlic and cigarette smoke. Joe leads me into his kitchen. We pass several glass display cases containing dozens of signed baseballs and three glowing plastic shrines to the Virgin Mary, Mother Teresa, and Frank Sinatra. Joe is short, five six or so, and when he walks, bounces like he's on a trampoline. His hair, close-cropped, was once blond but has since turned the color of ash. His skin is sallow and pockmarked; his nose is sharp, jagged, and a little too large for the rest of his face. His eyes are watery and red from whiskey and losing.

"How long have you lived in this house?"

"Fifteen years. A beautiful house. For that I gotta stop the gumbling."

He stands over a stove and sprinkles a fingertip of salt into a pot of pasta.

"You have quite a collection of baseballs."

"That is nothing. You'll see downstairs. This is *second* collection."

He grins. A backdraft of smoke pours out of his nose. "I go on the show. You know, the ookshun."

"Oh, auctions, sure."

Joe shakes his head.

"So Arnie's in L.A. You can't hear him anymore."

"No. That is bad. You like it veergin olif oil?"

"Yes, thank you."

Cigarette dangling from his mouth, Joe tosses a salad with a fork and spoon. He places it on the table, which is draped with a plastic, checkered tablecloth, set for one.

"Let me ask you something, Joe. Do you really gamble like you say?"

He lowers his voice. "Last vick I lose two thousand." He shrugs. "How you can go on?"

"Do you bet just sports?"

He sucks in his breath with the ferocity of someone about to dive underwater. "Tree hundred sixty-five days a year. Bissbull, besketbull, footbull. Colleges, pros, boat. Do you know what this is? You asking Got to help you. He help you one day, but not tree hundred sixty-five days a year."

A woman passes through the kitchen.

"Hello," I say.

She smiles shyly, then glides into another room like a ghost.

"My vife. Beautiful vooman. You know how many times she take it tree thousand dollars and give to me? For the gumbling?"

Another shrug. Then a shiver. "She's sick over it."

"Is this your only vice? You don't do drugs—"

"No. I don't do drugs. Never. I drink. Lot. I have problem. I'm alcoholic. If I drink, I no stop. And the gumbling, it put it more pressure on me."

"And that makes you drink," I say, not helpfully.

He removes the pot of pasta from the stove and ladles it into a bowl. He then removes a sauce from a skillet simmering with sautéed vegetables and gently pours that over the pasta.

"Here. A nice pasta. Primavera. I make for you."

"You share it with me."

"No. I eat already. And we got it Swiss chard with potato."

He dishes out a steaming plate of what looks like mashed potatoes flecked with spinach.

"Come, eat," Joe says. "I love cook. I am, how many years, a vaiter? I am forty-nine now, I vork since I am sixteen."

"Thirty-three years," I say.

"Cheese?"

With a flourish, he sprinkles freshly grated Parmesan over the pasta. "I gotta see if she got it some vine. I don't know. But I got it soda and if you vant beer, I go buy—"

"No, no, soda is fine."

I survey the feast in front of me. Pasta primavera, salad, warm bread, and steaming Swiss chard with potatoes. Joe rummages through his kitchen cabinets, exploring, removing bottles of olive oil and jars of spices.

"Mary!" he suddenly shouts into the other room. *"Mary!"*

"No, Joe, soda is fine, really. Sit down. Tell me how you got started calling Arnie."

He puts out his cigarette, sits down next to me, and lights another.

"I'm losing in gumbling and I need help. I've been listening, so I call Meester Arnie. I need *help.*"

I nod, sample what Joe the Waiter has made for me. The salad and Swiss chard are tangy and delicious. The pasta primavera melts in my mouth.

"Where were you when you called?"

"I be home," Joe says, waving away a curtain of smoke from

his cigarette. "I say, I have to try anything. I be down again two thousand dollars. He give me eleven vinner."

I'm not sure I've heard him right. *"Eleven* winners?"

Joe's face breaks into a grin. *"Eleven* vinners. Eleven and oh. I swear Got."

"Eleven in a *row?*"

"I swear Got. Next veek I no have like that. You know. You can't."

"So, wait, the next week you called and you said, Arnie, you went eleven and oh—"

"This be on radio. The people no believe."

"This is incredible," I say, referring to the Swiss chard.

"It's how we do. Swiss chard with potato and garlic. Try. You no like, you just leave."

"No, I love this."

I hear a rustle behind me and look over my left shoulder. The woman has reappeared. She holds a bottle of wine and one wineglass.

"This is vife. Mary."

"Very nice to meet you."

"He like it your Swiss chard." Joe smiles.

"Thank you," Mary says and bows her head. She is dressed in a light gray sweater and black slacks. She has a slow stride and a full figure and a warm, sad face. Her body is slightly bent.

"Croatian vine," Joe says, taking the bottle from his wife.

"I should get the recipe for this," I say, polishing off the Swiss chard. "My kids would like this. My wife would like this."

"Oh, yeah?" Mary laughs doubtfully.

"She excellent cook. See, we European. People here, come in, all the time. Sunday. She cook. Excellent. Thirty, forty people, nothing to her."

Mary stands silently over the kitchen counter and begins brewing coffee while Joe pours me a glass of wine the color of blackberries. I sip it. It's smooth and heavy, the kind of wine you could eat with a fork.

"Umm." I turn to thank Mary, but she's gone. I turn back to Joe. "Okay, well, what about the second time you called Arnie?"

"The second time, not too good. I lose. But I never blame Meester Arnie."

"But wait, Joe, I heard that. You didn't play all the games he gave you. You went off on your own."

He's caught. "Okay, I play half. Dot is truth. No for me anymore. I am out. I can listen. But I don't vant gumbling. I have beautiful house, beautiful vife. Is hard. But no more."

"Did you tell people you were calling the radio?"

"No. Nobody. Mary hear me because I be down in bussment. But vot happened, friend of mine, I no see him in four, five year . . . *he* call me. 'Joe, is this you?' He recognize my voice. Because my broke English." Joe laughs. "He always listen sports radio. He can't be*lieve* vot he heard." This breaks Joe up. "A lot of people think Arnie pay me."

"That's what I asked Arnie. Is Joe the Waiter real?"

"Now you meet Joe Vaiter. Vot is your opinion?"

"Real. Very real."

He bows his head.

"Some people call because they want to be heard on the radio."

"No. I call just for my desperation. I never call before. Never. I just vant be free from my sickness. Because is very hard. You know how you feel ven you sveating, sveating like mad? Especially ven you vork and you can see the TV over there and you can't stop it your vork to call? Like dot."

"How much do you bet?"

"A thousand dollars a day," he whispers.

"Whoa."

"The whole board. I bet every game. Every one. And reverses."

I look at him blankly.

"Like parlays. Only pay more, but you *lose* more."

"Let me ask you something about Arnie. Did you listen just for his picks or because you liked him?"

Joe looks offended. "I like him. I love Meester Arnie. But especial for the picks. He's got, em, beeg talent. A unique style. His voice. His everything. You never get bored vith him. He know vot he talk. Excited. Even if he no give pick, I listen him."

He starts to laugh again, choking on his own smoke.

"Ven he yell, he so funny. My, my, so funny."

Joe catches his breath, stubs out the butt in a saucer painted with a bouquet of lilacs. His face darkens.

"But for me, I think so I'm done. I no more sveating. Your shoulder . . . like tree hundred pound on your shoulder. And you go home. Empty. I no have any more feeling."

The silence hangs over us like a weight. I sip the deep black Croatian wine. Joe looks longingly at my glass. A room or two away I hear the sound of a sitcom. Joe glances in the direction of the canned laughter.

"I tole her I stop. She give me the money. Vatever I make it, I give her the money. She pay all the bills, everything. I never pay von bill. But ven I get beat, I no know vot to do. Thank Got for Meester Arnie."

Joe reaches an arm over his shoulder as if he's giving himself a hug.

"Have you ever met Arnie?"

"No. I vood like to meet him someday."

"What do you think he looks like?"

Joe smiles, and then, in the brown light of the kitchen, I think I see him blush. He moves his head from side to side slowly, then he closes his eyes.

"He's not tall," Joe says.

"Not tall." I nod.

Arnie is six one.

"Middle," Joe says. He laughs, embarrassed. He presses his thumbs against his eyelids.

"How old?"

"I think so he's . . . forty-five."

He's thirty-six.

"And I think so he's blond. Dot is in my mind. And he's got hair. Good hair over dere. Blond. Dot is what I see. I don't know."

Dark hair, thinning. Going on bald.

"Is he fat, thin?"

"No. He's thin. *Thin.* Dot I *believe.*"

Heavy, Joe. He's heavy. Like *very* heavy.

"Does he wear glasses?"

"Yeah, I believe he's got it glasses." Joe nods, filling in the description like a witness. Not too tall, thin, blond hair, glasses. Joe has just described Robert Redford.

"I am long, far avay? Tell me."

"Well . . ." I describe Arnie to him. Joe pinches his cheeks as I talk. I finish. He stares at the ashes in the saucer.

"He's big?"

"He's big," I say softly.

"No," Joe says. "He's thin. I believe he's thin. No big."

"Going bald," I say.

"No. Good hair. Blond. I believe he's *blond.* Dot I believe."

I pick at the remains of my Swiss chard, regretting that I've told him the truth.

Later, dishes cleared, Joe makes me Turkish coffee and on another floral-patterned saucer lays out a half dozen Croatian cookies. The cookies are crumbly and sweet, the coffee strong.

"You are a great cook and a great host," I say to Joe the Waiter.

He shrugs massively like he's doing a shoulder exercise. "Tomorrow I make it my vife spinach salad and breast of chicken."

"Sounds great."

"I be do it much better if I not be gumbling."

"You could go to Gamblers Anonymous. It works for a lot of people."

"Nah, I can do it by myself. I gotta stop and dot's it. Because I can no put in jeopardy everything. You know how many job I lose because of the gumbling? I tell you, one night, we be play cards, whole night."

"Poker?"

He nods. "Poker. The next day, on lunch, I'm so tired, I ask it customer, when I take it their order, 'How many cards you vant?'"

"No."

"I swear. I ask customer, 'How many cards you vant?' I swear *Got.*"

Joe Talaja takes me into his cellar. It is an East Coast basement, far from a California slab, two full rooms, finished and furnished, ideal for an in-law's apartment, kid's refuge, collector's retreat, or gambler's hideout. Jammed against one wall is a white-slipcovered sofa piled high with pictures of baseball, football, and hockey players. More pictures, some in frames, are stacked on several card tables. Many of the pictures have autographs, the result of Joe's either serving these players in restaurants or hunting them down on the street.

At the bottom of the basement stairs, Joe whisks aside a faded green curtain, revealing shelves of baseballs, boxes of baseball cards, autographed footballs, and piles of team T-shirts. It looks like the storeroom of a sporting goods store. I wander alone into the far room, where another table is strewn with half-framed pictures all over the top. Along the edges of the room are display cases stuffed with hockey sticks, baseball bats, autographed boxing gloves, and, yes, more baseballs. Hundreds of signed baseballs here. No, I'm low. At least a thousand.

Joe appears behind me and sighs. "I hef so much vork to do down here. Oh. Let me show you."

He opens a display case and pulls out a black baseball bat. "This is my Mets collection. See, I got it the block bot. The block bot they gave the player . . ."

His voice trails off, searching for the significance of the black bat. He twirls the handle and squints at the lumber as if the answer were carved into the sweet spot.

"Dot is '69, complete team with Jill Hodges."

"Mike and the Mad Dog were talking about him not getting into the Hall of Fame."

Joe puts a hand over his heart. *"Please.* I am so disappointed. He belong in Hall of Fame. He *belong* there."

I am witness to a transformation. The gambler in Joe is momentarily gone, replaced by a heartsick fan. Suddenly, in the strange cellar of this strange man, this compulsive collector and addicted gambler, I have stumbled upon the core of sports talk radio. It lies in the connection between host and listener. Joe the Waiter doesn't listen to sports talk because he gambles; getting winners was a bonus, a sign from God. He listens because of what sports means to his soul: the beauty of a game played by gods disguised as humans, regularly electrifying us with their gifts, occasionally devastating us with their frailties. Sports exist to spirit us away from both the mundane and momentous decisions that clutter and conquer us. When we are at a ballpark, stadium, arena, or in our living rooms cemented to our sofas in front of our big-screen TVs, we are, for those three flimsy hours, safe. And free. And as soon as the game is over, sports talk radio opens the phone lines so we can gloat, bitch, summarize, analyze, and relive those three hours all over again with guys who share our passion, our memories, and who appreciate our call.

Joe replaces the black bat into its case as if he's laying down a baby.

"How much does a bat like that cost?"

Joe purses his lips. He takes a long pause before he answers. "I vood say . . . is hard . . . ah-boat two thousand dollar."

We head into the other room, Joe pointing out signed pictures on the wall as we go.

"Dot is my Yonkees. Joe D and Mickey Mantle. I got it big sheet of Yonkee Stadium. A hundred seventy-five dollars I pay, he no vant sign. He say he's too beeg."

"Who?"

"Joe D."

I'm stunned. *"Noo."*

"I swear Got."

"That's too sad" is all I can say.

Joe begins rummaging through sections of his collection, pulling out photographs of boxing greats Joe Louis, Max Baer, and Ali. The amount of memorabilia in these two rooms is staggering.

"I got a lot," Joe admits.

Oh, *yeah.* Joe the Waiter is a sports-stuff pack rat. I wonder how much money he has spent at auctions and baseball shows accumulating all of this. I wonder how much it is really worth and how many of the signatures are genuine. Joe, hands on hips, surveys his sports-stuff empire.

"I know," he says finally. He hops back over to the faded green curtain, spreads it, and hands me a football.

"Signed by Stiff Yoonk," he says. "I vant you should bring Arnie, for Shea, his son. I never got it a gift for him. You bring."

"I can't," I say helplessly. "I can't fit it in my suitcase."

"No? No problem."

He slides the football back onto its shelf and pulls out a long rectangular box of baseball cards.

"How about this?"

"Yeah, I think so."

"Okay. And this." He hands me a tiny gray New York Yankees T-shirt. "I know he's a big Yonkee fan."

"I can take this, too."

"Okay. You take. And I believe he's *thin.*"

"Right. And blond."

Joe laughs, a crackle that dissolves into a cough.

"Well," I say, "I'd really better go. If I can just borrow your phone to call a cab . . ."

"No."

"No?"

"No cab." He smiles. "Mary take you."

In a clean, late-model Camry, we drive stealthily toward the city, Mary at the wheel, Joe in the backseat. Mary is an intense, focused driver, her eyes steady and straight, never wavering from the road. She speaks nearly perfect English with only a trace of an accent. She seems much younger than Joe, but there are wrinkles beneath her eyes, Rorschachs of strain that spread down her cheeks like spiderwebs. In the background, a radio station softly plays classic rock.

"So, Joe, you became a collector because of your daughter?"

"Yep," Mary says. "She started off with baseball cards and then he ended up with everything else."

Mary doesn't speak again for twenty minutes. From the backseat of his Camry, Joe carries on his own talk show. He rants about autographs he's gotten and missed, describing a rough encounter with Reggie Jackson, who refused to sign a ball for him at a sports show. He rails about the escalating cost of living in New York, complains about real estate prices going through the roof even in his precious Queens neighborhood. He segues into point-shaving and game-fixing. Like most gamblers, he is astounded at the accuracy of the Vegas linesmakers who repeatedly and maddeningly are able to predict games within a single point of the actual score. And then, as we cross the Fifty-ninth Street Bridge, past WFAN, on our way back into Manhattan, Joe talks again about his disease.

"The one thing is, listen, I know lotta bookies, nobody's broke. I know lotta people that lost the restaurant, they lost this, that lost that, from gumbling. Is hard beat them. Stay avay and dot's it. She's be happy. Ha, Mary?"

Silence. Eyes on the road, concentrating on one thing and one thing only: removing the stranger from her car.

"Mary?" The man of the house has spoken.

"Hmm?" she murmurs.

"You be happy, too?"

She refuses to speak.

"She never talk about it—"

Then, from the sheer depths of her being, a voice escapes, a rumble, with the power of a dam bursting.

"You've got to change your *life.* "

He's never heard this voice before. He swallows and whispers, "I do gotta change."

I don't know why I say anything, but I blurt out, "You can do it, Joe."

"I gotta. If I have different vife, I be on street long time ago."

"Believe me, you will," Mary says, a promise sneaking out through pursed lips.

"She loves you, Joe," I say, looking through the window, hating that I'm in the middle of this, wanting to jump out of the car at the next light.

"Old story." Joe sighs, and I can feel his breath on the back of my neck.

He settles back into the crook of the seat, studies the nightlife on the East Side of the city, twenty-somethings pouring out of bars, rowdy teenagers laughing as they cross the street against the light. The city that never sleeps. There is always someone awake to take your bet.

"I no have license," Joe says sadly, a regret, his tone suggesting this might be a blessing.

I watch Mary drive and I can see both the pain and the strength in her eyes. She is a modern survivor, a big-city success story, a woman from Croatia who came to this country with two suitcases, a husband, and no promises. She mastered English and got a job as a teller at a major New York bank. She learned computers and worked her way up through the system, arriving at a position now of challenge and responsibility. She raised two daughters, ran a house, and supported her husband, a hardworking, hard-drinking, high roller. She loves him, she is bound to him, but something inside her is unraveling, like a spool of thread. This I also see in her eyes.

"Stay," the Jackson Browne version, spills out of the car radio. We drive on Sixtieth Street over to Madison, then head up to Seventy-fifth. I make up my mind. I'm going to get off and walk the rest of the way.

"I luv everything," Joe says suddenly. "But I tell you, is hard for first generation in this country. Is hard. But I still believe I gotta chance for me."

I look at Mary. Eyes locked straight ahead. She sniffs.

"You've done well, Joe," I say. "You've both done well."

"I know. But I can do it much better."

He leans forward, grips the back of my seat with sudden, shocking urgency.

"Ask her vot she thinking how much I lost. *Ask her.*"

"I don't want to—"

"What do you think, Mary? Huh? Ten thousand? Fifteen? Twenty?"

"Are you kidding?" She laughs. "You think I'm a *fool?*"

"You know, this is good right here. I can get off here—"

"I come here vith nothing, two suitcases, ask it me that story. Now *dot* is story."

Stayyyy just a little bit longer.

Mary, her hands clutching the wheel, the blood drained out of them, turns to me as she drives. She speaks evenly, without emotion, as if she's under oath.

"You know, I didn't marry a gambler. All this happened later. Now"—she swallows—"he has a habit. And he has to stop that habit. Otherwise—"

And she starts to cry. She speaks loudly, believing, I think, that by raising her voice she can cover her tears.

"Otherwise he's not going to have me."

Why don't you stayayayyyy just a little bit—

"I'm telling him that, and I'm telling you that now. He's not going to have *me.*"

She pulls the car over.

"I stop," Joe whispers.

"One day at a time," I say lamely.

"I stop," Joe says again. "Mary, I stop."

She lowers her head. A tear drops onto the steering wheel.

Sayyy you willl.

XIII.

genius on hold
ONE TOO MANY

Saturday night at ten, after a nice dinner and a couple of drinks, Mike Thompson drives into work and cleans out his office. He carries the things that matter out to his car—a few framed and signed posters of logos for the stations he's turned around, and his most precious memento, a framed and laminated letter written in 1920 announcing the formation of the NBC Radio Network. The whole operation takes less than fifteen minutes. Hell, he could've kept the car running. But it's better this way. Now he can bypass the messy good-byes and avoid the inevitable sticky explanations. Yes, it's much better to escape like a thief in the night.

His departure is hardly unexpected. Rumors have been flying for weeks, hitting the streets, the radio Web sites, and landing with a clunk in the *L.A. Times.* Thompson, who'd been unhappy for months, had arranged his getaway well before anyone knew. He is heading back to Atlanta, a town he adores, a town he *understands,* and a town that loves sports talk radio, especially guy talk. Mike will be taking over and revamping WCNN (no relation to Ted Turner's CNN) and taking on Atlanta's other established sports talk station, The Zone. And this time he'll win.

"It was a mutual parting of the ways."

Thompson is tooling down the New Jersey Turnpike the Friday before he is to begin his new job. His voice, whipping in the wind, streams animated and carefree from his cell phone into my living room.

"Look, guy talk can work in L.A. It can work in any market. I just didn't have the time or opportunity to do it the way I wanted. I have twenty years in this business. I know what I'm doing. Believe me, it would've worked."

"So why didn't it?"

"To begin with, you need a better signal. Then you need to change those call letters. Everyone confuses KXTA in L.A. with XTRA in San Diego. Half the people filling out the ratings books don't know which station they're writing down. Kills you. You have to give the station a new name, a new identity. Call it The Ticket or The Score, something that says *sports.* You also have the West Coast baseball problem. The games are on at all different times. You can't find your host; you don't know what time he's on. Plus, you cannot do an hour-and-a-half pregame show. It's death. Finally, you have to upgrade the guests. If you have B- and C-list guests, it's a waste of time. You have to tune in for the host. If the host can't carry it, you're in trouble."

"Which brings me to Arnie."

"Arnie has talent. No doubt about it. It has to be nurtured, that's all."

"Aged like a fine wine."

"Exactly," Mike roars. "I don't know if his new bosses will do that or not. It's a very tough challenge out there. Very tough."

"Seems that—"

"Hey, man," Mike Thompson says, his voice suddenly crackling, "I'm losing you."

"Sky's the limit. I mean that. And Arnie is totally in the right place. Chicago was great, but L.A.? Endless possibilities."

Jason B., personal manager, is talking about the future of his newest client, the Stinkin' Genius. Jason B. handles comedians and actors. Arnie is his first and only sports client.

"I think Arnie is going to be the king of sports talk radio. I really do. And we can open a lot of other doors for him as well. Like voice-overs. You kidding me? That voice? That's a whole market for him. He's going to do very well there. Very well. I see him doing it all. Radio, TV. Have you seen his spot on the Channel 9 Sunday sportscast?"

"I have."

"And?"

"He comes across well."

"I know. He really does. I think he should have his own show. His own television show."

"That's where you come in, I guess."

"Exactly. Hey, have you seen his Web site? We don't even advertise it and he's getting ten thousand hits a week. That's unbelievable. Mostly football picks. Some personal stuff. Ten thousand hits a week. Can you believe that? I can see Arnie becoming like a Chris Berman, I really can. Sky's the limit."

"And what about radio? How's he doing?"

"Fine. He's doing fine. Of course, he'll have to adjust to the new program director, whoever that's gonna be. But he will. I have no doubt. Yeah, it's going real well on the radio."

"Good. With Thompson leaving and all, I wasn't sure."

"Why? What do you hear?"

• • •

Arnie Spanier is worried.

His concern is not being caused by any one thing. It's a million things, little annoyances swirling around him like minuscule gnats, nibbling at him, unsettling him, keeping him up nights, sending him straight to the fridge.

To start with, the ratings are iffy. In men thirty-five to fifty-four, Arnie's share has increased to 1.1 in the winter quarter, up from 0.6 since the fall quarter, which was before Arnie arrived. However, in the crucial men twenty-five to fifty-four demographic, Arnie's share is 0.9, exactly the same as the fall quarter, pre-Arnie, and significantly trailing Hacksaw's 1.5. In other words, the ratings haven't really changed, and Arnie has not dented Hacksaw.

"Thompson told me not to worry," Arnie says. "Now Thompson's in Atlanta. I'm worried."

Arnie also wasn't sure if Thompson, his program director, was steering him in the right direction. Thompson wanted more discussion of Arnie's personal life, fewer callers, less hard-core sports. Arnie didn't mind occasionally talking about Shea or Beth or having a woman come into the studio to give him a massage on the air, but he wanted to keep the emphasis on sports. In addition, Thompson constantly gave him pointers about his delivery, harping on him to modulate his voice and muffle his screaming. Arnie tried to split the difference, tried to satisfy his boss and please himself. It was getting nerve-wracking, and as a result he was working *tight*. Bad enough worrying about ratings; now he also had to worry about reviews from his boss.

Arnie was vulnerable. He had been taking continuous heat for bashing the Lakers, but he truly believed that the Lakers weren't as good as Portland and couldn't see Shaq, Kobe, and Phil bringing home the championship trophy. He was so positive they'd fall short that he offered to wash the cars of all Laker fans within earshot if the Lakers won the NBA title. When the Lakers won, the station set up a remote at a Studio City car wash. It was mid-June, hot and sunny, and a line of honking cars stretched nearly half a mile down Ventura Boulevard. Attired in a purple and gold Lakers away uniform, Arnie, grinning, huffing, and baking in the hot Valley sun for three hours, mopped and hand-vacked dozens of cars, a quartet of skimpily dressed Hooters girls splashing in a portable hot tub behind him, providing much needed visual relief. This remote far surpassed the one held on that bleak February afternoon at the gas station in the rain. At least three hundred people came, many snagging Arnie's autograph and picture. Still, Arnie wasn't completely satisfied. He felt there should've been even more people. And Thompson left after about twenty minutes. What was that about?

Whenever Arnie felt uneasy, he would take solace in how well the show was selling to advertisers. Commercials during his 3–7 P.M. show were flying out the door like Happy Meals. A few months ago Arnie's show had been ranked eighteenth in its time slot of commercial billing. This month the show had moved up to fourth.

"They have been selling the shit out of the show. Gotta admit that."

Arnie's voice is quiet, searching for the reason, looking for loopholes.

Partly, Arnie's feelings of inadequacy are fueled by his lack of acceptance by the local sports community. In February, Tom Hoffarth, writing in the San Fernando Valley's *Daily News,* ranked Arnie number one in his Bottom Five worst sports talk show hosts in L.A. Hoffarth suggested that Arnie's act would soon wear thin, and if all he did was bash the Lakers, his listeners would shortly abandon him. Arnie was, naturally, wounded by the article. In late July, Larry Stewart, writing in his weekly TV-radio column in the *Los Angeles Times,* scooped Mike Thompson's departure and asked: "Wonder what will become of Arnie Spanier? He epitomizes 'guy talk.'"

"I have a contract," Arnie answers Stewart defiantly, but the words come out almost like a question.

In September, all of the on-air talent and producers at KXTA are asked to play in a Lakers golf tournament and to attend the last Dodger home game of the season. Arnie, alone, is not invited. And when Arnie asks the newest Laker, Horace Grant, to appear as a guest on his show, he is told by Lakers media relations that Grant is not allowed to talk to him. Arnie's producer eventually interviews Grant, and Arnie plays the recorded spot, but the message is clear: as far as the Lakers are concerned, Arnie Spanier is off-limits.

Arnie talks about all of this on the air, trying to make light of it. His halfhearted attempt at comedy hardly conceals his pain. He begins expressing to friends that he's getting restless, tells Papa Joe Chevalier that he has his eye on the nine-to-one shift at WFAN, which leads into Mike and the Mad Dog.

"That is gonna be my shift someday. That is where I belong. I'm perfect for that slot. I would *kill* in New York. They don't appreciate me here."

Meanwhile, in Thousand Oaks, Beth puts the Spaniers' house up for sale. She wants a bigger space, has grown tired of the sameness of their suburban development, and has reached her limit with Gary, the neighbor who is no longer a novelty and has become a nuisance. She sees an opportunity to buy up and turn a good profit by taking advantage of the rising real estate market in the deep Valley. In the heart of Burbank, Arnie, with Thompson no longer coaching him from the sidelines, turns up the volume and keeps his personal life off the air. He also keeps an eye on the FAN, even contemplates calling Mark Chernoff to test the radio waters out by the Hudson.

In early October, Larry Stewart wounds him again. Stewart announces in his column that ABC Radio is about to purchase KRLA (1110-AM) and turn it into an all-sports station featuring ESPN Radio programming. Stewart also reminds readers of the impending launch of the new Fox Sports Radio Network, rumored to end up on KLAC (570-AM). These two stations would give Los Angeles a total of *five* sports talk radio stations. Ending his column, Stewart writes:

"How many sports talk stations does Los Angeles need? One **Arnie Spanier** is already one too many."

The bold print is his, not mine.

And then there is TV. For the past six months Arnie has appeared on L.A.'s Channel 9, doing a two-minute spot on *Sunday Sports Round-Up*, a weekly half-hour sportscast hosted by Alan Massengale.

"I just basically do my radio show for two minutes. At first there were about a hundred E-mails telling them to get rid of me. But things have calmed down," Arnie says from his makeup chair. He seems comfortable here, upbeat.

Standing next to him, the beautiful blond newscaster studies herself in the mirror as she removes a cluster of hot rollers from her hair. Behind her, a window air conditioner, dusty, ancient, creaky, wheezes and spits arctic air across the room.

Leticia, the woman about to apply Arnie's makeup, rummages through a metal drawer looking for a powder puff with Arnie's name on it.

"There is something to this TV thing, man," Arnie says. *"Hey, that was quite a home run! We'll take a break and we'll be right back!'* I wouldn't mind getting five hundred grand a year to do that. Don't have to take phone calls. No appearances. None of that crap."

"That's what these guys make?"

"Five, six hundred, something like that."

"I don't see your powder puff," Leticia says.

"It was there last week."

"I don't see it."

"The way I look at it, this town needs a character. Especially now. Somebody who stands out. I like to have fun and I am certainly a character. Why shouldn't it be me? Why shouldn't I take over this town?"

"Found it," Leticia says. "Way in the back. Do you just put on a base?"

"I don't know. Make me beautiful."

"She's does makeup, not magic," the blond newscaster says.

"Ha *haa!*" Arnie roars.

"Close your eyes."

Leticia deftly dabs his eyelids with the soft pink puff.

"*Ooh,* those eyebrows. I wish I had those," the blond newscaster says, never taking her eyes off herself.

"Yeah, I know. I shaved them once. Came back longer."

"No!"

"True. I couldn't believe it—"

The air conditioner gasps, dies, and all the lights go out.

For a moment, the four of us—the blond newscaster, the makeup woman, the sports talk radio host, and the writer—stand in darkness, in silence. Then:

"Ow! The roller!"

"This happened last—"

"I hope it's only—"

"You know what this is like?" Arnie's voice. Calm, even, clear. No rasp, no scream. "It's like being a sports talk radio host."

"What do you mean?"

"You're in the dark. Not knowing. Not knowing who's listening. You don't know if you're getting through, whether you're making sense, whether people like you, hate you. Nothing. You're in the *dark,* man. It's always night."

Suddenly the lights flicker, then return.

The air conditioner kicks back in, blowing freezing-cold wind all over us.

On Friday, November 3, the bomb drops. I hear through the talk radio grapevine that KXTA (1150-AM) plans to abandon its all-sports format and change to an all-finance format. The station will retain Dodger broadcasts but remove the rest of its on-air talent. The all-sports talk experiment begun in 1997 has failed.

Driving into the station one morning, Arnie asks, "If I get fired, am I still in the book?"

"You're on the cover," I tell him.

"Nobody listens to that station. *Nobody.* But I have to say, I love my new boss. You know what he told me? 'Try stuff. Go crazy. Don't be afraid to fuck up. Nobody's listening anyway.'"

"You're not leaving the station? What are you going to do, the Nasdaq update?"

"Well, the rumor is—" He pauses. "I'm moving over to Fox. Might change my time slot, too. I could be on twelve to three. It's all good. All good."

"This a done deal?"

"Pretty much. I might have a partner, too. We'll see."

"The Stinkin' Genius lives."

"You better believe it. Look, I've only been here nine months, and people tell me there's a good buzz about me. I know there is. The lines are lit all show long. The salespeople say they love me. My show is selling like crazy. It's not my fault the station's in trouble."

"So you're about to start a new chapter?"

"Looks that way."

"Stay tuned, huh?"

"Yep. What will happen this time? Will Arnie sell his house? Will Arnie make it on Fox Radio? Don't go away. You might have to rewrite the end of the book!"

Ha ha *haaa*.

I'm on hold.

One minute. Two. Getting antsy. I go over my take. It's solid. But is it too long? He could cut me off after my first point and I'll never get to what I really want to say. I'd better trim this.

Three minutes. Jesus. This guy can talk. Maybe it would be better to go with my second point first, the stronger point. I look over my notes. Yes, I have written notes. On a yellow legal pad, too, the tool of the sports talk trade.

The waiting is nerve-racking. Gets you thinking too much. That's what throws you off, then you stumble. Suddenly a click, and, jarred for a moment, I hear:

"Big Al! What's on your mind? Bring it."

"Two points I want to make!" I roar into the phone. "First, what's up with all these teams hiring managers who were former catchers turned broadcasters? Their role model, of course, is Joe Torre, who used to broadcast for the Angels."

"I remember that. He was pretty good."

"Buck Martinez and Bob Brenly are now big league managers. Bob *Brenly*? Are you kidding? Who's next, Elston Howard?"

A laugh.

See, Elston Howard's dead, so that worked.

"Point two. The Subway Series. The Mets are down three games to one. This is it. No tomorrow. Bobby Valentine, who's been out to lunch all Series, has to start managing *now*, as in this minute, before tonight's game even starts. He has to bench Perez and start Bubba Trammell."

"Trammell? He butchered that ball last night."

"He was nervous. First Series game. And Valentine should move Alfonzo to leadoff. Gotta generate more offense."

"I like it. Makes sense. Good take. You playing poker tonight?"

Okay.

I'm not on the air to a sports talk radio host.

I'm in my kitchen, talking to my friend Randy.

For the past year, without defining it as such, Randy and I have called each other at lunchtime as if we were doing a sports talk radio show. Sometimes he'll call me with a take and I'm the host. Other times I phone him. Call it method writing. An occupational hazard.

I actually did write out this World Series take. And I did intend to call one of the hosts I've come to know—JT or Eddie or Hacksaw or Mike and the Mad Dog. Last night I stayed up past midnight, listening to a parade of callers on JT's 9 P.M. to 2 A.M. show named Benny the Jet, the Sports Maven, the Big Chief, and Mr. Chardonnay. But I couldn't get myself to pick up the phone. I couldn't pull the trigger. Rather than waste the take, I called Randy.

Why couldn't I call last night? I'm not shy and I have no problem talking on the phone.

I think it's because my reason for calling was calculated. It was phony. The real callers I've heard across the country call sports talk radio because, I believe, they have to. They have critical information to share, an important opinion to express, or require insight into a particular game, one they are going to watch or bet. Sometimes they call just to hear themselves on the radio. And sometimes they call because they just need someone to talk to. But each one calls because it's part of his day, part of his life.

That's also why we listen. It's part of our day. Somewhere the President of Radio has figured this out. Sports talk radio has become *huge*. WFAN in New York, the first sports talk station, is now the highest-grossing radio station in the world, grossing over $50 million in ad billings over the last three years. Many major cities—Chicago, Phoenix, Miami, Atlanta—have three all-sports-talk radio stations broadcasting nonstop, around the clock. With ESPN Radio arriving on the airwaves just last week, Los Angeles now has *four*. According to *Forbes* (February 1999), "Sports radio stations are the hottest gig in broadcasting."

Used to be I'd hear rap music everywhere. Especially from boom boxes in the afternoons at the village green where skateboarders gather to run circles around each other and suck down those disgusting smoothie drinks that look and taste like a field. Now the boom boxes spew sports talk. Wherever I go—the gas station, coffee place, cleaner's, my local pub—I hear the voices from sports talk radio. Voices of guys I know. It's amazing and unnerving.

I end with a question, one I posed to myself a year ago:

What defines great sports talk radio?

The answer is . . . *urgency*.

You *have* to listen. You make an appointment to tune in and you are always reluctant to tune out.

The hosts in this book know this. They are always in search of urgency. The best of them are talented enough to create it.

When I began this book, I read a quote that pissed me off. Howard Manly, the radio-TV critic of the *Boston Globe*, wrote of sports talk radio:

"If saying stupid things was a crime, there would be no talk radio."

I doubt Mr. Manly had listened to as much sports talk radio as I now have. If he had, I don't think he would have said that. Sports talk radio hosts, at least the ones I met, are not the stereotypes some people imagine. They are not uneducated thugs who wander into radio stations to disgorge incoherent sports opinions off the tops of their thick heads for four hours at a crack. They are intelligent, funny, knowledgeable, prepared, opinionated, passionate, full of energy and warmth, and maybe just a tad wacky. In other words, guys you'd want to hang out with.

Each guy also believes he makes more money than everybody else in the country, or if he doesn't, he should, and that he has, by far, the biggest TV.

It was a helluva trip.

AUTHOR'S NOTE AND ACKNOWLEDGMENTS

In the world of sports talk radio, things change.

A couple of significant changes:

In the year from November 1999 to November 2000, One-on-One Sports, which I listened to religiously, went from a lineup of John Renshaw, Peter Brown, Papa Joe Chevalier, and Arnie Spanier to Jay Mariotti and a partner, Nestor Aparicio, and Papa Joe. Arnie moved to L.A., Renshaw moved into his basement, then to Florida, and Peter Brown moved to weekends. In early 2001, One-on-One Sports became Sporting News Radio.

In late November 2000, ESPN radio debuted in Los Angeles. I mention this because I finished writing the book the week before ESPN arrived. I missed out on hearing the radio voices of Tony Kornheiser, Dan Patrick, and Joe McDonnell. These are voices I now respect and enjoy and may have wanted to include in *Sports Talk*. The timing just wasn't right.

I could not have written this book without the cooperation, enthusiasm, hospitality, and openness of Arnie and Beth Spanier, Eddie and Judi Andelman, JT the Brick and Julie Tournour, Mike and BeBe North, Chris Russo, Mike Francesa, Lee Hamilton, Papa Joe Chevalier, Mike Thompson, John Renshaw, Richard Gerwitz, Joe the Waiter, and "Mary." *Sports Talk* is really your book, and I thank each of you for your generosity of time and spirit.

My first draft of the book was nearly seven hundred pages. I had to make cuts. I was forced to eliminate several hosts I interviewed and hung out with, talented guys whose company I truly enjoyed but whose stories I just could not include. They are Jay Mariotti, Peter Brown, Scott Ferrall, Nestor Aparicio, and Steve Carbone.

Also, sincere thanks to Dale Arnold, Mark Chernoff, Lee Hammer, Jason Wolfe, Chris Carlin, Bob Gelb, Brian Blackmore, Matt Nahigian, Mike Schneider, Mike Ogulnick, Eric Spitz, Vic Jacobs, and Rick Scott.

My deepest appreciation to Sean Carroll for paving the way, and to Mark Gentzkow for your time, your insight, and for keeping it going.

Some writers hang out in coffee shops or bars. I hang out at Village Books in Pacific Palisades, California. Thanks to Katie, Jeff, Mia, Lea, Connie, Amy, and Lionel for letting me in.

Thanks to my parents, Jim and Shirley Eisenstock, and to my brother Jay Eisenstock, whose sports talk radio knowledge was invaluable. Thanks to my cousins David Wilson for sending me newspaper clippings about sports talk radio and Richard Rustin for wining and dining me in New York.

David Ritz, I owe you. Thanks to you, I'm here doing it every day.

Thanks to everyone at Pocket, particularly to Luke Dempsey for jumping into the breach with great energy, humor, and intelligence; Suzanne O'Neill, assistant editor second to none; and Judith Curr for continued support and enthusiasm.

This book lives because of my New York Giants: Wendy Sherman, an incomparable agent but an even better person and friend, and Jason "Cutter" Kaufman, the smartest, funniest, and best editor alive.

I became a writer of books because of three voracious readers, keen-eyed editors, and indomitable spirits.

Bobbie, Jonah, and Kiva, thanks for everything.

Alan Eisenstock, 2001